Beyond
Behaviorism

Beyond Behaviorism

VICKI L. LEE
Monash University

90-1233

LAWRENCE ERLBAUM ASSOCIATES, PUBLISHERS
1988   Hillsdale, New Jersey   Hove and London

Lawrence Erlbaum Associates, Inc., Publishers
365 Broadway
Hillsdale, New Jersey 07642

Library of Congress Cataloging-in-Publication Data

Lee, Vicki L.
    Beyond behaviorism / Vicki L. Lee.
        p.   cm.
    Bibliography: p.
    Includes index.
    ISBN 0-8058-0115-4
    1. Behaviorism (Psychology)   2. Behaviorism (Psychology)—
—Philosophy.   3. Psychology—Philosophy.   I. Title.
BF199.L39 1988   88-320
150.19′43—dc19   CIP

Printed in the United States of America
10 9 8 7 6 5 4 3 2

CONTENTS

PREFACE

This book presents a statement of my past attempts to understand what academic psychology is about. By *academic psychology*, I mean the psychology pursued and taught at universities. That is, I think of academic psychology as the pursuit of psychological knowledge for its own sake, at least in the first instance. I accept that this academic pursuit is not unrelated to the professional psychology practiced in clinics, schools, and other places where problems of conduct must be dealt with immediately. However, my primary concern here is with the academic discipline.

As I recall, my attempts to understand what psychology is about began in 1971 when I was an undergraduate at the University of Auckland in New Zealand. Of course I had tried to understand psychology before that time, but trying to understand psychology is different from trying to understand what psychology is about. My attempt to understand psychology as an undergraduate was a matter of trying to understand the psychology presented in textbooks and in prescribed journal articles. However, trying to understand what psychology is about amounts to finding a detailed explanation of why we need a psychology at all. It requires that we build a step-by-step account of the domain and problem that ordinary knowledge bequeaths to a pristine science of psychology.

In 1971 when I first started puzzling over the problem of what psychology is about, I could not have written this book. But by 1979, when I graduated with a PhD in psychology, I had an intuitive grasp of the core of what I have written now. Still, I could not have written the book then either. I had to do a great deal of reading and thinking first. Finally, in late 1985, I made a commitment to write for 3 months. If I had not made that commitment, I would still be reading and thinking, because, certainly, I had taken on an endless task. The pressure of other work forced me to put the manuscript aside after 3 months. I began writing again late in 1986, and this time, I finished the first draft. Late in 1987, I worked on the manuscript once more and tried to sharpen the argument and improve the prose. I have now let the manuscript go, and I believe that it represents the best statement I can make at this point in time about what I consider to be the continuing process of trying to understand the essential nature of psychology's special domain and problem.

The title of this book, *Beyond Behaviorism,* will surprise some of my colleagues, because most of them probably think of me as a behaviorist. In fact, I am not a behaviorist in the generally-accepted sense. As I understand it, *behaviorism* usually means a stimulus–response psychology associated with reductionist and mechanistic presuppositions about the nature of psychology's subject matter and task. In this book, I insist that psychology must abandon behaviorism. It might seem that this insistence is old-fashioned because other contributors to the literature of psychology have already frequently and vigorously denounced behaviorism. The difficulty arises because behaviorism is more easily denounced than abandoned. Indeed, we can find behavioristic presuppositions in the very psychology that openly rejects behaviorism. These presuppositions invite further inquiry. Should psychology persist with its behavioristic orientation? If not, why not? In this book, I insist that psychology as a whole is still behaviorist in orientation and that we should explicate and fully abandon our behavioristic presuppositions.

Psychologists also need to move psychology beyond behaviorism in the sense of desisting from dismissing a genuine alternative to behaviorism *as* behaviorism. This alternative is known as *radical behaviorism.* Despite its name, it turns out that it is not a behaviorism at all. That is, radical behaviorism is not a behaviorism in the commonly understood sense of a stimulus–response psychology. However, the name *radical behaviorism* leads many psychologists to equate radical behaviorism with the behaviorism they ostensibly reject. In doing so, they reject radical behaviorism, and they miss the contribution it makes to psychology as a whole. In fact, radical behaviorism has much in common with other critiques that have unsuccessfully sought to turn academic psychology away from stimulus--response behaviorism and toward a psychology of human action. I know that many psychologists will greet this possibility with disbelief, if not mirth. I can ask them only to consider the present argument, which emphasizes the contribution of radical behaviorism to the task of developing a psychology of human action. As I understand it, radical behaviorism centers on and explores the ramifications of one key idea—that the subject matter of psychology consists of human action and that human action constitutes a subject matter in its own right. In this book I try to show that much follows from this key idea and that none of it is consistent with stimulus–response behaviorism.

I want to comment on the way that I have written this book. First, I do not present this book as a finished product, but as a provisional report of work in progress. I hope other psychologists will consider the book with the same constructive attitude that I have taken in writing it. I hope they will take from this book whatever they find useful in building a conceptually systematic science of human conduct. Second, I have tried to write the book in a way that connects with nonspecialist knowledge. My insistence on making that connection reflects my belief that a genuine science of psychology will emerge step-by-step out of ordinary (i.e., nonspecialist) knowledge and that it will provide a compelling account of this step-by-step emergence. Third, I have referred to many papers that most psychologists would probably consider to be dated. It seems to me that many of these older papers contain more wisdom about the problems under discussion than any knowledge I have encountered in some of the more recent literature. I refer to these papers in part to draw the reader's attention to them. But I also refer to them in order to highlight the fact that a small minority of psychologists has long considered the issues raised here but has been unsuccessful in changing our collective attitude. Fourth, I accept that this book omits various areas of scholarship and research that could bear on its argument. An example is the philosophic literature on the theory of action. Another example is the literature of philosophic anthropology. The fact is that I have written this book as a psychologist and as a psychologist whose home base has been the literature of operant psychology. In a domain as vast and diverse as human conduct, there is only so much that one person can do. I freely admit that I have not done everything that could be done. But I hope that what I have written is sufficiently intelligible and interesting that it will invite other scholars to extend the argument.

Many people have contributed to the writing of this book, although most of them have done so unknowingly. My intellectual debt to W. F. Day, C. B. Ferster, I. Goldiamond, M. Sidman, and B. F. Skinner is obvious to those readers who know their work. Other sources of my current understanding of what psychology is about are apparent from the references I cite. In this connection, I want to thank W. K. Honig for his stimulating commentary on the first draft of this book.

CHAPTER 1

Psychology as Protoscience

LITERATURE OF CRITICISM

Academic psychology has a literature of criticism that is diverse and far-reaching. This literature contains criticisms of specific problems, such as the lack of cumulative progress in psychology (e.g., Koch, 1975; Leary, 1980), the flight from naturalism (e.g., Schoenfeld, 1972), the abundance of jargonized commonsense masquerading as scientific knowledge (e.g., Bode, 1922; Joynson, 1974, pp. 6–13; Shwayder, 1965, pp. 4–5), and the lack of relevance to practical concerns and to daily life (e.g., Ades, 1981; Gaylord-Ross, 1979). The literature contains criticisms of specific fields, such as developmental psychology (e.g., Cairns & Valsiner, 1984), cognitive psychology (e.g., Allport, 1975; Sampson, 1981), social psychology (e.g., Cartwright, 1979; Elms, 1975), and educational psychology (e.g., Ausubel, 1968; Shulman, 1970). The literature also contains criticisms of particular approaches to psychological inquiry, including behaviorism (e.g., MacKenzie, 1977), cognitivism (e.g., Coulter, 1982; Hamlyn, 1981; Skinner, 1977), and humanistic psychology (e.g., Koch, 1971), as well as criticisms of psychology as a whole (e.g., Howard, 1986; Hudson, 1975; Giorgi, 1976, 1984; Joynson, 1974; Koch, 1959, 1971, 1973, 1981; MacLeod, 1965; Sarason, 1981).

The literature of criticism does not concern particular techniques and theories. Rather, it concerns the goals, methods, and achievements of psychology. More fully stated, it concerns what psychology is about, what it is trying to do, how it proposes to do it, and how much progress it has made so far. The literature of criticism expresses uncertainty and despair among psychologists concerning these matters. Indeed, the literature suggests a discipline that is replete with confusion, malaise, doubt, disillusionment, and mutual antagonism, and which lacks enthusiasm, commitment, and shared direction.

The literature of criticism does not enjoy favor in academic psychology. On the contrary, psychologists most often ignore it. Moreover, introduc-

1

tory textbooks present psychology as a science making indubitable progress. There is no space dedicated to the doubt and despair evident in parts of the psychological literature. Perhaps such doubt and despair have no place at an introductory level. Yet, the neglect is more widespread. This is evident if only because academic psychology seems to continue as before, unaffected by the criticism. Indeed, the conservative majority often seem to dismiss the critics as a disaffected minority.

For whatever reason, the critical literature has had little effect on the academic mainstream. Some writers (e.g., Carver, 1978; Gergen, 1978; Mishler, 1979; Sherif, 1979) have noted that, despite massive criticism, traditional practices have persisted in psychology. Examples include the persistence of group-statistical research designs, the persistence of a decontextualized approach to human behavior, and the persistence of a commitment to physiological reductionism. The persistence of traditional practices does not reflect the recency of the criticisms. The relevant literature dates back to the early years of this century and gives psychology a long tradition of self-criticism. Of course, the unimpressive effect of this literature is open to interpretation. It might reflect the vacuity of the criticisms. Perhaps the critics do constitute only a disaffected minority that the mainstream can ignore with impunity. At the other extreme, perhaps psychology has become impervious to criticism, persisting in traditional practices despite much criticism. Either way, the criticisms need to be addressed in order to clear the way for a more constructive psychology. Ignoring the criticisms and continuing regardless can only permit doubts to linger about the nature, purpose, and achievements of our discipline.

DISUNITY

This book does not merely add to the literature of criticism. Psychology does not need another critique that offers no alternative to traditional practices. The present purpose is more constructive. It is to suggest a framework that offers psychology the core of unity it currently lacks. This lack of unity warrants discussion because it is at the heart of psychology's difficulties. The following discussion should establish the reasons why psychology urgently needs a unifying framework.

Many critics (e.g., Balz, 1940; Giorgi, 1976, 1985; Leary, 1980; Lee, 1985; Lichtenstein, 1980) have noted a lack of unity in psychology. This lack of unity does not amount to incompatible interpretations of particular experiments. More fundamental than that, it has to do with what counts as the subject matter of psychology, with what questions we should ask about this subject matter, with how we should go about finding answers to these questions, with the status of existing psychological knowledge, and with whether psychology can be a science. Psychologists do not agree upon these basic matters. They do not share a common understanding about the subject matter, task, method, and achievements of psychological inquiry. Critics refer to this lack of shared understanding when they speak of psychology's disunity.

Disunity in psychology does not amount to a lack of the theoretical integration that follows the subsumption of two or more laws under a single theory. Koch (1978) denied psychology the possibility of unity on the grounds that no discipline had achieved unity in this sense. But the theoretical integration of laws under a theory is an advanced stage of inquiry far beyond the current scope of psychology. Some writers (e.g., DeLucca, 1979; Skinner, 1972, pp. 295–313; Spence, 1956, pp. 18–19) have explained that in this sense, theory follows the identification of critical variables and the subsequent formulation of two or more laws. An example is Newton's integration of the laws of planetary motion and mechanics. Writers who deplore disunity in psychology mean something more preliminary than theoretical integration in this advanced sense. Giorgi (1985) gave the term *concinnity* to unity in the preliminary sense of having a shared perspective that allows us to integrate otherwise disparate findings. This shared perspective would permit us to relate the results of diverse projects to each other in a meaningful way. Psychology lacks unity in this preliminary sense. It has no unifying theme or organizing principle that will permit integration of diverse findings and guide further inquiry. Without this unifying theme, the work of individual psychologists cannot contribute to a cumulative body of knowledge of a common domain. Without that convergence of the contributions of individuals, psychology will not reach the level of conceptual development at which theoretical integration of two or more laws becomes an issue.

Some psychologists will deny that psychology has fundamental disunity. In defending this view, they might point to the apparent unity evinced over recent years in a leading journal of academic psychology—*The Psychological Review*. But the unity they point to in that journal is the unity of the mainstream. It is the unity of the orthodoxy of academic psychology. To equate that particular perspective with the whole of psychology is either to define that perspective as psychology or to ignore alternative perspectives or both. Furthermore, it ignores the scholarship of many critics who believe that, as a whole, psychology lacks unity.

This lack of a shared understanding about basic issues exists not only in psychology as a whole but also in the special areas of psychology. For example, Elms (1975) commented that although research in social psychology has increased in volume and complexity, our understanding of social behavior has not improved because social psychologists do not share a common outlook on their common domain. Elms referred to the work of Shulman and Silverman (1972), who studied citation indices to determine whether social psychologists share any unifying orientations. They concluded that only a small fraction of research in social psychology suggests the coordination that a common conceptual framework would provide. Cartwright (1979) also acknowledged the lack of theoretical integration in social psychology, as did Bethlehem (1984) and Farr (1978). Critics (e.g., Cairns & Valsiner, 1984; Masters, 1981) have offered similar criticisms of developmental psychology. In short, lack of unity has been noted in some specialized areas of psychology as well as in psychology as a whole.

As some writers (e.g., Giorgi, 1976; Mulkay, 1978) have pointed out, the issue of disunity in psychology is important because genuine sciences, such as physics and genetics, have a core of unity. In this sense, unity consists of agreements about many laws, about the results of many kinds of experiments, about what counts as a scientific explanation, and about how, in principle, to solve remaining problems and uncertainties. Agreements on these basic matters exist alongside disagreements about specific hypotheses because basic unity does not preclude diversity in other respects. The advanced sciences are not bland homogeneities without theoretical controversies and interesting problems. But, agreement on basic matters lets the work of many independent investigators converge in a single, advancing stream. Individual investigators can use the procedures, formulations, and findings of other investigators in their own work, and as a result they can relate their own procedures, formulations, and findings to a common framework. In consequence, the patchwork contributions of many independent investigators can converge into a single advancing stream. Psychology lacks unity of this kind. There are few if any definitions, principles, and explanations that all psychologists agree upon. Moreover, there is no common body of data that all psychologists agree they must deal with. As we shall see, psychologists do not agree on what counts as the proper subject matter of psychology.

SCIENCE OR PROTOSCIENCE?

Because it lacks unity, psychology is unlike the other sciences. Accordingly, the scientific status of psychology is open to doubt. Of course, introductory textbooks routinely describe psychology as a science. However, behind the impression given by that description there is much to discuss (e.g., Howard, 1986; Koch, 1974; Leary, 1980; Lipsey, 1974; Sloane, 1945; Snoeyenbos & Putney, 1980).

Those who defend academic psychology easily dismiss the debate about the scientific status of psychology as a matter for philosophers. Yet we should not dismiss the question of whether or not psychology is a science so quickly. Ziman (1978, p. 158) explained that scientific knowledge is our most reliable guide to action, such that in matters of science, scientists rightly claim authority unquestioned by nonscientists. Therefore, the issue of whether psychology is a science is important, not only for theoreticians but also for policymakers and practitioners. Do psychologists have access to special knowledge not available to nonpsychologists? Is that knowledge sufficiently reliable and extraordinary so that it counts unequivocally as scientific? Is it sufficiently reliable and extraordinary so that we can look to psychologists for information held with some confidence and that is not already available through ordinary (i.e., nonscientific) means? These are some of the questions we must address when we consider the scientific status of psychology. The questions of interest do not concern the sophistication of our statistics or the inaccessibility of our formulations to a nontechnical audience. Rather, the questions of interest are concerned with whether we have constructed formulations that both probe beyond what is already available to ordinary observers and survive the test of replication by a critical audience. In other words, the questions of interest center on the issue of whether psychology can offer a body of extraordinary and reliable knowledge. These are questions we cannot dismiss as beyond the concerns of psychologists.

Many critics have argued that psychology does not count as a science. William James (1892/1961, p. 335) insisted that the psychology of his time only amounted to the hope of a science. It was no more advanced than physics before Galileo or chemistry before Lavoisier. Sloane (1945) offered a similar conclusion. He said that modern psychology has produced a psychology no more advanced than the Aristotelian–Thomistic psychology of scholastic times. The recent literature suggests no change in how critics view the matter. For example, MacLeod (1965) described the idea of psychology being a science as a delusion, Fiske (1979) denied that psychology is yet a science, and Skinner (1980, pp. 71-72) concluded that there is not much science in modern psychology. Other critics (e.g., Cantril, Ames, Hastorf, & Ittelson, 1949; Koch, 1971; MacLeod, 1965; Sherif, 1979) have insisted that psychology is scientistic rather than scientific, in adopting the trappings of science—the laboratories, terminology, and mathematics—without yielding the fruitful concepts and the core of well-replicated findings that characterize the genuine sciences. These denials of scientific status are consistent with psychology's disunity concerning basic matters. After all, one mark of a science is a core of unity concerning past achievements and future strategies. How can psychology be judged as a science if it does not have a core of unity about these basic matters? Under these circumstances, we must argue the point and not just assume that psychology is a science.

Perhaps the critics should give psychology more time to develop a body of reliable and extraordinary knowledge. In fact, Spence (1956, pp. 1–4) acknowledged and rejected this possibility long ago. Certainly, as Lichtenstein (1980) remarked, it seems reasonable to ask how long we should go on accepting this explanation for the lack of unity and progress in psychology. In any case, if youth is a chronological matter, then psychology does not have a case, for it has been a science by declaration for over a century. Of course, the date of origin is controversial because psychologists have repeatedly founded psychology anew. This has been noted by some critics (e.g., Giorgi, 1976; Mischel, 1976). The date of origin that is most often accepted is 1879, when Wundt established the first psychology laboratory. This date of origin makes scientific psychology a century old. Unlike psychology, the other sciences were well-advanced by the end of their first centuries. An example is genetics, which was named early this century by Bateson and has made unequivocal progress since that time. Psychology does not offer reliable and extraordinary knowledge of the kind offered by genetics, physics, and the other advanced sciences. It does not have the core of consensus that these genuine sciences enjoy. In short, chronological youth excuses psychology's lack of progress only in the eyes of those blind to the progress made in the genuine sciences during their first centuries.

Consistent with doubts about the scientific status of psychology, some writers (e.g., Gaylord-Ross, 1979; Giorgi, 1976; Watson, 1973) have described psychology as preparadigmatic. By *preparadigmatic,* they mean a discipline lacking the core of unity that characterizes the advanced sciences. An alternative and perhaps less controversial term is *protoscience.* This means a discipline in the process of becoming a science. The term *paradigmatic,* though widely used by psychologists (e.g., Burgess, 1972; Palermo, 1971; Snoeyenbos & Putney, 1980; Staats, 1981; Warren 1971) is controversial (e.g., Shapere, 1964) and it seems better to avoid it. A protoscience, though lacking the conceptual unity of genuine science, lays the foundations out of which unity can emerge. As Farrell (1978) noted, although confusion and lack of discernible progress plagued chemistry between 1700 and 1770, the work during that time laid the ground for Lavoisier's breakthrough and, with it, the emergence of chemistry as a science. In short, the current state of confusion in psychology contradicts claims that psychology is a science but it does not preclude the eventual achievement of that status. Taking an optimistic stance, we might count psychology as a protoscience, properly engaged in tentatively exploring and clarifying the general nature of its domain. This stance is optimistic because we will know that psychology is currently protoscientific only if it eventually becomes genuinely scientific.

For the present, let us assume that psychology is properly described as a protoscience. The primary task of this discipline is to isolate and explore the rudiments of a common outlook on a common domain. We need to acknowledge the bootstraps nature of this task that faces a protoscience. We will know if protoscientific inquiries have been successful only once a genuine science emerges. Yet the emergence of a genuine science requires a common outlook that will permit independent investigators to contribute to a single, advancing body of reliable and extraordinary knowledge. Without that common outlook, the work of independent investigators will not converge in a single, advancing stream. That is, the bootstraps nature of the task arises because we cannot know we have a fruitful, common outlook until a body of reliable and extraordinary knowledge emerges. And such a body of knowledge cannot emerge until we have found a fruitful, common outlook.

This book presents the view that the rudiments of a common outlook are available amid the confusion and conflict that currently plague psychology. Identifying this core of unity will not solve the problems of psychology by immediately making the discipline unequivocally science. But at least this conceptual core holds the promise of identifying the strategic problems that might yield the reliable and extraordinary knowledge we expect from a science. This book also presents the view that a small body of reliable knowledge is already available. This body of knowledge is available outside the mainstream of psychology, and it is not widely recognized as psychological knowledge because of the blinkers of behaviorism. To recognize this body of psychological knowledge as such, academic psychology will have to identify and abandon these intellectual blinkers. In doing so, it may recognize both the potential already available for a common outlook on a common domain and the body of reliable knowledge we already have.

CHAPTER 2

Subject Matter

THE PROBLEM

The stated subject matter of psychology has changed historically. Early this century, most psychologists agreed that psychology was about human consciousness. By the 1920s, behavior had replaced consciousness. Watson (1913) heralded this shift in stated subject matter with his paper entitled "Psychology as the Behaviorist Views it." Other psychologists before Watson had also argued that behavior was the proper subject matter of psychology. An example is McDougall (1912) who defined psychology as the science of the behavior of living things. Another example is Angell (1913) who said that the word *behavior* represented the phenomena of interest to psychologists better than *consciousness.* Still, as Burnham (1968) noted, Watson excited much interest with his vigorous presentation, made when many psychologists were well-disposed toward the concept of a science of behavior. Psychology remained behaviorally oriented until the 1960s when the stated subject matter changed again. Psychology became the science of cognitive processes and the mainstream rejected behavior as its subject matter.

The shift in stated subject matter from consciousness through behavior to cognitive processes seems simple enough. But the apparent simplicity is misleading. For one thing, contemporary psychologists do not agree that their subject matter consists of cognitive processes. A minority continues to insist that psychology is about behavior. Second, despite the apparent simplicity of saying that psychology's subject matter consists of cognitive processes, psychologists find it difficult to specify that subject matter. A convincing explanation of why psychologists should study this subject matter and of how it is linked to observables has not been provided. In this respect, the concept of cognitive processes has something in common with the concept of behavior, which has received ample criticism (e.g., Coulter, 1982; Hamlyn, 1953; Roback, 1923) for its imprecision and ambiguity. In sum, there is disagreement, confusion, uncertainty, and vagueness concerning what psychology is about.

Uncertainty about the general nature of psychological phenomena brings psychology into disrepute. We must wonder about a putative science that cannot tell us what it is about with some precision, clarity, and consensus. We must also wonder whether disagreement, uncertainty, and evasiveness about psychology's subject matter suggests that psychologists do not know what they are trying to do. Pratt (1939, p. 1) raised this possibility long ago. In addition, the disagreement about the subject matter of psychology means that debate about other issues rests on an uncertain foundation. These other issues include the distinction between psychology and physiology, the possibility of physiological reductionism, the nature of psychological units, the relative contributions of phylogeny and ontogeny, and the place that inferential statistics have in psychological inquiry. Debate about these issues presupposes that psychologists can state the general nature of their domain. Furthermore, disagreement concerning the subject matter of psychology blocks the cumulative development of knowledge we expect from a science. This cumulative development depends on working agreements about definitions and rules of procedure among investigators. These agreements permit the work of many individuals to converge into a single advancing stream of knowledge. Psychologists need to construct a working agreement about the general nature of their subject matter. At best, disagreement about the latter issue is unlikely to facilitate progress. At worst, it seems likely to engender such confusion, ill-feeling, and controversy that progress becomes impossible.

The problem of what counts as psychology's subject matter, once pushed beyond nominations of consciousness, behavior, or cognitive processes, is a problem that most psychologists ignore. This neglect is evident in the persistence of queries and complaints about the problem. Early papers that typify this persistence include those by Hunter (1932), Balz (1940), and Walker (1942). Despite this early interest, the problem remains unresolved, and Feigl (1959) described it as psychology's greatest embarrassment. Indeed, comments by more recent contributors (e.g., Franck, 1982; Heinen & Stafford, 1979; Mueller, 1979) underscore the persistence of this problem. The neglect of this problem is also unmistakable in textbooks on research methodology. As Kvale (1976a) pointed out, these textbooks typically consider only the quantitative treatment of data and neglect the prior qualitative issue of what counts as a psychological datum. Certainly, psychologists rarely include the problem of defining their subject matter as a methodological problem. In traditional terms, only quantitative problems are deemed methodological problems. That is, methodological problems have to do with collecting data and not with thinking about the general nature of the subject matter. Yet clarifying the general nature of the subject matter is a methodological problem, if only because issues of *how* to measure follow qualitative clarification of *what* to measure. The logical priority of the qualitative problem has been noted by several writers (e.g., Cantril, Ames, Hastorf, & Ittelson, 1949; Platt, 1964; Somerville, 1941). But these discussions have had little or no impact on psychology as a whole.

LIMITATIONS

When stating the subject matter of psychology certain limitations need to be acknowledged at the outset. For one thing, we can never state any subject matter exhaustively. An exhaustive statement would require full and complete knowledge. Scientific knowledge is always open to correction and is never full and complete. As discussed by several writers (e.g., Bunge, 1967, p. 5; DeLucca, 1979; Ziman, 1978, pp. 92-93), it is fallible knowledge. This limitation can only block efforts to improve discussion about the general nature of psychology's subject matter if we neglect it. Fallibility is neglected when we dismiss approximations toward a common outlook on the grounds of their incompleteness. But, an initial framework is inevitably incomplete. It can only become more detailed and comprehensive as conceptual and empirical work progresses within it. To dismiss a promising framework solely because it does not answer all of our questions is to engage in something other than scientific inquiry.

A second limitation is the tendency to prescribe subject matters through nomination. Woodworth (1930) noted this prescriptive tendency. He preferred to look for a comprehensive definition of psychology to explain the work psychologists actually do. But there are limitations imposed upon this strategy by the lack of conceptual unity in psychology. If a psychologist is a person who teaches and conducts research in a psychology department, then the work of psychologists includes much we might intuitively exclude from the category of the psychological. Consistent with that, some critics (e.g., Hunter, 1932; Luchins & Luchins, 1965, p. 351; MacLeod, 1965) have noted that much inquiry conducted in university departments of psychology could be pursued in other departments of academic inquiry. The present argument takes a strategy different from that recommended by Woodworth. It looks for categories given in ordinary knowledge that are considered to be psychological, as opposed to physical, biological, or sociological. This strategy does not prescribe the subject matter through nomination, as in the declaration that psychology is about behavior or cognitive processes. Rather, it begins in a list of categories found in the way we ordinarily talk about human conduct. Chapter 3 begins to develop this alternative approach.

A third limitation is the problem of identifying a subject matter upon which all psychologists agree. This causes difficulty because only individual psychologists can contribute to the search for a clear statement of the psychological domain. Yet no single individual can state a consensual subject matter, since, by definition, consensus reflects a collective opinion. Individuals can offer statements for other psychologists to scrutinize and improve on, and a statement found useful by many psychologists might, through that usefulness, eventually enjoy consensual acceptance. Still, such acceptance will require time and sustained collective effort.

STRATEGIC PROBLEMS

Work aimed at explicating the general nature of psychological phenomena, if successful, would end in the identification of a strategic problem in psychology. A strategic problem is a problem that can guide inquiry beyond what ordinary knowledge already reveals. Chemistry found such a problem when it focussed on the weights of substances, and mechanics, when it focussed on times and distances. A strategic problem separates relevant from irrelevant variables and helps investigators uncover the invariant connections in the domain of interest. It directs the inquiry that results in the formulation of laws. This insistence upon a connection between strategic problems and laws will not be well-received by psychologists who reject the search for psychological laws as behaviorism. On the contrary, Franck (1982) explicitly said that psychology must find the laws of its domain if it is to be considered a science. Other writers (e.g., Sidman, 1960; Skinner, 1953, pp. 3–42, 1972, pp. 295–313) have offered the same insistence less explicitly. Certainly, comments by writers outside psychology (e.g., Bunge, 1967, p. 15; Feibleman, 1972b, p. 3; Russell, 1931, p. 45) strongly suggest that a discipline does not count as a science until it has uncovered the laws of its domain. Uncovering these laws depends on, and signals, the finding of a strategic problem.

Finding a strategic problem, logically, if not necessarily chronologically, precedes empirical inquiry. Somerville (1941) described the process in an account that deserves more attention. Ordinary knowledge hands over its *difficulties* to pristine sciences, but these sciences must formulate their own *problems*. Ordinary difficulties might need much scrutiny and recasting before orderly empirical solutions are possible. Somerville noted that ordinary difficulties are overcome only when the problem is properly formulated, or alternatively, once the proper problem is formulated. Other writers have referred to this matter as the problem of problemization (Cantril et al., 1949), the problem of finding the heart of the problem (Northrop, 1947, pp. 1–2), or the problem of finding answerable questions (Eisenberg, 1960). Identifying the proper problem is difficult. But it is also crucial, because no amount of empirical work will produce a body of reliable and extraordinary knowledge in the absence of a strategic problem.

Some psychologists will reject the logical priority given to formulating a strategic problem. The philosophic work required by the problem of problemization is not attractive to psychologists, most of whom seem more concerned with collecting data and designing experiments than with questions about the foundations of psychology. The neglect of these philosophic questions is more prevalent than it might seem. Certainly, critics (e.g., Chein, 1972, p. 54; Glass & Kliegl, 1983; Kvale, 1973; Lichtenstein, 1980; Llewelyn & Kelly, 1980; Roback, 1923) have long noted the widespread neglect of the basic matters on which empirical research in psychology is founded. These basic matters include the nature of units of description, the relation between psychology and other disciplines, and the relation between practice and research. To the critics, many psychologists seem unconcerned about having a systematic position with respect to these basic matters. More fundamentally, most psychologists seem unconcerned about finding a common outlook on a common domain that can provide an integrative framework for psychological inquiry. Stated less categorically, work directed toward clarifying the general nature of the subject matter of psychology does not have a prominent place in psychology. The lack of widespread interest in work of this kind doubtless reflects a desire to dissociate psychology from philosophy and, in the process, to make psychology scientific. In turn, this desire suggests a conception of science as dustbowl empiricism, devoid of any philosophic significance. It also suggests that the interdependence of philosophic and empirical techniques in science has gone unnoticed.

Philosophic problems and techniques have an indispensable and unavoidable place in scientific inquiry. Empirical work (observing) and philosophic work (reasoning) properly belong together. One kind of work serves and informs the other. In doing empirical work, we find out more about the world by looking at it. Empirical work deals directly with the subject matter. It engages us in making, recording, tabulating, and reporting our observations; in designing and conducting experiments; and in inventing new instruments of observation. Empirical work checks our formulations against the subject matter and enlarges the range of phenomena we have collectively observed. In doing philosophic work, we find out more about the world by clarifying the meaning of what we already know. Philosophic work consists of the reasoning used in such activities as stating research problems precisely, checking the internal consistency of formulations, finding contradictions and ambiguities, clarifying confusions, explicating unspoken assumptions, and deducing new statements from old ones. In these activities, we scrutinize our formulations. Thus the object of philosophic work is what we say and write about the subject matter rather than the subject matter itself. It clarifies our existing formulations and explicates their unnoticed implications. Stated otherwise, philosophic work within the context of scientific inquiry explicates and examines what we already know about the subject matter. Both empirical and philosophic work are required when we seek to expand our reliable knowledge of nature.

Psychologists who persist in taking an antiphilosophic stance might do well to consider Woodger's (1929/1967, p. 37) comment that Galileo was accused of having read more philosophy than physics. They might also consider Hutten's (1956, p. 13) comment that Mach's critique of the concepts of Newtonian physics eventually led to the relativity theory. In general, initiating and elaborating an experimental science of physics was as much a philosophic undertaking as anything else. Indeed, philosophic problems are unavoidable in science, as some writers (e.g., Bunge, 1959, p. 9; Kantor, 1969; Van Melsen, 1961, p. 13; Woodger, 1929/1967, pp. 1–3) have noted. We need to accept the task of dealing with these problems as an ongoing part of psychology. To denigrate inquiries that concern fundamental issues in psychology as mere philosophy is to miss the problem that psychology faces. In the end, that problem is a problem of natural philosophy. As Shimp (1984) indicated, the problem is to construct a theory, however rudimentary, of the subject matter of psychology.

CONCLUSION

We need to identify a strategic problem in the difficulties that ordinary knowledge raises about human conduct and experience. But, first, we need to accept the fact that the problem of what counts as our subject matter is a proper methodological problem. Acceptance seems unlikely or, at least, not easily won. As implied earlier, critics (e.g., Cantril et al., 1949; Chein, 1972; Koch, 1951; Kvale, 1973; Roback, 1923) have long deplored the avoidance of fundamental matters concerning the subject matter and task of psychology. Such critics have remained a small and unpopular minority, and their recommendations with respect to the importance of philosophic inquiry have had little effect on the work of most psychologists. Long ago, Bode (1922) insisted that psychology is obliged to define its problem and its task. Yet, psychology continues to evade this obligation and to devalue the work of those few psychologists who raise questions about the foundations of the discipline. Many psychologists seem to think they can solve the problems of psychology by continuing as before. But to believe that, is to overlook the nature of the problem; the problem of problemization. It is to find a strategic problem that will allow psychological inquiry to produce a body of reliable and extraordinary knowledge. James (1892/1961, p. 335) noted long ago that to find the heart of psychology's problem requires philosophic work such as that done by Galileo in physics and Lavoisier in chemistry. If psychologists continue as before, this philosophic work will remain undone. At least, whatever work is done will have little impact on mainstream practices. Psychologists not only need to conduct philosophic work aimed at clarifying the general nature of their special domain, but also to construct a professional environment in which such work will flourish.

CHAPTER 3

Origins

INTRODUCTION

When we discuss the scientific status of psychology, we presuppose an understanding of what science is. Without that understanding, we cannot deny or affirm the scientific status of any discipline. At least, we cannot make a reasoned presentation of our denials and affirmations. Consequently, we now need to explicate what we regard as science. Earlier in the discussion of unity in the sciences, some part of the required explication was offered. This chapter adds to this earlier discussion by developing the minimal notion that any discipline we deem to be a science offers some knowledge that is both reliable and extraordinary. The chapter discusses what is meant by "reliable and extraordinary knowledge." It also discusses the origin of this knowledge in ordinary knowledge and the origin, in principle at least, of scientific psychology in ordinary psychology.

EXTRAORDINARY AND RELIABLE KNOWLEDGE

Scientific knowledge is extraordinary knowledge. It is knowledge of phenomena beyond ordinary observation. Probing beyond ordinary observation is part of what we ask and expect of a science. We expect a science to tell us something more than we already know. We expect it to help us see something we would otherwise miss. Some writers (e.g., Shwayder, 1965, p. 3; Ziman, 1978, p. 159) have acknowledged this expectation. Certainly, as Feibleman (1972b, p. 51) noted, the sciences reveal much that ordinary observation cannot reveal. For example, ordinary observation does not reveal that oxygen exists or that water is a composition of two gases. Moreover, ordinary observation does not prepare us for seeing how water, metals, and rubber behave under high altitudes, heavy pressures, and other extraordinary conditions. In revealing something beyond what ordinary observation can already tell us, science provides a body of extraordinary knowledge.

If extraordinary knowledge is what we ask and expect of a science, then a discipline must probe beyond ordinary things to count as a science. But extraordinary knowledge is not enough by itself. After all, astrology, numerology, and witchcraft offer extraordinary knowledge, yet we do not respect them as sciences. Scientific knowledge differs from other bodies of extraordinary knowledge, if only because it is also reliable knowledge available to the anonymous observer and indifferent to whoever makes the observation; knowledge in relation to which all trained observers are equivalent. Reliability is established when an experiment has been replicated across experimenters and across laboratories. Only repeatable experiments, and the formulations they support, belong to the reliable knowledge of a science. This aspect of the nature of scientific knowledge has been discussed by many writers (e.g., DeLucca, 1979; Feibleman, 1972b; Johnston & Pennypacker, 1980; Ziman, 1976, 1978)

Scientific knowledge, therefore, is both extraordinary and reliable knowledge. For our present purposes, let us accept that characterization of scientific knowledge as one of our assumptions. Given an acceptance of that assumption, we can proceed to discuss the origins of bodies of scientific knowledge in ordinary knowledge.

FOUNDATIONS

Scientific inquiry begins with phenomena available to ordinary observers. Before the 17th century, all observers were limited to such phenomena. They could observe only what nature presented to their unaided senses. However, scientists soon developed the means to probe beyond what is available to unaided observation. They developed instruments of observation that probed beyond what nonspecialists could already see. These instruments of observation have included microscopes, telescopes, Geiger counters, and bubble chambers. They permit observations that are otherwise impossible. Science also probes beyond ordinary observation by systematically varying the conditions of observation. This systematic variation is the essence of experimentation. Experimenters vary the conditions under which they make their observations in order to determine how different conditions affect the phenomena of interest. For example, scientists might observe the behavior of water under conditions of high altitude, heavy pressures, and so on. In the process, they see how objects behave under conditions that nature does not ordinarily present or that nature does not present to ordinary observation. In sum, science starts in what nature presents to ordinary observation but soon probes beyond ordinary phenomena with experimentation and special instruments of observation, a matter noted by many writers (e.g., Cohen, 1949, pp. 57-58; Feibleman, 1972b, pp. 127-128; van Melsen, 1961, pp. 27-28).

Just as science begins with phenomena available to ordinary observers, so it also begins with a language available to ordinary speakers. As noted by several writers (e.g., Dewey, 1930; Furnham, 1983; Hunter, 1932; Koch, 1975; Quine, 1957; Shwayder, 1965, pp. 2-4), science begins with ordinary language.

Ordinary languages—English, French, Spanish, and the like—are the languages used in the daily interchange of people living within particular geographical boundaries. These languages are acquired incidentally in the course of daily life and are more talked with than talked about. In fact, ordinary language is so much a part of daily life that we scarcely think to talk about it. These languages embody our ordinary knowledge of the world, our shared understanding of the human world, and our shared understanding of how objects and events are related and grouped together in that world. An example of this shared understanding is the kinship knowledge embodied in the terms *parent, child, uncle, grandmother,* and so forth. Another example is the moral knowledge embodied in the terms *justice, rights, blame,* and *responsibility.* A final example is the physical knowledge implicit in the terms *tin, water, fire, earth.* In mapping categories and relations, ordinary language embodies an archaic natural philosophy. This archaic philosophy, bequeathed to us by past generations, is constitutive of the human world and foundational in our efforts to probe beyond what we already know.

Investigators in the pristine sciences adopt ordinary knowledge when they use ordinary language in the early stages of inquiry. The special terms and concepts of a science emerge step-by-step out of this terminological and conceptual foundation. Refinements are required because scientific inquiry probes beyond the phenomena available to ordinary observation. In the process, some borrowed terms are redefined. For example, the meaning of the word *force* in physics differs from its meaning in nontechnical contexts, as do the meanings of *body* and *energy.* Sciences also coin new words, usually from Latin and Greek roots, to name phenomena for which no ordinary terms exist. As Savory (1967, p. 41) indicated, word-making is an integral part of science because science probes beyond the concrete particulars available to ordinary observation, and therefore demands words in addition to those already available in ordinary language.

Scientific languages differ from ordinary language because their vocabularies consist of nonordinary terms and phrases and of ordinary terms and phrases with nonordinary meanings. They retain much of ordinary grammar and the vocabulary of concrete particulars in the domain of interest. A scientific language that consists entirely of introduced terms can make no contact with the world of ordinary observation. This contact is essential, because even if scientific knowledge probes beyond what is ordinarily available, ordinary knowledge still fixes the domain of inquiry.

For example, physical knowledge is about ordinary phenomena, such as the rising of balloons, the melting of ice, and the freezing of water. Furthermore, experimentation probes beyond ordinary observation but is still pursued at the level of ordinary observation. A scientific language, then, is an adjunct of ordinary language. It grows out of and retains many features of ordinary language, even as investigators add new terms to it and change the meanings of borrowed terms.

The origin of scientific knowledge in ordinary knowledge should not be surprising. After all, specialized inquiry can begin only in some preexisting body of knowledge. Without preexisting knowledge, no one can realize that something is missing or that questions need to be asked. This preexisting knowledge, if not already specialized itself, is inevitably the ordinary (i.e., nonspecialized) knowledge available to us prior to any systematic inquiry.

PSYCHOLOGY AND ORDINARY KNOWLEDGE

The step-by-step emergence of scientific knowledge from ordinary knowledge suggests that a scientific psychology must emerge out of an ordinary psychology. This conclusion requires that we ask whether ordinary knowledge includes an ordinary psychology. Many writers (e.g., Estes, 1959; Hamlyn, 1981; Hargreaves, 1980; Joynson, 1974, pp. 1–15; McDougall, 1922; Malcolm, 1971; Rippere, 1977; Ryle, 1949/1966; Scriven, 1956) have acknowledged such a psychology, giving it various names, including *commonsense psychology, lay psychology, naive psychology, folk psychology, concepts of mind, informal psychological theory, popular psychology, the psychology of common speech,* and *knowledge of persons.* The following discussion considers the general nature of this preexisting knowledge of psychological matters.

Ordinary Psychology

Ordinary psychology consists of culturally-shared ways of talking about what we do, say, think, and feel in the conduct of our daily lives. These ways of talking depend on a psychological vocabulary that includes terms such as *writing, tracing, touching,* and *hitting,* terms such as *remembering, hoping, expecting,* and *perceiving,* terms such as *personality, mind, memory,* and *emotion,* and terms such as *happy, affable, confident,* and *enthusiastic.* In addition to these vocabulary items, ordinary psychology includes truisms such as "absence makes the heart grow fonder" and "out of sight, out of mind."

The vocabulary items and truisms of ordinary psychology are something we talk with rather than about. In ordinary conversation, we readily say that a person is mean, kind, thoughtful, and the like. We readily attribute episodes of conduct to a person's intelligence, anxiety, personality, and so forth. This manner of talking does not puzzle us. On the contrary, it informs us. Even so, ordinary psychology usually remains intuitive and unreflected. In the process of getting on with life, we generally leave reflection about ordinary psychology to others, if we even notice the possibility of reflection at all.

Ordinary psychology also includes our practical know-how concerning how to act in particular situations. To live socially means that, to some extent, we influence, predict, and understand our own actions and the actions of others. Without this practical understanding, we could not live as we do. Beyond this ordinary (i.e., nonspecialized and perhaps unformulated) understanding of conduct, we have specialized bodies of know-how in particular domains of conduct that have accumulated through direct experience of how those domains work. For example, techniques of time-management have emerged through the accumulated experience of successful executives, strategies for teaching various subject areas have emerged through the accumulated experience of teachers, and so on. The appearance of individuals with special skills in particular domains has often been accompanied or followed by collections of recipes that prescribe effective conduct within each domain. Examples from Lakein's (1973) principles of time-management include "Don't waste time regretting failures" and "Concentrate on one thing at a time." Ordinary psychology includes recipes for how to train children, how to handle depression, how to obtain buyers for merchandise, how to manage mental fatigue, and other matters of everyday concern. Much of daily life consists of following and testing these recipes in managing our own conduct and experience. For example, we follow advice about childrearing, about managing our time, about preparing for an interview, and about managing our money. Generally, these recipes and the craft psychologies they formulate have arisen through empirical trial-and-error experience of how particular domains of human conduct work. They have arisen outside and exist independently of experimental psychology.

We also have the literary psychology found in novels, plays, biographies, poems, and the like. Literary psychology uses the words and phrases of ordinary psychology but often conveys the nuances of human psychology more effectively than is possible with ordinary talk. Conveyed empathically rather than intersubjectively, the psychology implicit in literature tells us a great deal about how to understand various modes of conduct, how to recognize the significance of certain acts, and so forth. Novelists and other contributors to literary psychology construct representations that can enhance the reader's understanding of how human beings act, think, and feel. Literary psychology amplifies and extends our experience of daily life, and explores, clarifies, and extends the more mundane parts of ordinary psychological knowledge. This has been discussed by several writers (e.g., Hebb, 1974; Holt, 1962; Joynson, 1974, p. 5; Koch, 1975; McDougall, 1922; Notcutt, 1953; Sederberg & Sederberg, 1975; Swartz, 1959; Wetherell, Potter & Stringer, 1983).

As a whole, ordinary psychology is not easy to pinpoint. For one thing, it is not static. On the contrary, ordinary psychology continually changes, as seen, for example, by historical variation in recipes for childrearing and by the historical emergence of trait names. Furthermore, ordinary psychology varies across cultures. For example, as Geertz (1975) noted, the Western concept of a person as a bounded unit containing a personality, a memory, and so forth, is an unusual concept when seen in cultural perspective. Moreover, individuals within a culture talk about people with varying levels of skill. For example, the precision with which we talk about conduct and in our insightfulness in seeing the broader context of a person's actions varies. Despite these difficulties, it is clear that much ordinary knowledge of human conduct and experience exists ahead of academic psychology. Indeed, if academic psychology ceased to exist, we would carry on our daily lives unaffected. We would continue to know much about human conduct and experience, and we would pursue our lives the same as before. The question that now arises concerns how academic psychology has dealt with this preexisting knowledge of human conduct and experience.

Rejection of Ordinary Psychology

Despite its ubiquity and abundance, psychologists generally overlook or disparage ordinary psychology. This attitude reflects an unspoken assumption that only scientific knowledge is worth taking seriously. Accordingly, many psychologists seem to see their task as a matter of providing a laboratory-based account that will replace ordinary psychological knowledge. In pursuit of this task, psychologists typically offer a morass of data, while prohibiting further discussion about ordinary psychology, an orientation consistent with their antiphilosophic stance. Recipes for successful living are no less ignored or disparaged. Psychologists most often dismiss these recipes as superficial aphorisms that at best await testing by the approved methods of empirical research. Literary psychology invites similar disregard or disparagement. Most psychologists seem to regard the possibility of turning to literature for insights into the psychology of human beings as absurd.

The tradition of rejecting or ignoring ordinary psychology reflects a scientistic attitude that elevates scientific knowledge and denigrates other knowledge. This attitude unnecessarily polarizes the sciences and the humanities. Reflecting this polarization, many psychologists reject the psychological knowledge that arises from outside mainstream psychology, and many humanists deny the possibility of a scientific psychology on the grounds that such a science would threaten empathic views of human nature. But scientific knowledge is a particular kind of knowledge that does not threaten or properly compete with other kinds of knowledge. The scientistic elevation of laboratory-based knowledge leads psychologists to miss other kinds of psychological knowledge, including the ordinary knowledge out of which a scientific psychology should properly emerge. Psychologists use ordinary psychological knowledge as an unacknowledged resource, but in leaving this borrowing unacknowledged and unexamined, they fail to fully extract the insights already available about the general nature of human conduct and experience.

The special characteristics of scientific knowledge that distinguish it from other kinds of knowledge need some discussion. Scientific knowledge is, most centrally, reliable and extraordinary knowledge. It is knowledge available to the anonymous observer and knowledge beyond what is already available to the ordinary observer. These characteristics of scientific knowledge impose constraints on scientific inquiry that are not imposed on nonscientific inquiry. For example, science must deal with phenomena that occupy time or time and space; it must use consensible terminology; it must either use techniques for varying the conditions of observation or rely on the concepts and principles of other sciences that use these techniques; and so on. Science works under these constraints because it seeks formulations based on experiments that the members of a large, critical community can replicate.

In contrast, the nonscientific disciplines can proceed unfettered by demands for replication. Freedom to proceed unfettered by these demands does not make the humanities inferior to the sciences. As DeLucca (1979) explained, science and nonscience have different ends and use different means to pursue those different ends. Consistent with that, nonscientific and scientific accounts have different starting points and develop their concepts in different ways, such that no nonscientific system can overthrow any scientific system, and vice versa. Furthermore, one person can hold both scientific and nonscientific beliefs at the same time without contradiction. Moreover, neither scientific nor nonscientific knowledge can tell us all there is to know about the world. We need to recognize and clarify the differences between scientific and nonscientific knowledge. At the same time, we need to avoid elevating one kind of knowledge above the other.

Jargonized Commonsense

We must take ordinary psychology seriously if we wish academic psychology to go beyond the ordinary and on to extraordinary knowledge of psychological matters. As things stand, critics (e.g., Brener, 1980; Hargreaves, 1980; Joynson, 1974, p. 13, p. 60; Shwayder, 1965, pp. 4–5) can insist that academic psychology offers much jargonized common sense. Bode (1922) gave succinct expression to this criticism. He described psychology as "the science that explains what everyone knows in language that no one can understand" (p. 252). In other words, unlike the genuine sciences that use technical terms to express extraordinary matters, psychology commonly uses technical terms to express matters of ordinary experience. This language that gives technical expression to matters of ordinary knowledge is known as *jargon.* In particular, jargon consists of terms that sound more technical than the ideas they express.

An example is "the neurological impress method" (e.g., Kann, 1983), that refers to a procedure for increasing fluency in reading, by having student and teacher read aloud simultaneously. Another example is the term *reinforcement,* when it is used as a synonym of *reward,* rather than in its technical sense. Other examples come from Bandura's theory of self-efficacy (e.g., Bandura, 1977, 1982), which Smedslund (1978) translated into nontechnical language without loss of meaning. For instance, the central concept of self-efficacy translates as a person's belief in what they can do. Less obvious examples noted by Koch (1959) consist of adjectival extensions of the word *behavior.* Examples include *language behavior, perceptual behavior, conscious behavior, motivated behavior,* and *response behavior.* If these terms refer to anything in the domain of conduct, they must refer to actions, such as speaking, asking questions, giving instructions, looking at things, talking about one's own conduct, and so on. Terms such as *language behavior* allow psychologists to avoid giving consensible expression to the concrete particulars of interest. More specifically, these terms give unnecessary and pretentious translations of the more consensible language of action.

Jargon is not peculiar to psychology. Indeed, as Cohen (1949, pp. 85–86) remarked, the academic disciplines have long set themselves apart from ordinary thought by using jargon. Around the end of the 18th century, academics changed from Latin to the vernacular. Prior to this time, persons who spoke and wrote Latin were considered learned no matter what they said or wrote. However, academics speaking and writing in the vernacular had to do more than merely speak or write to deserve their reputations. The dual strategy of introducing nonordinary terms for ordinary ideas and of using ordinary terms in nonordinary ways set academic work apart from ordinary thought once again. The pursuit of terminological extravagances allows academic writers to talk in expert tones about matters of ordinary experience. Even worse, they can talk in expert tones about nothing that exists in nature.

CONCLUSION

There is nothing wrong in starting systematic inquiry in what we already know. That origin is expected and necessary. The pity of it is that academic psychology neither explicitly accepts the need for that origin nor explores what ordinary psychology suggests about the general nature of a scientific psychology. Certainly, we should not expect academic psychologists in one breath to denigrate ordinary knowledge and in the next to offer a jargonized version of what they denigrate. We should expect inquiry to start in what is known and deliberately to surpass it. We want an academic psychology that can provide extraordinary knowledge and that can link its extraordinary knowledge step-by-step to the foundation given in ordinary psychology. To clear the way for a psychology that pursues extraordinary knowledge, we should exorcise formulations that give merely the illusion of extraordinary knowledge. These formulations delude psychologists more than anyone else. They also obscure the need to examine ordinary psychology and to search for and find in it strategic concepts and problems. The present attitude that offers jargonized common sense while denigrating ordinary psychology ensures that an extraordinary psychology will emerge only by accident, if at all. Without clarifying ordinary psychology, we might never know with any confidence whether subsequent advances do in fact probe beyond what is already known.

Rejecting ordinary psychology is easy given the failures of academic psychology. A comment by Skinner (1971, pp. 5-6) exemplifies this rejection. Skinner compared the development of psychology with the development of physics and biology. Greek thinkers had psychological, physical, and biological theories. Modern physics and biology have surpassed this early knowledge, such that Greek scholars would require much preparation to understand modern discussions in physics and biology. Psychology has not advanced in the same way. Skinner suggested that this lack of advance indicates that something is wrong with the thinking about human conduct that past generations have bequeathed to us. There is another possibility. Perhaps we have misunderstood the nature of ordinary psychology. Perhaps we have failed to recognize the strategic concepts that ordinary psychology contains. Certainly, trying to make sense out of ordinary psychology for the purposes of scientific inquiry seems better than dismissing it as misleading and wrong. Ordinary psychology is constitutive of our experience of conduct and it is not easily set aside. We need to examine ordinary psychology. If systematic psychology is anything like the other sciences, then it will have its foundation in ordinary knowledge. It is difficult to imagine what origin a science of psychology could have other than in ordinary knowledge of psychological matters. Consequently, we need to make that origin explicit and give a step-by-step account of how our specialized knowledge grows out of its origin.

CHAPTER 4

Consensible Reality

INTRODUCTION

The notion that scientific knowledge is both reliable and extraordinary suggests a direction we might take in our attempt to clarify the subject matter of psychology. This notion suggests that psychology must identify categories that hold the promise of leading to a body of reliable and extraordinary knowledge. Identifying these strategic categories may seem impossibly difficult. Apart from anything else, the task is a bootstraps operation. We can know our categories are strategic only once work done within the constraints set by those categories produces a body of reliable and extraordinary knowledge. This complication does not free us to collect data relevant to any interesting set of categories in the hope that a body of reliable and extraordinary knowledge will eventually emerge. On the contrary, we can find further guidance in another characteristic of scientific knowledge. This characteristic deals with the origin of bodies of scientific knowledge in classifications of concrete particulars.

This chapter discusses the general nature of classification. It emphasizes that identifying or constructing a classification is the first step in bridging the gap between the concrete particulars of ordinary experience and the abstractions of science. The discussion prepares the groundwork for Chapter 5, which argues that scientific psychology properly begins in the conceptualized particulars given by the action terms of ordinary language.

CLASSIFICATION

Much classification has already been done by the past generations who have bequeathed us ordinary language. In English, all words, other than proper nouns, designate classes. *Cat* designates a kind of animal, *bus* a kind of vehicle, and so on. That is, *cat* does not name a particular cat.

Instead, it names any cat or, better, cats as a kind or class. The word names a particular cat if this designation is indicated by linguistic markers (*this cat, my cat,* etc.). All ordinary descriptions presuppose the classification embodied in ordinary language. This classification imposes a generic order on our experience, which itself is particular and concrete. We see particular cats, particular trees, particular thunderstorms, and so forth. Even so, we use class names when talking about these concrete particulars, and in the process, we identify the particulars as members of the named classes. It follows that we classify every particular in the process of talking about it. The class-particular structure of ordinary language makes this process of classification unavoidable.

Classification is the first stage of scientific inquiry. A classification embodies the classes or kinds of particulars that constitute the subject matter of a science. Such a classification is presupposed in further work, because without a classification, a science has nothing to theorize about. The classification specifies the classes of categories that require further inquiry. Subsequent formulations are meant to elaborate and deepen the description given in the initial classification. The account is elaborated by reformulating the initial classification, by identifying classes of classes, by abstracting the properties of limited classes of the subject matter, and by identifying invariant connections among these properties.

A pristine science invents a new classification or, alternatively, adopts a preexisting classification. Exemplifying the first possibility, early biologists spent much time observing and classifying the particulars of interest to them. Indeed, zoology and botany were exclusively taxonomic in their early stages. Much time and effort were spent observing and classifying because ordinary language did not provide a sufficient classification of the particulars of interest. In contrast, a domain that ordinary knowledge has already classified presents investigators with the task of identifying classes, and particularly strategic classes, that will occasion empirical work that has orderly (i.e., replicable) results. Physics exemplifies the second possibility. Ordinary language already provided a classification of the physical world (tin, water, air, and the like), and this classification provided the foundation for experimental work.

Finding an initial classification requires the inspection of particulars rather than experimentation, as well as attention to kinds rather than to amounts. In other words, finding an initial classification is the work of natural history rather than of experimental science, and it is a qualitative task rather than a quantitative one. Thus, the first task of a pristine science is not to perform experiments and to elaborate mathematical theories. It is to identify the kinds (i.e., classes) of concrete particulars that constitute the special domain of the science. The enthusiastic pursuit of experimentation and mathematics without first dealing with this qualitative task is scientistic rather than scientific. Although it might lead to an impressive collection of data, mathematics, and speculation, there will be no compelling linkage to a well-specified classification of concrete particulars. Indeed, any demand for such a linkage will typically perplex or prompt claims that providing such a linkage is properly the work of philosophers and not of psychologists.

CONCRETE PARTICULARS

A concrete particular is anything we can regard as a single entity. My computer is a concrete particular, as is my going to lunch today, the tree in my backyard, the wave that my friend just surfed in on, and the ringing of my telephone just now. So, a concrete particular is anything we can identify directly by pointing to it, by touching it, or both. At least, a concrete particular is something we can point to or touch in principle. This caveat lets us include members of extinct species, craters on the far side of the moon before 1960, and so on. These items are concrete particulars even if they are no longer observable or once were not observable. It also permits us to include phenomena that only trained observers can point to or touch, as well as phenomena we might point to or touch if we had the appropriate techniques and instruments. Concrete particulars, therefore, consist not only of the phenomena of daily life but also of phenomena available to human observers through special instruments of observation. In sum, concrete particulars consist of items we can point to or touch in principle if not in practice.

More can be said. First, concrete particulars are located in time or in time and space. Events are concrete particulars that occupy time, and objects are concrete particulars that occupy time and space. Givón (1979, pp. 314–322) explained that the distinction between events and objects has to do with the relative stability in time of these particulars. Objects, such as trees and dogs, are sufficiently stable in time so that we experience them as they occupy space. Events, such as a bolt of lightning or a wave, do not have the properties of location that we attribute to objects. They do occur in particular places, but we cannot act on them as we can act on objects (e.g., pick them up, weigh them, touch them, push them). Second, concrete particulars are unique. No tree is the same as any other tree, no thunderstorm is the same as any other thunderstorm, no human being is the same as any other human being, and so on. Indeed, each tick of a single watch is unique because no two ticks can both be simultaneous with a third tick. By definition, concrete particulars occur only once, or have only one instance. Third, concrete particulars have been called *concrete objects, individuals, individual cases, confrontable things and events,* and *singular events.* All these terms are appropriate in that a concrete particular is particular, individual, confrontable (in principle at least), and singular.

Concrete particulars are the starting points and the end points of scientific inquiry. Scientific inquiry starts in concrete particulars and constantly returns to them. Writers refer to this cycle when they say that science begins and ends in observation. This statement does not deny that presuppositions guide our observations. It just reminds us that observations are made at every stage of scientific inquiry and that scientific inquiry never divorces itself from observable phenomena. This commitment to observation is what we mean when we say that science is empirical. In empirical inquiry, we find out about the world by looking at it, and we share our discoveries by pointing to what is there. Empirical work deals with, and is in itself limited to, the concrete actualities that fill time or time and space.

We can think about single particulars (e.g., a tree) and about collections of particulars (e.g., a forest). Glass and Kliegl (1983) used the term *object field* to refer to a collection of particulars. For example, all the particulars in my room constitute an object field, as do all the events that occurred today in my graduate seminar, or all the events that occurred today on my way to work. Although these examples are bounded by narrow temporal and spatial boundaries, an object field is not necessarily this narrow. An object field might consist of all the particulars that geology takes as its domain, of all the particulars that astronomy takes as its domain, and so on. Balz (1940) used the term *nature* for the total collection of particulars. Nature, in this sense, consists of a vast collection of particulars that have existed, that now exist, and that will exist in the future.

SPECIES-INDIVIDUAL STRUCTURE

As Van Melsen (1961, p. 95) pointed out, nature has a species-individual or class-particular structure because every particular is both an individual and a member of a class or species. For example, every actual fall belongs to the class of falling, every actual dog belongs to the class of dogs, and every actual thunderstorm belongs to the class of thunderstorms. Restated, the concrete particulars identified by a classification are conceptualized particulars. They belong to classes or species, and we see them as both individuals and members of these generic entities. This dual status of particulars gives every natural domain a species-individual or class-particular structure. In fact, a species-individual structure pervades the whole of consensible reality. It pervades the whole of the reality that independent observers can share relatively unambiguously. In other words, it pervades the domain of which we can have reliable knowledge.

If we did not impose a species-individual structure on the world, we would have no reliable knowledge because reliable knowledge is knowledge of a species-individual structure. It is knowledge shared among the members of a group of investigators. The data reported by individual investigators contribute to reliable knowledge once many independent observers have observed the reported phenomenon for themselves. Other investigators cannot observe the concrete particulars observed by the original investigator. Instead, they see other concrete particulars of the same class. Thus, a single particular does not recur, but other instances of the same class do. Reliable knowledge depends, therefore, on the class-particular structure of natural phenomena.

A species-individual structure is implicit in ordinary language in that the class names of ordinary language identify classes (species, kinds) and particulars (individuals). As it emerges conceptually out of ordinary language, a pristine science automatically imposes the species-individual structure of ordinary language on its subject matter. Imposing such a structure on the domain of interest is one of our unspoken assumptions in building upon a foundation given in ordinary knowledge. It is an assumption we should make explicit, particularly when we look for guidance from the other sciences in our attempt to clarify the subject matter, task, and method of a science of psychology.

CONCRETE PARTICULARS
AND ABSTRACT ENTITIES

Consensible knowledge goes beyond concrete particulars to the abstract inhabitants of natural domains. Quine (1957) noted that these abstract entities include classes of particulars. Unlike concrete particulars, classes cannot be found in time or in time and space. We cannot point to them or touch them as we can point to or touch a concrete particular. Furthermore, classes are not collections of concrete particulars. For example, the class of cows is not a herd of cows, the class of trees is not a forest, and so on. Rather, a class is a logical, theoretical, or abstract entity whose members might consist only of possibilities. We can speak of a class that is an empty set; for example, the class of walking on the moon with bare feet. Classes, therefore, belong to our formulations and not to the concrete dimension in which we find the particulars that constitute our observables.

Even so, we can suppose that abstract entities such as classes belong to consensible reality and that consensible reality has two tiers—a concrete tier and an abstract tier. The contrary practice of equating consensible reality exclusively with the total collection of particulars assumes an ontology that does not admit the abstract inhabitants of natural domains. This practice would limit us to natural history; or to whatever we can observe without performing experiments. As well, it would deny an ontology taken by Quine (1957) from the sciences as they exist. Only the following items exist in a tentative ontology of the domain of reliable knowledge: particulars, properties of particulars, relations among properties, classes of particulars, and classes of classes, classes of classes of classes, and so on. The ontology is partially apparent in the concept of the species-individual structure of reality, which gives particulars and classes of particulars a basic place in consensible reality and in our formulations of it.

APPEARANCES AND REALITY

We sometimes distinguish between appearances and reality. This distinction is another way of acknowledging that consensible reality comprises concrete and abstract dimensions. Appearances consist of what we can point to or touch. Appearances are available to us through inspection. They comprise the vast collection of actualities that constitute the concrete dimension of a natural domain. Reality, on the other hand, consists of the underlying patterns, the hidden variables, processes, and mechanisms that connect the otherwise disconnected particulars of a natural domain.

The terms *appearance* and *reality* suggest that only the abstract parts of natural domains are real. This suggestion demerits efforts to start inquiry where it should start: in the conceptualized particulars that constitute the concrete dimension of natural domains. Theorists impatient with modest beginnings can use the distinction between appearances and reality to dismiss efforts to unequivocally link our formulations to concrete particulars. They can dismiss these efforts because they do not deal with reality. In the process, they dismiss attempts to firmly tie theoretical psychology to a set of conceptualized particulars.

Theorists of a different persuasion dismiss so-called reality as a theoretical fiction and insist that inquiry must stay with appearances. This view excludes the abstract tier of natural domains. In doing that, it removes our reason for conducting science, unless we only want to confirm what ordinary observers can already see, in which case we would support natural history but not experimental (or nonexperimental) science. The task of experimental science is to probe beyond appearances in order to illuminate the patterns that underlie fields of particulars. We cannot uncover these patterns without performing experiments because the patterns underlie all the possibilities in the domain. Observation of the domain as nature presents it to us can reveal only the current actualities and not all the possible actualities in that domain. In sum, it seems better to insist that we are after reliable knowledge, that the reliable knowledge is always of abstract entities, and that abstract entities belong to consensible reality no less than do concrete particulars. In any case, we cannot avoid abstract entities, because as long as we deal with conceptualized particulars, we make a tacit commitment to the concrete and the abstract as indissoluble dimensions of consensible reality.

OSTENSIVE DEFINITIONS

Both consensible reality and the language of science are two-tiered. One tier of a scientific language consists of terms that designate concrete particulars. The other tier consists of terms that designate abstract entities: magnitudes, relations, classes, classes of classes, and so forth. However, a scientific community does not accept every abstract term. Abstract terms that do not have some definite relation to concrete particulars are not scientific terms. As Feibleman (1972b, p. 87) insisted, science moves toward the abstract and away from the concrete, but it moves toward abstractions with some definite relation to the concrete.

Science achieves this admission of abstractions that square with the concrete through its insistence that some of the terms that constitute a scientific language must have ostensive definitions. Ostensive definitions are the foundation of any terminology. We provide an ostensive definition by pointing to a particular thing while saying its name. For example, we point to a pencil while saying "This is a pencil." More specifically, we define a term ostensively by pointing to a concrete particular that instances the class that the term names. For example, we point to actual instances of the class of pencils. Pointing is our best way of clarifying the meaning of a term and of conveying the meaning to someone else. Certainly, this is the way we teach children to name particulars. An adult names the particular and points to it, the child repeats the utterance, and so on. Curtis (1985) called this interaction *ostensive teaching.*

DeLucca (1979) discussed the fact that a term whose meaning we can convey by pointing has empirical content. Terms without empirical content convey nothing about consensible reality. Terms not susceptible to ostensive definition have empirical content but only through their connection to one or more ostensively defined terms. We can connect abstract terms that have empirical content back through deductive paths to other terms that refer to concrete particulars. In brief, terms and the concepts they represent have empirical content if connected, either directly or indirectly, to concrete particulars which we can touch or point to.

A science needs a stock of ostensively defined terms just as much as a collection of concrete particulars to theorize about. Ostensively defined terms occur at the interface of the subject matter of the science with the empirical language of the science. As Feibleman (1972b, p. 83) explained, they occur at the point where activities involving the concrete particulars of a science turn over into the empirical language of the science. In other words, ostensively defined terms connect the particulars, classes, and relations that constitute our subject matter to what we say about that subject matter; or, to our formulations of the subject matter.

A stock of terms with ostensive definitions has logical priority over terms with nominal definitions. Nominal definitions equate one term (the *definiendum*) with a longer expression (the *definiens*). An example of a nominal definition is the statement that " 'wrench' means a tool for turning nuts and bolts." The definiendum ("wrench") is equivalent in meaning to the definiens ("a tool for turning nuts and bolts") and allows us to talk about the same particular or the same class of particulars more economically. A stock of ostensively defined terms lets us offer definienda with empirical content. So, the definition of "wrench" might occasion the question "What is a nut?", whereupon we can point to a nut or to several nuts (Curtis, 1985). That is, we can define *nut* ostensively. If we could not do that or could not define *nut* nominally with a definiens consisting of other ostensively defined terms, then we could not eventually point to what we are talking about. Our statements about wrenches would have no empirical content.

Ostensive definitions are essential in science if only because abstract propositions must be restatable as questions about concrete particulars. Without such restatement, propositions about abstract entities would have no empirical significance. We cannot directly submit abstract formulations to empirical test. After all, empirical work deals only with concrete particulars, even if conceptual work probes beyond the particulars to classes, magnitudes, relations, and sets of relations (i.e., abstract entities). We distinguish untestable speculation from useful theorizing by insisting that useful theorizing depends on abstract concepts that we can unequivocally link to concrete particulars. The linkage does not depend on commonsense intuition. It must be as explicit and as compelling as possible given the state of our knowledge, which, of course, always remains fallible and open to improvement.

BACK TO CLASSIFICATION

A science begins, logically if not chronologically, in conceptualized particulars that we can define ostensively. In other words, it starts in a classification of concrete particulars. If classification is the first stage of scientific inquiry, then we must ask if psychology has a classification that will identify its subject matter and tie its theorizing to a domain of concrete particulars.

The disagreement among psychologists over their subject matter suggests that no such classification exists or that psychologists do not agree on how to classify their domain. In fact, psychologists do not even agree that classification has logical priority over theory. Indeed, they seem oblivious to the logical priority of classification. To neglect the problem of classification seems bizarre in a discipline that so urgently seeks scientific status. But this neglect is consistent with the empiricist orientation that allows psychologists to plunge into experimentation and quantification without prior qualitative work. A discipline that equates scientific progress with data, mathematics, and theory can easily dismiss the qualitative search for fundamental categories as irrelevant and unscientific. In the end, the difficulty is that psychologists equate scientific knowledge with the more obvious aspects of science—the mathematics, laboratories, technical terminology, and so forth. They want to design experiments, analyze data, and construct theory without doing the necessary preliminary work. Indeed, they do not recognize this preliminary work as scientific. Yet without a foundation in strategic categories, further work stands on uncertain foundations and is likely to require much recasting once the work of classification is done.

This neglect of the problem of classification has certainly contributed to psychology's lack of progress. In this regard, Scriven (1956) commented that psychological laws have been harder to find than physical laws. Of course, the difficulty might arise from the impossibility of finding psychological laws or from the complexity of psychological phenomena. Psychological laws also might have been harder to find because psychologists have omitted the essential preliminary of classification. Until we explore this possibility, we should not conclude that we cannot find psychological laws. In fact, without an accepted classification of psychological phenomena, we cannot agree upon the psychological phenomena for which we supposedly cannot find laws. In sum, psychology needs a classification that will identify its special domain and that will provide the foundation both for integrating what we already know and for guiding further inquiry.

CHAPTER 5

Acts as Raw Materials

BORROWED CATEGORIES

Ordinary language has an extensive vocabulary that enables us to talk about the acts, feelings, traits, needs, and other characteristics of persons. Psychologists accepted this psychological vocabulary when they adopted terms such as *reading, running, touching,* and *writing,* terms such as *thinking, hoping, recognizing,* and *remembering,* and terms such as *intelligence, memory, personality,* and *emotion.* This borrowed vocabulary provides categories not invented by psychologists but instead bequeathed ready-made by past generations of the ordinary (i.e., nonspecialized) community. The categories identify and roughly classify a domain of particulars ahead of systematic inquiry, and intuitively, this domain counts as psychological. Some writers (e.g., Dewey, 1930; Ryle, 1949/1966, p. 57, p. 302) have explicitly claimed this domain as psychological. Certainly, it is hard to imagine what other domain a science of psychology could have that other sciences have not already claimed.

Despite the abundance of categories borrowed from ordinary language, psychology has not built a body of reliable and extraordinary knowledge. This deficiency might have arisen because psychologists disagree over which categories are fundamental and which are trivial. For example, behaviorists reputedly start in action terms (*running, looking,* etc.) and reject other psychological categories as prescientific fictions. Cognitivists start with terms such as *memory, intelligence, attention,* and *perception,* and dismiss action terms as representing mere behavior. Perhaps psychology's difficulties stem from this lack of agreement about the categories that inquiry should start in. Alternatively, perhaps the problem is that psychologists have too readily accepted ordinary categories. Perhaps the categories need more sustained and serious philosophic scrutiny than psychologists have collectively given them. Engaging in this philosophic scrutiny does not require that we criticize and exclude categories that contradict some apriori prescription concerning the proper domain of psychological inquiry. It requires that we thoroughly examine each kind of category for what it might reveal about the general nature of psychological phenomena.

ACTION TERMS

Although psychologists have borrowed a diverse vocabulary from ordinary psychology, for the moment, let us consider only the vocabulary of action verbs. This vocabulary includes *running, reading, writing, touching, holding, sniffing,* and *driving,* among other words. By considering only these action verbs we can exclude the words Givón (1979, pp. 336–337) described as verbs of consciousness or of cognition (*know, think,* etc.), emotion (*fear, hope,* etc.), and intent (*want, intend,* etc.). It also excludes the psychological nouns (*memory, mind, intelligence,* etc.) and the various trait names (*optimistic, shy, extraverted,* etc.). Excluding these other parts of our psychological vocabulary does not deny that they identify categories of psychological interest. Rather, the exclusion is made to let us concentrate for the moment on the action verbs.

In ordinary conversation, action verbs usually appear in longer expressions such as "driving the car," "writing a letter," "talking with friends," "doing the shopping," "phoning to make a dentist's appointment," and "playing with a jigsaw puzzle." Let us refer to action verbs and to these longer expressions generically as *action terms.*

Many action terms designate events we can point to, in principle if not in practice. In this respect, events such as stepping off the curb, opening a door, and turning the page of a book present no difficulty. They have limited extension in time and we can point to them as they occur with little effort. Other events identified by action terms have greater extension in time; for example, driving to work, interviewing a student, giving a lecture, and spending the day at the office. In principle, we could continue to point to events of this kind while they occur. But, in practice, we might choose to point to the starting points and to the end points of these events. Action terms, therefore, designate events, rather than objects, and these events are those that we usually attribute to particular persons. For example, we usually say that John (or someone else) is talking with friends, doing the shopping, or driving to work. The attribution notes that one person rather than another is engaged in doing the talking, the shopping, or the driving. It implies that we need to consciously think of acts as events that persons engage in or perform.

Action terms provide psychology with natural units of description. We can identify and count successive instances of driving to work, writing a letter, purchasing food, and other such units of conduct. Consistent with this, some writers (e.g., McFall, 1982; Schoenfeld & Farmer, 1970;

Skinner, 1953, p. 93) have acknowledged that units of behavior are readily available for the purposes of psychological inquiry. Newtson and his colleagues (Newtson & Engquist, 1976; Newtson, Engquist, & Bois, 1977) reported some research relevant to the notion that we can identify natural units of conduct. They asked subjects to watch a motion film and to press a button each time the actor ended one act and began another. The number of different acts identified and the points chosen to delineate one act from another were reliable when subjects were retested 5 weeks later. Newtson concluded that his subjects saw a series of discrete units with beginnings and endings and that there was a reasonable degree of consensus about these units across different observers. This conclusion agrees with our ordinary experience of conduct as a series of events (Jones sitting at the table, looking at the menu, ordering a meal, and so on). It also agrees with the proposition that ordinary language contains categories that provide natural units of conduct. At least, it indicates that ordinary language has categories that provide a starting point for psychological description.

Action terms seem pedestrian when considered in the broader context of our entire psychological vocabulary. On those grounds, it is tempting to exclude action terms from serious consideration when we are looking for a fruitful starting-point for psychological inquiry. However, we should consider action terms more seriously if only because they serve indispensable pragmatic functions in interpersonal communication and in self-management. We use action terms when answering the question "What are you doing?", when describing the details of how we spent our day, and when trying to manage our own behavior (in writing "to do" lists, in managing our time, and so on). More generally, we use action terms when talking about the things we do in daily life; that is, about the actual events of conduct. We use action terms when we talk consensibly about daily matters, in ways that let listeners share relatively unambiguously in what we have done, in what we are doing now, and in what we plan to do later. This consensible talk concerns itself with actual events (e.g., "I did 6 hours of study today") and not with abstract formulations of those events (e.g., "I am unmotivated"). Consensible talk also belongs to scientific inquiry which requires consensibility as a prerequisite to the task of replicating experiments across independent laboratories. On these grounds of consensibility, action terms have an advantage over the less tangible items of our psychological vocabulary. Using action terms would compel us to talk about actual events. Through that means, we would ensure that our formulations, however abstract they eventually become, must deal with the concrete realities of conduct in the end. An argument in favor of this starting point is developed in later chapters.

ACT

Psychologists have used various terms to refer to the events of interest. One term, *a behavior*, has the disadvantage of unusual usage because it prefixes a mass noun with an article. The result is usage akin to "a sugar" or "a milk." *Behavior* has a disadvantage as a result of its ambiguity. The word covers acts and bodily movements, such that "a behavior" could just as easily suggest a movement as an act. Because we want to distinguish movements from acts, a term without this capacity for ambiguity seems preferable. Another term, *response,* suffers to the same degree from its origins because it continues to carry its original meaning of a muscular or glandular reaction of the body to a physical stimulus. But an act is not a muscular or glandular reaction; this will become obvious later.

Another term we might consider is *act.* This term has the disadvantage of a prior technical meaning. Some psychologists (e.g., Nissen, 1950; Spence, 1956, pp. 42–43) have used the term to mean an equifinal class of behavior; a class of behavior defined by an end-result. However, we could disregard this prior usage and take *act* to mean only an episode of conduct given by the action vocabulary of ordinary language, with no commitment at present to anything more than a list of examples. But, the term *act* bears an additional disadvantage because it suggests a punctate event. It suggests an event such as stepping across the curb more than an event such as writing a letter or spending the day at work. One solution would be to use Murray's (1951) term *proceeding* (p. 436) for every act with temporal extension. Murray gave the example of a pianist playing a sonata from start to finish. But adopting *proceeding* would expand our terminology unnecessarily. In addition, it would require a decision about the temporal properties that distinguish acts from proceedings. Regardless of how extended in time that event is, let us adopt *act* as the term for any event of conduct. Acts include punctate events such as opening a book, posting a letter, and shaking hands, as well as temporally extended events such as reading a research paper, conducting an experiment, and driving home from work.

Another disadvantage of the term *act* is that it can exclusively connote those items of conduct in which behavior operates directly upon the physical environment with the result of producing or preventing changes in it. That is, *act* can implicitly exclude listening, thinking, reading, and the like. Brown's (1982) comment about "learning by listening or reading rather than [by] acting" (p. 26) suggests an underlying concept of acting as exclusively nonverbal or physical. Beidel and Turner (1986) noted that cognitive therapists similarly tend to restrict their concept of behavior to public acts of this kind. The present concept is broader. It includes acts that clarify situations and acts whose primary effects are upon the person who acts.

An act, then, is any event of conduct that ordinary language has a name for. At least, let us accept the list of acts (opening a book, posting a letter, etc.) as primary and this generic description of an act as an approximation to a more adequate formulation of the contents of such a list. As well, let us use the term *act* for the items on this list and desist from using the more usual but nonetheless misleading terms, *behavior* and *response.*

ACT AND ACTION

We need to distinguish acts from actions. We use action terms when talking about acts as concrete particulars of conduct (e.g., "I spoke to John today"). We also use these terms when talking about kinds, classes, or types of acts and when making comments about them (e.g., "Speaking to John is usually worthwhile"). The latter usage of action terms as the names of classes occurs when, for example, we talk about speaking in general or about speaking as a kind of act. Let us use the term *action* for the generic entities, kinds, classes, or types implied by such discussions and, indeed, by the action terms themselves. Doing so allows us to distinguish particulars of conduct (acts) from classes of conduct (actions). Shwayder (1965, pp. 31–32) used this terminological distinction, noting that *act* has to with particulars whereas *action* deals with generic entities or types. In order to clarify this important distinction, acts and actions require separate discussion.

First, consider the status of acts as concrete particulars. Having that status implies that acts are actual events that have occurred, that are now occurring, or that will occur. It also implies that acts are events to which we can attach temporal markers. We can say when each act occurred. Moreover, having the status of a concrete particular implies that each act is unique. In this respect, an act is like any other particular. Thus, an act will not recur, if only because it has a unique temporal marker. The same can be said for a thunderstorm, a wave, a tree, and so on. Consequently, an act is an actual episode of conduct that is dated and unique. It has a starting point and an end point in time, and once it has occurred, it will never occur again.

Second, we must consider the status of actions as abstract entities. An action term unaccompanied by linguistic markers that tie it to an actual event does not name a single act. For example, "phoning the doctor" could name any instance of phoning the doctor. It only names a single particular if temporal markers are given or implied (e.g., "I phoned the doctor last week"). An action term without temporal markers could name any act of its class. Even so, an action is not an empirical collection like a herd of cows or a forest of trees. It is a logical, theoretical, or abstract entity whose members might consist only of possible instances rather than of actual instances. So, we can speak of an action that is an empty set (e.g., the action of walking on the moon in bare feet). In sum, we cannot point to an action as we can point to an act, and we cannot necessarily point to all or any of the instances of an action: An action is an abstract entity.

CONDUCT

We also need a term for talking about actions generically. Relevant to this, Shwayder (1965, p. 22) commented that we have a large vocabulary in English for talking about what people do, but we have no term for talking about the phenomenon of interest as a whole. He suggested that this deficiency has occurred because we have not yet developed ways of thinking abstractly about human action.

We could chose to use the word *behavior* as a generic term for action. However, this word is ambiguous between activity, movement, and action. The ambiguity conceals the distinction between bodily activities, on the one hand, and action, on the other. As it is explained in Chapter 9, we must make this distinction between movement and action in order to see action as a subject matter in its own right. Furthermore, as it is used outside psychology, *behavior* always means the behavior of something; for example, the behavior of stars, of soils, or of genes. Using the word *behavior* in psychology encourages usage of the expression "the behavior of organisms," which in turn suggests that the behavior of interest to psychology is the behavior of organisms. Actions are grounded in the behavior of organisms, but they involve something more than the behavior of organisms. As it is argued later, the expression "the behavior of organisms," when used to represent the subject matter of psychology, conceals the emergent nature of conduct and perpetuates the mistaken tradition of locating psychological phenomena in the organism. We would do well to avoid using the word *behavior* to represent the subject matter of psychology.

This book uses the term *conduct* as a generic term for the units identified by the action terms of ordinary language. This term is not without its difficulties, and these require some discussion.

First, the term *conduct* might suggest that we assume all actions are performed consciously and with deliberation. Indeed, Hadfield (1923/1964, p. 87) used the word *conduct* to designate behavior governed by and directed toward a consciously held end or purpose. He contrasted conduct with behavior, which according to him, is not governed by a stated purpose but by hereditary and environmental variables. Thus, Hadfield used the terms *conduct* and *behavior* to express a distinction made elsewhere between two ends of a continuum of awareness. This continuum of awareness reflects our tacit recognition that some acts are performed without awareness, others with the awareness that they are being performed but not why, and so on. We could restrict usage of the term *conduct* to one end of this continuum of awareness. But we would still need a generic term to cover the whole of action. It seems more reasonable to use *conduct* to cover human actions generically, without commitment to the extent of awareness present before, during, or after the performance of an act. In other words, *conduct* is used here with indifference to the presence or absence of awareness.

Second, *conduct* draws attention to the value-laden nature of our subject matter. Parmelee (1924, pp. 1–2) chose not to use *conduct* because of the ethical connotations of the word. The use of *conduct* has the advantage of making the ubiquity of values in the subject matter of psychology explicit. As some writers (e.g., Notcutt, 1953, p. 233; Peters, 1960; Skinner, 1969, p. 76) have acknowledged in various ways, our statements about conduct are always value-laden. Much of what we say expresses or presupposes judgments of good versus bad, right versus wrong, normal versus abnormal, successful versus unsuccessful, stupid versus smart, mature versus immature, skillful versus unskillful, and so on. The intrusion of these judgments into our statements about conduct is plain when we speak of someone meeting a standard; for example, adjusting to a situation, solving a problem, conforming to the rules, adapting to the environment, or improving or deteriorating according to some criterion. Success depends on what the observer considers to be successful, correct, appropriate, normal, and so forth. Our statements about performance, learning, development, and the like, are unavoidably laden with values in the sense of judgments about what counts as right or wrong, acceptable or unacceptable, and so on. This ubiquity of values in conduct should not disturb us. As we shall see later, conduct comprises behavior (read, bodily activity) and results, and is always value-laden because some results amount to the meeting of standards and because all results are susceptible to judgment by the actor and by observers as good or bad, right or wrong, successful or unsuccessful, and so on. In short, values are inevitable and ubiquitous constituents of our subject matter. Using the word *conduct* for our subject matter tacitly acknowledges this inevitability and ubiquity.

WORKING HYPOTHESIS

Let us make the assumption that acts constitute the raw materials for a science of psychology. In particular, consider the assumption that public acts constitute those raw materials. We can make this assumption while admitting that public acts do not constitute the whole of our subject matter. In order to understand what is meant by this admission, we need to consider the continuum that ranges from refraining-from-acting to actual performances of acts that might be public or private.

Some acts are public because independent observers can see them occur. For example, we can watch a person close a door, work on a crossword puzzle, or cross a road. In a different case, such acts can be available to an independent observer in principle though not in practice. For example, a person might work on a crossword puzzle while he or she is alone and is therefore not available for observation by others. On this occasion, the act is public in principle but not in practice.

Other acts are private, for the reason that only the actor can detect them. Examples include daydreaming, imagining what a future event will be like, and privately rehearsing what to say next during a conversation. These private acts are bequeathed to a science of psychology by the categories of ordinary psychology no less than are public acts.

Ordinary language also suggests the additional category of inchoate or incipient acts; for example, in the expressions "being about to turn right," "feeling inclined to go to the picnic," and "being on the point of speaking." Inchoate or incipient acts have to do with a readiness to act, with an increased probability of acting given the opportunity, or with a disposition to act. This notion of a disposition to act suggests that in conduct we must deal with a continuum from the absence of a disposition to act, through an increasing disposition to act, to actual occurrences. That is, the categories bequeathed by ordinary language to a science of psychology suggest that this science must not only deal with the actual occurrences of conduct (i.e., acts), but also with dispositions to act.

To make matters more complex, we must also consider refraining-from-acting. The notion of refraining is available in the ordinary ways we talk about conduct. For example, we speak of refraining from lighting a cigarette or of refraining from interrupting while another person is speaking. The notion of refraining from acting suggests not only the nonoccurence of an act, but also a disposition to not-engage in an act that might otherwise occur if the actor did not refrain. Some writers (e.g., Best, 1978, p. 81; Brand, 1971; Ryle, 1979; Schutz, 1954) have discussed the act of refraining and have mentioned the concept of a negative action in this regard. The availability of this notion of refraining-from-acting to ordinary thought suggests that a science of psychology must deal with refraining-from-action as well as with engaging-in-action.

Taken together, these considerations indicate that conduct does not constitute a subject matter that consists only of publicly available events. It does not consist only of events that actually occur and that are available to observation by the anonymous observer. Conduct seems more like a field of probabilities ranging from negative strength (refraining) through nonoccurrence to actual private or public occurrence. Both Skinner (1953, pp. 62-63) and MacCorquodale (1969) have discussed the latter notion.

We need to recognize the complexities brought into our subject matter by private acts, by dispositions to act, and by acts of refraining. But, even while recognizing these complexities, we can still take the actual events seen publicly in actual occurrences as our proper starting point. Doing so does not exclude private acts, dispositions, and acts of refraining. It uses public acts as the starting point for our metatheoretical inquiries because they are the public particulars of the psychological domain. They are the perceptually obvious parts of this domain that we can point to and share in relatively unambiguously. The working agreements that psychology needs are more likely to arise if we take public particulars as our starting point. At the very least, we should attempt to extract information from our preexisting knowledge of public acts before we consider the categories of ordinary psychology that are less available to scrutiny. Admittedly, this strategy requires an unhurried stance that is unusual in psychology. However, we must take such a stance if we want to determine whether ordinary psychology contains the strategic concepts that a science of psychology needs.

CHAPTER 6

Means and Ends

INTRODUCTION

What can we do with a subject matter that consists of acts? Most obviously, we might list the acts that a particular person engages in, count their frequency of occurrence in particular settings, and so forth. In doing so, we might gain much valuable information about how particular persons conduct themselves. But we would not probe beyond what is already available to ordinary observers. To probe beyond appearances, we need to know something about the structure of conduct. In fact, psychologists already have rudimentary knowledge of the structural patterns in their domain. This knowledge provides the foundation for probing beyond the appearances of conduct and for making sense of the body of reliable knowledge already available. The present chapter develops an account of this foundation by discussing both the ubiquity of end results and equifinal classes in conduct and the nature of actions as entities that comprise end results and equifinal classes.

END RESULTS

We identify a particular act as that act by the end result of bodily activities. Household chores provide compelling examples. We wash our clothing, do the dishes, and prepare meals, among other things. We would not say we have prepared a meal unless a meal has been prepared, we would not say we have done the dishes unless the dishes have been done, and so on. At least, we would not say these things and expect other members of our verbal community to agree with us. Unless we achieve the end result, we have not engaged in the action. Harré (1982) acknowledged the importance of end results in this respect. He said we identify the action of nailing by the result of two objects being fixed together. Alston (1974) also noted that end results, or, in his terms, *success-*

conditions, identify an action as that action. For example, we identify the action of baking a cake by the coming-into-being of a cake. In brief, we rely on end results to identify the actual actions that a person performs.

We can make a further claim — that the language of action is a language of end results. Guthrie (e.g., Guthrie, 1959; Guthrie & Edwards, 1949, p. 67) presented this view. He emphasized that the language of action is about what we get done, what we make, and what we achieve. It is not about the movements we engage in to get things done, made, and achieved. For example, the arrival of guests at dinner is the important thing rather than how they get to dinner, whether it be by walking, driving, or some other means. In this context, all those behaviors count as getting to dinner. Similarly, a letter can be handwritten, typed, dictated to a secretary, and so on. "Writing a letter" covers all these behaviors indifferently (Guthrie & Edwards, 1949). English has a vast collection of action terms such as "writing a letter," "getting to dinner," and the like. Their number and diversity reflect the number and diversity of end results that the English-speaking community recognizes as critical. English also includes many terms that let us talk about the results of behavior generically. These terms include *effect, end, goal, success, failure, consequence, outcome, result, achievement, accomplishment, purpose, reward, punishment, advantage, disadvantage, gains, losses, benefits,* and *costs.* The number, diversity, and importance of these terms is not inconsistent with the description of the language of action as a language of end results.

POSTURES AND MOVEMENTS

We achieve end results through the activities of our bodies. In this context, *activity* designates the expenditure of energy of any part of the body. The bodily activities that most obviously produce end results consist of two classes: postural activities and movements.

Postural activities support, balance, and right the body according to the laws of physics. Such activities occur when, for example, a person who is standing, raises his or her left leg off the ground. Through the mediation of reflex mechanisms, the body moves to the right, the center of gravity shifts to a position vertically above the center of the right foot, and an upright posture is maintained. More technically, postures are composites of the positions of all the joints of the body at any one time. Sleeping and resting postures require little muscular activity. Standing still and other static postures require groups of muscles to work statically to stabilize the joints. Walking, running, and other dynamic postures require constant adjustments of posture to meet the changing conditions that result from movement. Movements are superimposed on a postural background, and they provide proprioceptive and other stimuli that elicit postural adjustments. In sum, while it is at rest or in motion, the body holds various positions that depend on the postural reflexes and on gravity and other mechanical forces that act on the body.

Movements are motions of body segments around the joints. The body segments consist of the head, the trunk, and the upper and lower extremities. The joints are the junctions between bones that afford stability and mobility to the body. An example of a movement is extension of the forearm in which the triceps muscle contracts and the lower arm straightens. The muscles attached to the bony core of the body segments provide the motor force that moves the segments. Gravity and the various external mechanical forces that act on the body also contribute to bodily movement. The permissible kind and degree of movement of a segment around a joint depends on how the joint is built and on the number and type of ligaments that hold the articulating bones together. More simply, a joint acts as a hinge that permits two or more bones to move in relation to each other and that, at the same time, limits the motion possible. For example, distal finger and toe joints have one ligament on each side of the joint so that motion is possible in only one plane. Gross movement of the whole body through space depends on the more molecular movements of the body segments around the joints. (Postures and movements are discussed in texts on human movement; e.g., Kendall & McCreary, 1983).

Bodily activities, and particularly postural activities and movements, are essential if a human being is to produce one of the end results identified by the action vocabulary of ordinary language. But, even so, postural activities and movements are not the units of interest to psychologists. On the contrary, many if not most actions include something more than bodily activities.

INSTRUMENTALITY

Postural activities and movements provide the means by which we act upon the world and produce end results. This direct action upon the world is fundamental to phenomena of psychological interest. Some psychologists have used the concept of effectance motivation to express this acting of individuals on their environments. But the concept seems to imply that the individual is passive unless driven into action by internal drives. Clearly, the concept reflects the assumption usually attributed to behaviorism (e.g., Hitt, 1969; Hunt, 1969; Sampson, 1981): Human beings are passive unless acted upon. Without that assumption, psychology would not need the concept of effectance motivation. Contrary to the assumption of passivity, effectance of the body in producing end results is a given in a subject matter consisting of action. Consistent with this rejection of passivity, Skinner (1957, p. 1) has emphasized that we act on the environment and change it. The present view follows Skinner. It stresses that human beings act directly on the world. Dewey (1922/1957, pp. 118–119) also promoted this concept of a human being as a biologically active entity. Likewise, Bruner (1972) acknowledged that we act on the world and change it, and that we develop instruments to amplify our effectiveness. In short, the effectance or instrumentality of the body is something psychologists can assume. It is implied by the assertion that psychology's subject matter consists of actions.

Psychology needs to shift conceptually from the implicit assumption that individuals are passive-unless-acted-upon to the assumption that they act directly upon the world. The assumption of passivity is partly derived and mistakenly borrowed from the stimulus–response model of reflexology. The assumption leads us to think of human beings as entities that environmental stimuli prod into action. On the contrary, human beings as biological organisms constantly act on their surroundings and on their own bodies while they are awake. The assumption of passivity also arises because of the traditional emphasis in psychology on perception rather than on action, as seen in the contemporary interest in the organism as an information processor. This emphasis gives no place to human beings as biological organisms that act on themselves and on their surroundings — producing change, preventing change, clarifying situations, and meeting standards. Viewing this acting upon the world as fundamental will require a substantial change in the way psychologists think about their subject matter and task.

REACTIVITY

The body and its parts are instrumental in effecting end results in various contexts, and, in turn, these contexts are reactive or nonreactive to the body and its parts. An example of a nonreactive context is a locked door when someone tries to push open the door without first unlocking it. Simply, reactivity has to do with whether bodily behavior can change its surroundings. Reactivity also has to do with how much behavior (intensity, temporal extent) is required to produce or prevent change. Furthermore, it has to do with what kind of behavior (form) and with what timing (pauses, duration) is required. That is, the objects, persons, and agencies that provide the context of an individual's behavior require not only the occurrence of behavior but also the occurrence of behavior with certain quantitative and qualitative properties. In short, reactivity is a property of contexts, just as instrumentality is a property of the body. Indeed, instrumentality of the body and reactivity of contexts are two sides of one coin.

The concept of context is different from the concept of environment. In psychology, we usually contrast the environment with the organism or with the behavior of an organism. The implication is that the environment consists of everything beyond the boundary provided by the skin of the organism. Skinner (1974, p. 73) implied agreement with this interpretation when he said that the environment is located outside the body. Consistent with this, other usages have treated the concept of environment as designating the various settings of a person's behavior. For example, one group of investigators (Brown, et al., 1979) said that *environment* means the places in which people live, work, play, eat, and so on. Similarly, Wahler, Berland, and Coe (1978) said that an individual's environment consists of various settings such as "at home alone," "at home with parents," and so on. However, Bijou (1971) noted that the behavioral concept of environment departs from this ordinary usage of the word. The behavioral concept designates conditions that actually affect behavior, and these conditions occur outside *and* inside the body. Likewise, Smith (1983) observed that Skinner's concept of environment includes conditions inside the body.

A comment by Schacht and Nathan (1977) illuminates the inconsistency between the ordinary usage and the behavioral usage of the term *environment.* They noted that we can think of the terms *organism* and *environment* as conceptual devices such that, for example, the tissues which surround a neuron constitute its environment even though at another level we assign those tissues to the organism and not to the environment. Following through the implications of this statement, we might accept that all variables relevant to behavior, whether they are located inside or outside the organism, constitute the environment for matters of psychological import. This possibility deprives us of the ordinary meaning of *environment* and does not help us make the conceptual shift we need to make—from the dualism of behavior (or organism) and environment to the dualism of means (behavior) and end results. We should consider the alternative strategy of retaining the ordinary meaning of *environment* while introducing another term for the environment (in Schacht and Nathan's sense) of the behavior that is a constituent of conduct. Let us use the term *context* to designate the environment of the behavior that is a constituent of conduct. The body as a whole has a context and so does each body segment (forefinger, forearm, etc.) and each set of body segments (arm and hand and fingers, trunk and legs, etc.). In other words, context consists of the surroundings of the bodily unit of interest (the body as a whole, the legs, etc.).

We can consider the nature of instrumentality and reactivity in terms of this concept of a context. Instrumentality is always of the body, but reactivity is of the body and of objects outside the body (i.e., of the context of the bodily constituents of the action of interest). Instrumentality and reactivity imply a distinction similar to Murray's (1951) distinction between an actor and an alter. The actor is the subject and the alter is the object of the action. The object of an action might be part of the actor's body, as in nail-biting, cleaning the teeth, brushing the hair, and the like. Thus, the context of our acting-upon need not be the environment in the sense of the world outside our skin. A psychology that starts self-consciously with actions rather than with organisms would give the distinction between actor (subject) and alter (object) greater salience than the distinction between behavior (organism) and environment. It could retain the term *environment* in its ordinary sense of the various settings of conduct. As is discussed in Chapter 13, the latter distinction between behavior and environment derives more from the stimulus–response model borrowed from reflexology than from the concept of an action as a means–end unit. The dualism of behavior and environment does not direct us to the means–end structure of conduct, and it makes stimulus–response thinking difficult to abandon if only because it directs us into thinking about behavior (response) and environment (stimulus) instead of about means and ends.

CHANGES, PREVENTIONS, AND CLARIFICATIONS

Our bodies are instrumental in producing change. For example, we water the garden and change the state of the garden from dry to wet, close a door and change its state from open to closed, and so on. In these cases, our bodily activities produce change, and the change adds something to the existing situation, takes something away from it, or both. For example, turning on the heater adds warmth and takes away cold, watering the garden adds water and reduces dryness, and so on. Either way, behavior changes the situation.

Behavior can also prevent change. For example, we water the garden and prevent the plants from dying, we change the topic of conversation and prevent our listener from leaving, and we continue working and prevent the change in our standard of living that would follow losing our job. In this way, we maintain the present situation or prevent change in it as an end result of our activities. We need self-consciously to include prevention of change among the end results of behavior because it is easy to overlook prevention of change as an end result. In overlooking it, we miss the full range of ways in which bodily behavior can be effective psychologically.

Bodily activity is instrumental in producing and preventing change through both physical and nonphysical (symbolic) means. Some end results are physically related to bodily activity. For example, walking towards an object reduces the distance between the person and the object, reaching for the object makes physical contact more likely, pushing and pulling the object changes its position, and so on. As Skinner (e.g., 1953, p. 261; 1957, p. 1; 1974, p. 89) noted, in these examples behavior is related directly, mechanically, spatially, or geometrically to its results. Other end results do not have a physical connection to behavior. I can tell a colleague that a research paper is worth reading and increase the chance that he or she will read it, I can ask my assistant the time and he or she will tell me, and so on. In these examples, although behavior is effective, it is not effective through physical means. It is effective because the audience has been trained to be reactive to it. MacCorquodale (1969) noted that we have traditionally thought of this type of behavior as symbolic. (This symbolic [or verbal] behavior was discussed by Skinner [1957] in his book *Verbal Behavior.*)

Clarification is another end result of behavior. Some behavior has the critical result that it clarifies a situation. Reading a map is one example. It clarifies a situation and increases the chance of a person getting to a destination. Another example is looking at a traffic light, seeing it is green, and accelerating through the intersection. In these examples, reading the map and looking at the traffic light are acts whose critical results consist of clarification. The clarification might lead to behavior that has physical results. For example, the acceleration of a car through an intersection takes it from one momentary location to another. However, we need to notice the clarification itself as a kind of result. Behavior that can clarify includes manipulating objects; consider turning on a light to read at night or adjusting the focus of a television set. Skinner (1957, p. 416) explained that such behavior also includes gross movements of the body, such as moving the head to reduce the glare, and more subtle acts of attending. The important thing about these acts of observing is the resulting clarification, not the details of the bodily activities that produce the clarification. The individual who does the observing has been called *an observer,* whereas the terms *actor* and *agent* refer to the individual who acts (e.g., Langford, 1971). Although this distinction is useful, it must not conceal the nature of observing as a kind of acting that requires bodily activity and end results.

EQUIFINALITY

There is usually more than one way to achieve a particular end result. For example, I might get to work today by walking, cycling, driving, and so on. As another example, I might obtain a copy of a research paper by writing for a reprint, by taking a copy from a journal held in the library, and so on. Also, I might reduce the glare of the sun by putting on my sunglasses, by shielding my eyes with my hand, and so on. In brief, there is usually more than one good way to do something: We can usually achieve the same end result through a variety of alternative means. This availability of alternative means to a single end is apparent to ordinary observers. It is expressed in the proverb "There is more than one way to skin a cat," and it is commonplace in human experience.

Psychology has not missed the phenomenon of interest, which is plain by the multiplicity of terms that refer to it. We equate items of behavior on the basis of a common end result, and, in doing so, we get an equivalence class, a class of generically identical instances (Schoenfeld & Farmer, 1970), a generic class (Ferster, 1979), an act (e.g., Nissen, 1950; Spence, 1956), an operant (e.g., Skinner, 1953, p. 65), or a functional class (Moore & Lewis, 1953; Churchman & Ackoff, 1947; Kitchener, 1977). The phenomenon of equivalence has been called *the intersubstitutability of motor skills* (Tolman, 1959), *response equivalence, behavioral plasticity* (Chiszar & Carpen, 1980; Muenzinger, 1928; Ringen, 1976), *action-constancy* (MacKay, 1982), *motor variability* (Hebb, 1949), *motor equivalence* (MacKay, 1982), and *equifinality* (e.g., Abelson, 1981; McFall, 1982; von Bertalanffy, 1951). The members of an equivalence class have been called *class equatable events* (Schoenfeld & Farmer, 1970), *functionally equivalent episodes* (Ferster, 1979), *variants* (Keller & Schoenfeld, 1950, p. 179; Schoenfeld, Harris & Farmer, 1966), *paraphrases* (Bruner, 1972), *responses, consequence-defined responses,* and *kinematic variations* (Higgins & Spaeth, 1972). The following discussion uses *equifinality* for the phenomenon of interest, *equifinal class* for the relevant classes, and *variants* for instances of the classes.

Psychologists have long acknowledged equifinality, equifinal classes, and variants. Indeed, many theorists, inside and outside psychology, have emphasized that behavior of psychological interest consists of continued, persistent and varied effort toward some end result. Supporting the primacy of end results is a series of experiments performed in the 1920s and 1930s (e.g., Lashley & Ball, 1929; Lashley & McCarthy, 1926; MacFarlane, 1930; Wickens, 1938) that showed how subjects learn results and not movements. For example, MacFarlane (1930) found that rats trained to run through a maze continued to perform correctly when the maze was filled with water and they had to swim through it. In a similar experiment, Wickens (1938) found that subjects trained to extend their index finger to avoid shock flexed that finger when their hand was turned over. In that manner, they learned to move their fingers away from the shock pad rather than to perform a particular movement. Experiments of this kind suggest that subjects learn to produce end results. On these and the other grounds previously discussed, many psychologists (e.g., Bruner, 1972; Hunter, 1932; McDougall, 1912; McFall, 1982; Murray, 1951; Russell, 1938, pp. 1–2) have acknowledged that behavior of psychological interest is coordinated in a way that produces end results and that psychological invariances are found in end results and in the equifinal classes they define.

This long history of interest in equifinal classes might suggest that equifinality now has a central place in psychological formulations. Indeed, Chiszar and Carpen (1980) commented that psychology has specialized in the theoretical interpretation of this phenomenon. Asserting this specialization suggests an explicit and shared recognition of equifinality among psychologists in addition to a deliberate and fruitful interpretation of it. Yet Hebb (1974) felt able to comment that psychological theory has not handled equifinality with success, and Jessor (1958) commented that equifinality has been taken for granted. Skinner (e.g., 1953, pp. 64–65, 1957, pp. 16–17) has made it plain that his interest is in equifinal classes and not in particulars as such. Still, critics have missed this commitment to equifinality because of the way in which operant psychologists sometimes discuss it. Specifically, operant psychologists sometimes defend their interest in equifinal classes on the grounds that acts are nonrepeatable events. But single instances are scientifically important only as interchangeable members of classes, and our concern with classes follows more from the generic and equifinal nature of our subject matter than from the uniqueness of the single instance. Indeed, emphasizing the class rather than the instance is compatible with what Skinner has written (e.g., Skinner, 1953, p. 64–65, 1957, p. 16–17). It highlights an interest in equifinality that operant psychologists share with many other psychologists. Regrettably, the critics have missed the central place given to equifinality by operant psychologists. As well, the central place given to equifinality through the history of psychology is often missed by operant psychologists, some of whom have identified equifinality as a specific contribution of operant psychology. In fact, considering the diversity of terms reviewed earlier, equifinality has long been acknowledged by other psychologists. As Hebb (1974) suggested, the problem is that we have not dealt with it adequately. We still need to fully explore the ramifications of equifinality for the general nature of a science of psychology.

BEHAVIOR AND RESULTS

Psychologists tend to identify equifinal classes as the units of psychological interest. Stated differently, interest falls primarily, if not entirely, on a unit that consists of the means to an end and not on a unit that comprises means and end as an undifferentiated whole. For example, Harré (1982) said that an action is a means to an end. The terms used by some theorists to designate psychology's subject matter reflect this emphasis on the means to an end. Terms such as *goal-directed behavior, purposive behavior,* and *teleological behavior* suggest that psychology is about behavior that has goals, purposes, ends, or effects. Consistent with this, some theorists have interpreted psychological terms such as *intelligence, personality,* and *mind* in terms of equifinality. For example, Edwards (1928) said that intelligent action is one of an indefinite number of possible responses, unlike reflexive behavior. McDougall (1912, p. 46) said that we do not hesitate to talk about mind or mental activity when we find equifinal classes. These terms and formulations encourage us to think that equifinal classes constitute the subject matter of psychology. The view taken here is that this notion is more incomplete than wrong. A more complete view places the equifinal classes together with the end results that define them so that the basic units of psychological interest encompass an equifinal class and an end result.

Consistent with the more complete view, some writers have explicitly included both the equifinal class and the end result in the units of interest to them. For example, Murray (1938, pp. 54–56) formulated an action as a unit that comprises an actone and an effect. An actone amounts to the mechanisms, means, ways, or modes of behaving. It has to do with the questions, "How is it done?" and "What means are used?" The effect is the effect produced or how the situation after the actone differs from the situation before. It has to do with the question "What is done?" Brand (1970) also included end results as part of the units of interest. He said that actions include the effects of bodily movements. For example, the pencil's raising is part of the action of picking up a pencil along with the bodily movements that have that effect. From (1960) also included means and ends (for him, purposes) in psychological units. He said we see movements and purpose as undifferentiated wholes. In seeing someone sit on a chair, hang up his or her coat, or light a cigarette, we do not experience purpose as something separate from movement or as some-thing behind it. We see what people do. In other words, we see the bodily activities and the end (or purpose) together-at-once. Parsons and Shils (1951) also included means and ends in the units of interest to them. They said that when an action is performed, behavior is oriented toward an end or a goal, it takes place in a situation, it involves the expenditure of energy or effort, and the energy expenditure is regulated. For example, driving a car to the lake to go fishing counts as an action. Going fishing is the end, the situation comprises the car and the road, energy is expended in getting to the lake, and the expenditure of energy is regulated because driving is an intelligent way to get to the lake (Parsons & Shils, 1951).

Although the discussions we have considered differ in detail, all of them include means (how something is done) and ends (what is done, outcome, goal, etc.) in the units of psychological interest. The discussions suggest that psychology properly deals not only with purposeful behavior, goal-directed behavior, and the like, but also with the purposes, goals, and so forth. Moreover, the discussions suggest that the purposes, goals, or end results are internal to the units of interest. This explicit inclusion of end results in the units of interest will seem trivial at first sight. But it has important ramifications for how we think about psychological phenomena.

ORGANIC NATURE OF CONDUCT

Walker (1942) noted that once the end-results of behavior are recognized as important psychologically, there is no telling where to stop in our descriptions. End results extend out into the future, so that whatever counts as an action (means *and* end) on one level becomes a means to an end at another level. It depends on which action we are concerned with. Howarth (1980) provided an example. Consider the action of fixing a lid onto a box. Hammering nails into the box is an action when considered by itself, but it is also a means to the end of putting the lid on the box. Seen this way, an action is a holon, in Koestler's (1978, p. 27) sense of an entity that is itself a whole but that participates as part of a larger whole. Moreover, an action might participate as part of two or more larger wholes and contain two or more less global actions itself. Any particular item in this organic system is embedded in a network of overlapping and interlocking actions.

Implying acceptance of the organic nature of conduct, we could say that if a person in New York kills another person in California by sending poisoned candy, then the locus of the act extends from New York to California. In saying this, we are discussing the act of killing a person in New York by sending poisoned candy from California. Davis (1979, p. 36) objected to this interpretation, which he attributed to Dewey. Davis asked if it was not more reasonable to say that the consequences of the act of sending candy occurred over that distance. But this objection does not consider that actions conjoin means and end and that whether we treat the receipt of candy as internal or external to an action depends on the action with which we are concerned. Allport (1936/1937) made this point too. He said that end results or purposes have no place except in the act itself. However, Allport seemed to exclude any end result or purpose not present at the point of observation. Thus, he approved "chopping wood" but rejected "chopping wood to build a fire" as an acceptable description in psychology. The second description implies a teleology that Allport would not admit. Allport, therefore, recognized that end results are intrinsic to the units of psychological interest, but he excluded units whose end results are not adjacent to behavior in time.

Expressions such as "chopping wood to build a fire," "studying to pass an examination," and "phoning to make an appointment for a haircut" are commonplace in ordinary discourse. They exemplify a pattern that we might describe as "A in order to B." Expressions that exemplify this pattern spell out the temporal extension of an act across a means and an end that might have considerable separation in time. Appropriately, Guthrie (1959) noted that action language is purposive. In this context, *purposive* means that action language is a language of end results, however separated those end results might be in time from the bodily behavior that they depend upon. Some writers (McDougall, 1928; Muenzinger, 1927; Russell, 1938, p. 2, 9) have insisted that using purposive language is the only intelligible procedure if we are to have a psychology at all. But many psychologists seem uneasy about the prospect of using a purposive language and particularly about using expressions that spell out the means-end structure of conduct. The reasons for this uneasiness need some discussion.

First, the format "A in order to B" seems to posit a causal condition acting backwards in time from the future. It suggests, for example, that the future event of letting your friend in causes you to open the door now. Alternatively, it suggests that a purpose or intention located inside you directs your behavior. So, your intention to let in your friend leads you to open the door. This apparent explanation restates the original statement and adds nothing useful to what we already know. On the contrary, it confuses the matter by clouding the means and the end that the original statement ("I opened the door to let in my friend") identifies. We do not need to make inferences about organocentric contents. Instead, our inferences are properly directed to our subject matter which consists of behavior-in-context. If purposes or end results are located anywhere, they are located in the means–end units of conduct that the language of action identifies for us. That is, purpose, in the sense implied by the "A in order to B" format, is neither an external cause operating backwards from the future nor a cause inside the organism. We can reject those two interpretations of the concept of purpose and still accept purposive language. We can accept that purposive language is the language of end results (or of goals, purposes, outcomes, etc.) and that end results, together with the relations they enter into with behavior, are constituents of action (i.e., of behavior-in-context).

Second, some psychologists might feel uneasy with purposive language because they believe that using this language is somehow unscientific. Psychologists who assume that their subject matter should be described with the language of the physical sciences might feel particularly uncomfortable with purposive language. A commitment to the language of the physical sciences might indicate that we should provide psychological explanations using the language of atoms, molecules, and the like. In fact, Davis (1953) explicitly recommended a physical psychology that would provide explanations of that kind. As McDougall (1928) insisted, using the language of atoms, molecules, and the like, would be unintelligible from the point of view of conduct. Sometimes the assumption that psychologists should use the language of physical science seems tantamount only to an insistence upon using a consensible language; a language that independent investigators can share in unambiguously. If so, then we should speak of consensible language, because to insist upon the language of physics is tacitly to espouse a physicalism that has no place in psychology.

The "A in order to B" format does not exhaust purposive language. *Studying, driving, reading,* and the like, also name units that comprise means and ends. They name end results and imply the occurrence of bodily behavior that has those results. End results can be had only through bodily behavior, and so action terms always imply units that comprise means and ends. For example, "opening the door" names a unit that comprises a means and an end no less than does "opening the door to let a friend in." With the action of opening the door, the means and the end are not spelled out in the name of the action. The end result is closely bound to the behavior, and the means and the end have a unity that makes them hard to see as constituents of the action. Nonetheless, the action has these two constituents.

Similarly, end results bound closely to behavior are easily missed when we think about conduct. An example given by Ferster (1979) is the pressure of a ball on a seal's nose contingent on the behavior of balancing the ball. Another example is seeing that a word is spelled correctly or incorrectly immediately after writing it (Lee & Sanderson, 1987). Results closely bound to behavior are difficult for us to see *as* results. For example, when asked about the result of a child cycling, we tend to think of the child getting places, gaining approval of friends, and the like. We tend to overlook the immediate changes in the direction, speed, and balance of the bicycle that are coordinated with changes in the positions and movements of the body together with changes in the terrain. Likewise, we tend to forget that one result of talking is hearing ourselves, that one result of writing is having the chance to be our own reader, that one result of looking in a mirror is seeing ourselves, and so on. In overlooking these results bound closely to behavior, we tend to overlook the instrumental nature of all behavior of psychological interest. We think of doodling, singing while alone, looking at paintings, and the like, as performed for their own sakes. Often that way of thinking does not recognize doodling, singing while alone, and so forth, as actions that comprise equifinal classes (i.e., means) and end results.

CONCLUSION

Explicating the rudimentary structure of actions takes us further in our task of characterizing the general nature of the subject matter of psychology. The discussion has suggested a subject matter that comprises a vast number of different actions at various levels of generality, with each action comprising two constituents, a means and an end. These constituents are internal to the unit we count as an action, although a particular action might also have an end that is external to it *and* internal to another (higher-order) action. The subject matter of interest, then, comprises at least the various ends that actors pursue and the means by which these ends are pursued. The multiplicity of means and ends, and the overlapping and interlocking nature of this subject matter are implicit in the concept of conduct as organic. Of course, this characterization of psychology's subject matter is rudimentary. Still, it suggests something about psychology's task. That task is to deal, both conceptually and empirically, with human effectiveness and lack of effectiveness and with the reactivity and nonreactivity of contexts. As we shall see later, the task is to deal with these problems directly and explicitly, and not via the mediation of organocentric abstractions (intelligence, memory, etc.) that obscure the means–end structure of conduct. The obfuscation engendered by those abstractions has enabled psychologists to avoid the problems they need to solve in order to deal with the two basic properties of their domain: first, that we get things done, made, and achieved only through bodily effort, and second, that what we can get done at any one time is constrained by the reactivity of the past and present contexts of our efforts.

CHAPTER 7

Contingencies

INTRODUCTION

The concept of the contingency provides the starting point for operant psychology. It has much in common with the concept of an action as a means–end unit. However, operant psychologists seldom acknowledge the similarity between the two concepts, and those psychologists who do discuss means and ends do not see that contingencies have to do with means and ends. Consequently, we seldom recognize or exploit the contribution of operant psychology to the problem of developing reliable knowledge of means–end units. The present chapter sufficiently develops the concept of the contingency to show that it does relate directly to means–end units. (Details of operant methodology and research can be found elsewhere, in texts [e.g., Cooper, Heron, & Heward, 1987; Ferster & Culbertson, 1982; Honig & Staddon, 1977; Johnston & Pennypacker, 1980], in review and discussion articles [e.g., Buskist, 1983; Harzem, 1984; Hineline, 1984; Michael, 1984; Schmitt, 1984; Skinner, 1986], and in the primary literature.)

CONTINGENCIES

A contingency is an if-then relation between behavior and end result. In discussions about contingencies, the word *behavior* designates an equifinal class and never a single episode, and it covers bodily activities (i.e., movements and postural activities) and acts. Examples of contingencies include the following: If you exceed the speed limit, your chance of getting a ticket increases; if you talk, you hear your own voice; and if you brush your teeth using peppermint toothpaste, you get a peppermint taste. The existence of a contingency means that unless the behavior occurs, the end result does not follow. Expressed differently, the behavior is required if the end result is to occur.

A causal relation is at the heart of the contingency, in the sense that the behavior makes a difference. It produces something that *would not* otherwise occur or prevents something that *would* otherwise occur. Of course, any particular instance of an equifinal class is not a necessary condition for a particular end result. It is only a sufficient condition in that some other instance of the class could produce the end result. Still, the end result depends on the occurrence of *some* member of the class, and, in this sense, the relation between behavior and end result is causal. Causal efficacy of this kind requires the effort of bodily activity. A contingency, then, is a work requirement, as noted by Hineline (1984), or a task, in the sense discussed by McFall (1982). Skinner (1969, p. 7) commented that the concept of the contingency represents the phenomenon that Tolman and Brunswik (1935) identified when they spoke of the "causal texture of the environment" (also see Brunswik, 1943). Similarly, Kendall, Lerner and Craighead (1984) alluded to contingencies when they spoke of individuals meeting contextual presses, as did Brown (1982) when she spoke of the implicit demands of schools. In sum, contingencies are the work requirements we must satisfy to get anything done, made, or achieved and to meet the standards (i.e., performance criteria) held by ourselves and by others.

The concept of the contingency is not extraordinary. Still, the ordinary nature of the concept does not mean we are necessarily aware of every contingency. Nor does it exclude the possibility that some contingencies are ineffable (i.e., beyond verbal formulation). As explained later, radical behaviorism, the philosophy of operant psychology, assumes that many acts are shaped and maintained by contingencies of which we are not aware. It assumes that the contingencies of which we are aware constitute only a subset of the total number of contingencies. Even if some actual contingencies are unavailable to awareness, the concept of the contingency still has many ordinary instances and is well-connected to ordinary experience through them.

Operant psychologists assume that contingencies are present in the human world independent of our theoretical formulations and empirical interventions. They assume we already participate behaviorally in contingencies and that this participation affects our subsequent performance. This formulation sees individual organisms as one ingredient of psychological phenomena. Consider the following explanation: Operant psychologists see a human being initially as a biological organism born into a human group. The organism has a supply of behavior (i.e., movements and postural activities) sensitive to contingencies, and this behavior is available for shaping by contingencies maintained by the physical environment and by other members of the group. Segal (1972) commented that the behavioral repertoire that emerges through this process depends on preexisting units determined by the phylogenetic history of the species. She noted that other writers (e.g., Kimble & Perlmutter, 1970; Skinner,

1969, pp. 172–217) have also suggested that the phenomena of interest to psychologists have their origin in this phylogenetically determined activity of the organism. Activity of this kind is the gross physiology of an anatomy in Skinner's (1969, p. 173) sense, and it presumably reflects the conditions under which the species has evolved (Skinner, 1969, pp. 172–217). Contributing to the theme discussed by Segal (1972), Thelen (1981) noted that a human infant engages in rapid, repetitious movements of the limbs, torso, and head. Infants kick, wave, rub, bounce, and sway. Thelen reviewed evidence that suggests that these motor units are transitional between earlier, uncoordinated activities of the body and the activities of interest to psychologists. Most important in the present context, Thelen commented that this neuromuscular coordination provides the infant with the means to have effects upon his or her physical and social environment. We must remember, of course, that the behavior that has these effects is an ingredient in, and not the whole of, the subject matter of psychology.

The other ingredient of psychological phenomena consists of various systems of contingencies. Each human institution arranges and maintains a system of contingencies. It makes demands on performance ("if you do this, then that will happen"; to achieve that end, you must do this"; and so on). Both the taxation department and its demands on performance and a university and its demands are examples. As Skinner (1977; 1980, pp. 298–299) asserted, particular objects, such as a bicycle or a piano, also maintain systems of contingencies. When riding a bicycle, if I turn the handle in the direction of the fall (behavior), then I break the fall (end result), and so on. As a final example, social groups also maintain contingencies, as is implied by expressions such as "the psychology of more" and "the psychology of winning." For example, the members of some social groups allocate much effort to acquiring material possessions, and this behavior has social as well as material results.

Operant psychologists, therefore, see human beings as behaviorally immersed in systems of contingencies, many of which are maintained by other people. These contingencies shape and maintain human performance so that each human being becomes the locus of a repertoire of acts that at any one time is more or less large and differentiated. Contingencies together with their cumulative effects on performance constitute the phenomena of psychological (as opposed to physical, biological, or sociological) interest. This notion that contingencies and organisms are constituents of psychological phenomena is discussed more fully in later chapters.

Given that contingencies are constituents of psychological phenomena, we cannot understand conduct without knowing about the systems of contingencies in which human beings participate. Consequently, the task of understanding conduct cannot be undertaken exclusively in a laboratory, because we need to describe the actual contingencies in which people participate behaviorally. Describing these contingencies is a task that belongs to psychology but also extends to anthropology, law, sociology, and other disciplines. Some of this descriptive work has already been done, by Skinner (e.g., 1953, 1957, 1968), Harris (e.g., 1977, 1981; also see Lloyd, 1985, Vargas, 1985), and others. No matter who pursues this task, a psychology without knowledge of the actual contingencies of the world cannot offer a comprehensive account of conduct. Still, that limitation does not exclude laboratory work intended to uncover the structure of conduct. This laboratory work is what operant psychologists have concentrated on.

Laboratory work in operant psychology concentrates on the search for reliable relations known as *functional relations*. A functional relation is identified when a change in an independent variable results in a change in a dependent variable. The independent variable is the variable the experimenter manipulates. The dependent variable is the variable the experimenter records to determine what effect, if any, the independent variable has on it. In pursuing functional relations that involve the performance of individual subjects, contingency-oriented psychologists follow the strategy of proof and counterproof recommended by Claude Bernard (1927/1957, pp. 53–57; also see Thompson, 1984). This strategy requires experimenters to show that a change in the dependent variable occurs in the presence of the independent variable and does not occur in the absence of the independent variable. Feibleman (1972b, p. 223) remarked that the relation of "if A, then B *and* if not-A, then not-B" is the essence of a causal law. Skinner (1972, p. 307) commented that relations of this kind are the basic facts of the experimental sciences. As we shall see, the basic facts arrived at through experimental work in operant psychology are functional relations between contingencies (independent variables) and the effects of contingencies on performance (dependent variables).

REINFORCEMENT AND PUNISHMENT

The exploration of the effects of contingencies on performance has revealed some invariances. At center are two qualitative invariances known as *reinforcement* and *punishment*. These terms mislead because of connotations carried over from their origins in ordinary language. In operant psychology, they have technical meanings, gradually acquired through the better understanding of the invariances. *Reinforcement* names a relation in which a contingency operates and behavior increments or is maintained because of the contingency. *Punishment* names a relation in which a contingency operates and behavior decrements or continues to be suppressed because of the contingency. Goldiamond (1975a) recommended the terms *increment* and *decrement* when discussing the effects of contingencies, but we often use *increase* and *decrease* instead. We need to emphasize that reinforcement and punishment do not explain anything, and they do not constitute theories. They are two functional relations, nothing more or less.

Some writers have described operant principles as principles of behavior-environment relations. For example, Catania (1973b) said that *reinforcement* names a relationship between behavior and environment. Similarly, Hineline (1980) said that operant psychology offers statements which relate behavior to environmental events. Wahler and Fox (1982) said that we focus on behavior-environment relationships, and Buskist (1983) said that operant research has revealed relations between behavior and environment. These examples are not exceptional. On the contrary, describing operant principles as formulating relations between behavior and environment is commonplace. This traditional way of describing these principles is a source of confusion. The principles name relations between contingencies and performance, and they are better described as relations between contingencies and performance.

We need to note that contingencies are the basic, independent variables in operant research. Weingarten and Mechner (1966) commented that critics might challenge the notion that contingencies are independent variables. They might object that the consequential event (i.e., end result) can occur only if the designated behavior occurs, with the consequence that the dependent variable (behavior) contaminates the putative independent variable (contingency). Weingarten and Mechner rejected this alternative interpretation and insisted that consequential events are not the independent variables in operant research. Contingencies have that status because they are the variables under the experimenter's control. Certainly, the status of contingencies as independent variables is clear when the procedure of noncontingent reinforcement is used in experimental research to exclude alternative explanations of the incremental effects of a contingency. When this procedure is used, the consequential event is still delivered. Only the experimental contingency is no longer present. This removal of the experimental contingency underscores the status of contingencies as independent variables. In general, the consequences of behavior are important only in directing us to contingencies. As Skinner (1957, p. 432) noted, our interest in *consequences* is an interest in the *contingencies* into which consequential events enter with behavior.

It is worth noting that operant psychologists distinguish nonverbal from verbal contingencies and nonsocial from social contingencies. Noting these distinctions, albeit briefly, points to the variety of contingencies that we must consider in a contingency-oriented psychology. First, *nonverbal contingencies* are work requirements in which causal efficacy depends on a physical relation between behavior and end result. Examples include turning the car steering wheel with the resulting change of direction and walking toward the door with the resulting change in the proximity of the body to the door. Second, *verbal contingencies* are work requirements in which the end result is mediated by a listener or a reader. Skinner discussed work requirements of this kind in his book *Verbal Behavior* (1957). Sundberg and Partington (1982, 1983) provided a bibliography of relevant empirical research, and Michael (1984) provided a review. Lee (1984) provided some clarification of the concept of a verbal contingency. As some writers (e.g., MacCorquodale, 1970; Richelle, 1976) have noted, this clarification was necessary because the concept has not been well-understood by critics (e.g., Chomsky, 1959). Third, *nonsocial contingencies* are contingencies in which the behavior of only one organism participates. Examples include opening a door or reading one's own writing. Fourth, *social contingencies* are contingencies in which the behavior of two or more organisms participate. Skinner (1953, pp. 297–312) has discussed contingencies of this kind, and several writers (e.g., Molm, 1981; Molm & Wiggins, 1979; Schmitt, 1984) have discussed the relevant experimental research.

It is also worth noting that operant psychologists speak of operant behavior which is, by definition, behavior that has end results and whose subsequent occurrence is affected because past behavior had these end results. To say that behavior has end-results implies that a contingency operates. So, by definition, operant behavior is behavior that participates in one or more contingencies. As well, again by definition, it is behavior affected by its participation in those contingencies. Therefore, in order for behavior to count as operant, both criteria must be met. Although sometimes only the first criterion is mentioned when we define the term *operant behavior,* as Burgess and Akers (1966) noted, omitting the second criterion misses the concept of operant behavior. It leaves us only with behavior defined by its results; that is, with an equifinal class. The concept of operant behavior encompasses not only equifinal classes but also the incremental, decremental, maintaining, or suppressing effects that past and present contingencies have on subsequent performance. Consequently, there are two classes of operant behavior, one class in which contingencies support and maintain behavior, and another class in which contingencies suppress behavior. The terms *reinforcement* and *punishment* name the functional relations that identify the two classes. Following Catania (1973a), we can use the terms *operant* and *stoperant* to designate these two classes of operant behavior. At this point, we can insist as Smith (1983) does, that operant psychology is about operant behavior and not about behavior of any other kind. All other behavior falls outside the scope of operant psychology. This abstracting out of a circumscribed domain is consistent with practice in the other sciences.

SYNTHESIS AND ANALYSIS OF ACTIONS

Contingencies let us synthesize actions. To have an action, say the action of pressing a button for points, the relevant contingency ("if button pressing, then a point, but not otherwise") must operate. If that contingency does not operate, then the action of pressing a button for points could not occur, by definition. As well, button pressing must increment over its level before the contingency was instituted, and the increment must occur because of the contingency. Otherwise, we could not say that the action of button pressing for points is occurring. The operation of a contingency and the resulting increment of the behavioral constituent (e.g., button pressing) of the relevant action (e.g., button pressing for points) is what the concept of reinforcement refers to. That is, the concept has to do with the basic structure of an action which consists of the contingency and of the behavioral constituent of the action that the contingency supports.

The behavioral constituent of an action becomes increasingly unitized with repeated reinforcement. Stated differently, with repeated success the variability of an operant declines. The term *stereotypy* refers to this behavioral sameness across successive occurrences of an operant. Many studies (e.g., Antonitis, 1951; Pisacreta, 1982; Schwartz, 1981; Vogel & Annau, 1973) have demonstrated stereotypy within such behavioral dimensions as duration, latency, rate, and sequence. This production of a stereotyped unit of behavior does not necessitate an inflexible repertoire. Extinction increases variability, instructions can prompt people to vary their behavior, and contingencies can require variability (e.g., Pryor, Haag, & O'Reilly, 1969; Schoenfeld, Harris, & Farmer, 1966; Schwartz, 1982). But stereotypy does suggest that contingencies unitize behavior, albeit in a way that retains the potential for variability and, thus, for the adjustive effects upon performance of new contingencies.

Stereotypy of the behavioral constituent of an action is also observed in studies that fall under the law of practice. As Verhave (1967) commented, this law restates the commonsense observation that practice makes perfect. As traditionally understood, contingencies are not apparent in practice, whereas they are salient in reinforcement. The distinction between reinforcement and practice is exemplified by a child playing the piano to avoid parental disapproval (reinforcement) as opposed to playing the piano for the sensory effects of striking the keys (practice). The parental disapproval is easy to see and seems contrived, whereas the sensory effects of playing the piano are easily overlooked and seem natural. The distinction between reinforcement and practice is arbitrary. It reflects the peculiar history of psychology and not the nature of the contingencies maintained by objects, persons, and agencies outside the laboratory. Operant psychologists have typically concentrated on contrived contingencies and cognitive psychologists on automatic contingencies, albeit without acknowledging them as such. With contrived contingencies, the experimenter controls the critical result and therefore the contingency. With automatic contingencies, the critical result is controlled by the performance. In each case, the units of psychological significance have been characterized as eventually displaying routinization, automaticity, modularization, or stereotypy but also as showing a continuing fluency, equipotentiality, and flexibility. These properties have been acknowledged by operant and nonoperant psychologists alike (e.g., Bruner, 1973; Connolly, 1977; MacKay, 1982; Schoenfeld, Harris, & Farmer, 1966). They reflect the increasing stereotypy of behavior with repeated reinforcement and the variability induced by extinction and other variables. The important factor is the contingency and its capacity to create, maintain, and recreate units of behavior. Psychology might gain much if we could use the concept of an incremental contingency to integrate the laboratory phenomena of practice and reinforcement.

Synthesis is an obvious feature of operant research. But operant psychologists also analyze actions. That is, they take them apart or dismantle them. Analysis is implicit in the principle of extinction. This principle states the relation between the cessation of a contingency and a resulting decrement in the behavioral constituent of the action. Studies of sensory extinction (e.g., Rincover, 1978; Rincover, Cooke, Peoples, & Packard, 1979; Rincover & Devany, 1982) provide interesting examples. One example is the case of a child who spent much time spinning a plate. Observation suggested that the child was listening to the noise made by the spinning. To test this hypothesis, the table top was carpeted to eliminate the auditory effects of spinning. The action of plate spinning ceased immediately. In this example, the action of spinning a plate to make a noise was taken apart by terminating the contingency between spinning and noise. Studies of delayed sensory feedback also provide examples of analysis as opposed to synthesis. Goldiamond, Atkinson and Bilger (1962) discussed these studies from an operant perspective. Behavior produces sensory effects that can in turn occasion subsequent behavior. For example, when we speak, we hear our own speech, which can occasion further speech. Similarly, when we draw, we see the products of our drawing, and they can occasion further drawing. Studies of delayed sensory feedback introduce a delay between behavior and its sensory effects. For example, in delayed auditory feedback, subjects wear earphones that present their own speech to them with a delay controlled by the experimenter. This procedure separates speaking from the sensory effects it produces and that occasion further speaking. Most studies of delayed sensory feedback report disruption of the behavior. However, Goldiamond and others (1962) reported recovery of speaking when their subjects spoke with auditory delay for longer periods of time. Other sensory effects of speaking ordinarily blocked by the auditory effects might have consequated the behavior and occasioned subsequent behavior.

As discussed to this point, analysis and synthesis have to do with positive actions or with actions whose instances are performed. Philosophers (e.g., Best, 1978, p. 81; Brand, 1971; Ryle, 1979, pp. 105–119; Schutz, 1954) have also discussed the concept of a negative action. This concept derives from the observation that we refrain from performing some acts. For example, we might refrain from speaking when it would interrupt a person who is speaking to us. Refraining is something other than doing nothing, so refraining from interrupting is something more than not speaking. Refraining suggests a disposition to act (e.g., to speak), otherwise we would have nothing to refrain from. It also suggests the effort of bodily activity with the end result that we refrain from performing an act we are disposed to perform. In addition to this immediate end result, refraining doubtless has other results; for example, avoidance of frowns, objections, and the like, contingent on interrupting a speaker. Thus, refraining from performing an action involves bodily effort and an end result no less than does performing an action.

The principle of punishment in operant psychology relates to the concept of a negative action. This principle states a functional relation between the operation of a contingency and the resulting decrement in the equifinal class whose members are consequated. *Punishment* names this functional relation, wherever it is found. This functional relation seems to constitute the structure of a negative action. Suppose we wanted to establish the negative action of refraining from button pressing. There would have to be some disposition to engage in button pressing at the outset. Otherwise, we could not talk about refraining from button pressing. To establish this disposition, we could institute a contingency (e.g., button pressing for points) that would increment and maintain button pressing. To have the subject refrain from button pressing, we would have to institute another contingency with decremental effects upon the performance of button pressing. This arrangement in which a decremental contingency is superimposed over an incremental contingency is what the principle of punishment designates.

This discussion about the analysis and synthesis of actions highlights one aspect of operant psychology that other psychologists reject. They reject what they see as an interventionist psychology centered around the use of contrived contingencies. The emphasis on analysis and synthesis gives the experimental techniques of operant psychology much in common with the experimental techniques of the other experimental sciences. Experimental scientists create the phenomena of interest to them whenever they can. Moreover, they make new chemicals, new proteins, and so forth, in their pursuit of the structure of the domain of interest. Without constructing new units, experimental scientists would be limited to the actualities that nature presents. They could not make the observations required in order to formulate the structural patterns that underlie all the possible actualities in the domain of interest. Similarly, operant psychologists construct units of behavior, and, in doing so, go beyond the actualities given in nature in order to study the structural patterns that underlie action.

In making the units of interest, operant psychology has a craft base missing elsewhere in psychology. Kvale (1973) commented that this craft base makes operant research an important exception to the triviality of much psychological research. An important aspect of operant psychology is the convergence of craft techniques with speculation about the general nature of conduct. The history of genetics exemplifies this convergence of craft and speculation in the other sciences. In genetics, breeding techniques, developed through centuries of practical experience, converged with speculation about the mechanisms of inheritance. Psychology as a whole has been peculiar among the sciences in lacking a craft base (e.g., Bass, 1974; Luchins & Luchins, 1965, pp. 375–376). This lack did not arise because craft techniques were unavailable. Rather, such techniques were unfashionable in a psychology with more esoteric concerns. Operant psychology, with its emphasis on techniques for creating units of behavior, departs from the passive tradition that restricts much of psychological research to actualities. It would be a mistake, however, to think that operant psychologists make units of behavior exclusively for the sake of doing so. On the contrary, craft techniques contribute by helping us separate relevant from irrelevant variables and by opening the way to the concepts and principles that a science properly seeks. Craft techniques also contribute by obliging us to ground our speculation about the nature of conduct in the everyday reality of the craftsperson and, thus, unequivocally in conceptualized particulars.

N-TERM CONTINGENCIES

The previous discussion has considered only two-term contingencies. But there are also three-term contingencies. The concept of the three-term contingency takes into account the occasion on which a consequence is contingent on behavior. Many two-term contingencies operate only on some occasions and not on others. This differential operation of contingencies is a familiar part of ordinary experience. For example, a red light is an occasion on which accelarating through an intersection has a higher chance of resulting in a collision. On the occasion of a red light, the particular two-term contingency is more likely to operate. A two-term contingency together with the situation under which it operates constitutes a three-term contingency. Such a contingency is stated, "if occasion, then if behavior, then consequence" (Sidman, 1986a, 1986b).

Some writers have treated the term *contingency* as meaning a three-term contingency. For example, Goldiamond (1975b) restated Skinner's description of a contingency in this way: Contingencies consist of the behaviors on which certain consequences are contingent both in relation to each other and to the conditions under which the behavior-consequence relationship holds. Goldiamond also said we must analyze conditions, behavior, and results; in other words, contingencies. Similarly, Ringen (1976) said he took the relationship among situation, behavior, and consequence to be what operant psychologists call a *contingency.* Other writers (e.g., Skinner, 1968, p. 4; 1969, p. 23; 1971, pp. 73–74; 1973) have also taken the term *contingency* to mean a three-term contingency. Departing from that, other writers have treated *contingency* as meaning the two-term contingency of behavior and consequence. For example, Catania (1973c) presented what he called a *behavior paradigm,* consisting of SD(R:SC). He said that the expression (R:SC) represents the relation of behavior to consequences, a relation called a *contingency.* It translates as meaning the effect of the behavior on the probability of the consequential event. Catania said that the paradigm as a whole represents a contingency that operates in the presence of a specified occasion (SD). In short, Catania used the term *contingency* in the sense of a two-term contingency. Skinner (e.g., Skinner, 1953, p. 85; in Evans 1968, pp. 19–20) has also used the term in that sense.

This apparent inconsistency in usage of the term *contingency* reflects a historical shift since the late 1930s from two-term to three-term contingencies. Early work in operant psychology defined behavior by its effect on the environment; for example, by the closure of a switch. There was no consistent relation between behavior and other events, so theorists did not have to relate behavior to anything other than its consequences. In other words, as Sidman (1978) pointed out, behavior was defined independently of the situation in which it was consequated. But, as noted by Schick (1971), Skinner has increasingly emphasized discriminative behavior and three-term contingencies in his writings, and usage of the term *contingency* has shifted, with some inconsistencies appearing.

The relation of two-term contingencies to the occasion on which they operate can be more complex. Specifically, other aspects of an occasion can indicate which of two or more three-term contingencies is currently in effect. For example, the time on my watch (e.g., after midnight) might correlate with the absence of the contingency of a ticket (consequence) upon accelerating through an intersection (act) with a red light (one aspect of the occasion). Similarly, if I am about to leave my car (one aspect of the occasion) and if the car lights are on (another aspect), if I turn off the lights (act), then I will avoid a dead battery later (end result). In these situations, the three-term contingency operates only on some occasions and not on others. The resulting discrimination is called a *conditional discrimination.* The whole situation constitutes a four-term contingency in which behavior has a result on a particular occasion conditional on the relation between two aspects of that occasion.

Sidman (1986a, 1986b) recently clarified the operant paradigm in light of this extension beyond the three-term contingency. This clarification admits n-term contingencies and organizes the findings of operant psychology under successive levels of increasing complexity (two-term, three-term, four-term, etc.). Briefly, the paradigm begins with the *two-term contingency* and with two functional relations, reinforcement and punishment. This level of complexity includes the parameters of reinforcement and punishment; for example, schedule, delay, alternative contingencies, and amount of the reinforcer. It also includes extinction and stereotypy. The level of the *three-term contingency* includes the phenomena of discriminative control which link the behavioral phenomena of the two-term contingency to the occasion on which the contingency operates. This level also includes the process of conditioned reinforcement which expands the number and variety of end results that can participate in incremental contingencies. Furthermore, the level of the three-term contingency includes second-order schedules (See Keenan, 1986) that permit contingencies to maintain large amounts of behavior despite infrequent end results. The level of the three-term contingency also includes chaining which can produce long and intricate sequences of behavior. The level of the *four-term contingency* includes conditional discriminations in which performance depends on the relations among two or more aspects of the occasion for behavior. This level also includes stimulus equivalence in which the establishment of one conditional discrimination leads automatically to others. Sidman discussed the further possibility of five-term through n-term contingencies. He suggested that contingencies, the functional relations that contingencies enter into with behavior, and the phenomena emerging from those functional relations (e.g., chaining, stimulus equivalence) constitute the structure of our subject matter.

The research that led to Sidman's (1986a, 1986b) summary of psychological structure started with nonhuman subjects. As shown by Nevin (1982), human beings were sometimes included as subjects but their participation in operant research was relatively insignificant. In the 1960s, operant psychologists increasingly extended their work to the socially important behavior of human beings. This extension resulted in the field known as *applied behavior analysis*. Initially, this field was intended only to extend empirical work in operant psychology to socially important behavior. The emphasis quickly changed from curiosity-oriented research to mission-oriented research, because of pressure from practitioners and agencies for practical results. The trend away from discovery and towards cures, however trivial and transitory, has led to much criticism of applied behavior analysis (e.g., Cullen, 1981; Deitz, 1978, 1982, 1983; Hake, 1982; Michael, 1980; Pierce & Epling, 1980). In particular, the critics have expressed doubt about the knowledge base that applied researchers have to apply. The empirical trial-and-error of much applied behavior analysis and the poverty of its conceptual base underscore this lack of basic knowledge. Concurrent with these criticisms, there is a renewed interest in basic research using human subjects (e.g., Baron & Perone, 1982a, 1982b; Buskist, 1983; Buskist & Miller, 1982; Hake, 1982). Such research is a new direction in operant psychology, with special interest being shown in human social behavior (e.g., Schmitt, 1984), in human verbal behavior (e.g., Michael, 1984), and in how human beings extract statements of contingencies which in turn affect their performance (e.g., Baron & Galizio, 1983; Lowe & Horne, 1985). These extensions, together with the paradigm summarized by Sidman (1986a, 1986b) and the philosophic clarification provided by Day (e.g., 1976, 1980, 1983), among others, hold the promise of a very different psychology from that which currently informs applied behavior analysis.

CONTINGENCIES AND MEANS-END RELATIONS

Contingencies are basic independent variables in operant research, and they constitute the primary objects of interest to operant psychologists. This interest in contingencies contradicts statements that operant psychology is about behavior, unless the term *behavior* means operant behavior in the technical sense. Behavior is of interest in operant psychology only to the extent that it participates in contingencies and is affected by them. Indeed, this interest is implicit in Smith's (1985) notion that operant psychology is about operant behavior and nothing else. Alternatively stated, operant psychologists are interested in contingencies and in the effects of contingencies on performance, instead of in bodily behaviors (i.e., movements and postural activities) as such. This interest establishes that a contingency-oriented psychology is a psychology of action and not a psychology of bodily activities. Indeed, some writers (e.g., Hunt, 1969; Kitchener, 1977; Shwayder, 1965, p. 18) have already noted the apparent similarity between the concept of an action and the concept of operant behavior. But this view is not widely held. Certainly the connection between contingencies and means–end units has been obscured by some of the ways in which we talk about contingencies.

First, we often describe contingencies as environmental variables. We speak of *environmental contingencies, outer contingencies, external contingencies,* of contingencies as outside the organism, of contingencies as properties of the environment, and so on (e.g., Bandura, 1974; Goldiamond, 1975b; Lundh, 1981; Schnaitter, 1975; Skinner, 1957, p. 31; Waller, 1977). But many contingencies span organism and environment; for example, the contingency between the behavior of closing a door and the closing of the door. In consequence, contingencies are not environmental variables, in the traditional sense of a variable located outside the skin of the organism. Other statements treat contingencies as interactions of behavior and environment (e.g., Harzem & Williams, 1983; Parsons, Taylor & Joyce, 1981; Skinner, 1969, p. 97). For example, Skinner (1969) spoke of "the interaction between organism and environment represented by the concept of contingencies" (p. 97). Although some contingencies span organism and environment, the concept of the contingency does not seem well-formulated as designating an interaction of organism and environment. The contingency implicit in daydreaming illustrates the difficulty, as does the contingency implicit in nail biting. In nail biting, for example, changes in the configurations of the nails follow the behavior of nail biting. Indeed, nail biting, as an action, comprises both the bodily behavior that produces the changes and the changes in the nail. Without the changes, the action might be only putting the fingers in the mouth, sucking the fingers, or something else. Formulating the concept of the contingency as designating an interaction of organism and environment makes actions such as nail biting and daydreaming seem anomalous. No such anomaly arises when we concentrate on means and ends or on equifinal classes and end results rather than on behavior and environment in a psychology of action.

Second, we easily think of contingencies as involving only explicit reward. Thus, the stereotypical contingency is between lever pressing by a rat and the contingent delivery of food or between studying by a child and the contingent delivery of praise and tokens. Stated differently, it is easy to restrict contingencies to contrived contingencies. Contingencies *are* contrived for the purposes of experimental research and for applied ends. Some contingencies bind behavior and results together such that the performance controls the results, so it makes good sense to contrive contingencies for experimental research. Also, sometimes it is useful to contrive contingencies in applied settings to establish the behavior we want. Indeed, without such contingencies, we might not get the behavior we want. Just because contrived contingencies are often used in operant research does not mean that the operant concept of a contingency is limited to contrived contingencies. On the contrary, operant psychologists include as contingencies the relation between speaking and hearing one's own voice, between spinning a top and hearing the whirring noise, and so forth. In addition, operant psychologists (e.g., Skinner, 1982; Vaughan & Michael, 1982) have contrasted these automatic contingencies with the contrived contingencies typical of behavior modification and of other deliberate attempts to change performance. Equating the concept of a contingency exclusively with contrived contingencies prevents us from seeing the ubiquity of contingencies in conduct. In particular, it prevents us from seeing sensory consequences and other consequences closely bound to behavior. We need to recognize that contrived contingencies do not constitute the entire universe of contingencies.

REPLICATION

In order to grasp the essential message of radical behaviorism, we need to do a great deal of work to eliminate our misconceptions about contingencies and to fully explicate the concept of a contingency as a work requirement. Radical behaviorism, the philosophy of operant psychology, centers around a commitment to a contingency-oriented psychology. Mentioning this commitment is the most direct way of describing radical behaviorism. As Day (1976, 1983) noted, it *is* an attempt to deal with psychological matters in terms of contingencies. In that spirit, Skinner (1967) described radical behaviorism as a working hypothesis about the nature of the subject matter of psychology. He said that radical behaviorists believe that this working hypothesis will lead to a successful science of psychology. That science will be a psychology of acts, of means-end units, or of contingencies.

The concept of replication is also central to radical behaviorism. Replication has to do with the repeatability of an experiment and its results. This repeatability is important because the reliability of scientific knowledge is established by the replication of experiments within a particular laboratory and subsequently across laboratories. Replication is implicit in the concept of a functional relation which in turn is implicit in the principles of reinforcement and punishment. A functional relation is demonstrated only if a change in the independent variable results in a change in the dependent variable. This demonstration requires that we systematically manipulate the independent variable. The experimenter presents the independent variable, removes it, presents it again, and so on, until it seems likely that changes in the dependent variable occur because of the presence and absence of the independent variable. The repeated production of this effect increases our confidence that we have identified a functional relation in a particular experiment. When other experimenters also find this relation, we become more confident that it is a reliable relation in the subject matter.

The knowledge accumulated by research in operant psychology is based on systematic replication. Systematic replication extends beyond direct replication, in which an experiment is repeatedly exactly. In systematic replication, we repeat the procedures of earlier experiments and add to them. The process has been described in detail by Sidman (1960) and by Johnston and Pennypacker (1980). Essentially, it amounts to repeatedly demonstrating a functional relation in new experimental contexts. For example, Skinner originally demonstrated performance under fixed-interval schedules using a few subjects. Since then, performance under fixed-interval schedules has been used in studying conditioned reinforcement, delayed reinforcement, chaining, temporal discriminations, conditional discriminations, and the effects of human verbal behavior on schedule performance. Each successive experiment has confirmed the original finding and added to it. Our confidence in the resulting body of knowledge depends on the repeatability of the experiments and on their usefulness as guides in conducting further experiments that reveal replicable patterns in our subject matter. And all of this depends on the self-corrective process of scientific inquiry. Moreover, it accepts that scientific inquiry proceeds step-by-step, starting with simple relations and increasing in complexity only as our capacity to obtain orderly results increases.

The strategy followed in operant research is consistent with that followed by the other sciences (e.g., Sidman, 1956; Skinner, 1972, pp. 295–312). But it departs from the research strategy of traditional psychology, which depends on large groups of subjects and on inferential statistics. In addition, a subject matter consisting of acts and contingencies departs from the traditional formulation of psychological phenomena as consisting of organocentric processes. On both these grounds, the body of well-replicated findings that operant psychology offers is not recognized by mainstream psychology as constituting a body of reliable knowledge about psychological phenomena. This difficulty is philosophic. It arises from differences among psychologists concerning what they count as psychological phenomena, and also from differences in how they conceptualize scientific inquiry. The fact is that research based on the metatheoretical foundation of the two-term contingency has produced a body of well-replicated findings. This result suggests that the concept of the two-term contingency does have strategic significance. The primary difficulty is to persuade all psychologists that this knowledge is psychological and that we would do well to build on this firm foundation step-by-step and to fully explore the ramifications of the concept of the two-term contingency for psychology.

CHAPTER 8

Radical
Behaviorism

INTRODUCTION

As we have seen, operant psychology is a contingency-oriented psychology. As such, it is a psychology of means–end units or, as understood here, a psychology of action. To an outsider, a psychology of action or of contingencies might seem unremarkable. But, within the context of academic psychology, operant psychology *is* remarkable. It is the only approach to psychology that takes contingencies explicitly and directly as the basic units of interest. In exploring the nature and effects of contingencies, operant psychology has become separated from the rest of psychology. Because of that separation, many misconceptions about operant psychology are expressed in the psychological literature. This chapter discusses the separation and the misconceptions.

OPERANT PSYCHOLOGY

Operant psychology has become separated from the rest of psychology. It has its own media and its own research traditions.

The media of operant psychology consist in part of academic journals which publish original contributions. *The Journal of the Experimental Analysis of Behavior* (JEAB) was founded in 1958. It publishes experimental work that centers on the behavioral and discriminative effects of contingencies. Much of this work uses nonhuman subjects, but, as Nevin (1982) noted, JEAB has always published some work using human subjects. Human operant research published in JEAB and elsewhere is listed in bibliographies prepared by Buskist and Miller (1982a, 1982b). In 1968, another journal, *The Journal of Applied Behavior Analysis* (JABA) appeared, in response to the need for an outlet for applied work in operant psychology. The journal *Behaviorism,* which appeared in 1972, concentrates on radical behaviorism, the philosophy of psychology associated with operant research. Another journal, *The Behavior Analyst,* appeared in 1978. It concentrates on conceptual, methodological, and professional issues. These four journals represent the core of operant journals, though several other journals also publish relevant material. Wyatt, Hawkins, and Davis (1986) provided a useful list of these other sources in their survey of the editorial policies of behavioral journals.

The media of operant psychology also includes many books. Michael (1980) listed early contributions, including Keller (1954), Keller and Schoenfeld (1950), and Sidman (1960). Michael noted that books on operant psychology are now too numerous to easily list. Among them are books written by Skinner. Epstein (1977) provided a bibliography of Skinner's books and papers. Skinner's first book, *The Behavior of Organisms* (1938), republished his early laboratory work. A later book, *Science and Human Behavior* (1953), was written for an undergraduate course in psychology at Harvard University. This book used operant concepts to interpret human behavior and social organization, including government, education, and religion. It is a detailed and comprehensive statement of Skinner's position. Other books published by Skinner include *Walden Two* (1948), *Verbal Behavior* (1957), *Beyond Freedom and Dignity* (1971), and *About Behaviorism* (1974). Operant psychology, then, has its own media. Operant psychologists contribute to these media, they use them to guide their own work, and they base their teaching on them.

Operant psychology has its own research traditions. It is the research tradition that gave rise to the knowledge of psychological structure summarized by Sidman (1986a, 1986b). The most salient aspect of this research tradition is that it deals with action directly as a subject matter with a structure that consists of contingencies, the functional relations that contingencies enter into with performance, and the various phenomena that emerge from these functional relations. As noted before, the basic independent variables in this research are contingencies and the basic dependent variables are dimensions of performance, including rate, duration, and interresponse times. Experimental research in operant psychology is a search for the independent variables that account for changes in the dependent variables. As it was explained in Chapter 7, a relevant independent variable has been identified when a functional relation is demonstrated. Functional relations are demonstrated by using individual subjects or by treating a group of subjects as an individual. They are checked and rechecked through the process of systematic replication described by Sidman (1960) and by Johnston and Pennypacker (1980).

Operant research is not restricted to empirical work. It also includes much philosophic and conceptual work (e.g., Branch & Malagodi 1980; Day, 1976, 1980, 1983; Deitz 1986; Deitz & Arrington, 1983, 1984; Hineline 1980; Lee, 1981, 1983; Malagodi 1986; Schoenfeld, 1972,

1976; Staddon, 1973) that aims to clarify the terms and concepts of operant psychology and of psychology as a whole. This scholarly work makes an important contribution to operant psychology by explicating unspoken assumptions and by exploring the ramifications of progress made in empirical research. Kvale and Grenness (1967) noted that work of this kind confronts the persistent philosophic problems that most psychologists dismiss as matters of armchair psychology. Marr (1984) insisted that work aimed at resolving these philosophic problems holds the key to significant progress in psychology as a whole. Indeed, such work is an essential part of research in psychology as it is understood by radical behaviorists.

RADICAL BEHAVIORISM

Operant psychology is associated with the philosophy of psychology known as *radical behaviorism*. Although B. F. Skinner initiated radical behaviorism, contrary to what outsiders might think, it is no longer exclusively the work of Skinner. Many writers now contribute to radical behaviorism. Moreover, radical behaviorism is ongoing, continually evolving, and internally disputatious. It is not an established dogma that requires its followers to spend their time interpreting the texts of its founder. Even so, we do need to explicate Skinner's writings. Skinner's writings are difficult, particularly because the difficulty is easily missed. As one writer commented, reading Skinner's work is like skating over thin ice. His writing is easy to read but difficult to understand. Skinner's contributions deserve careful study so that we can build on his insights and convey them to our students and to other psychologists. After all, Skinner has more fully and more explicitly explored the implications of a contingency-oriented psychology than any other psychologist. It would be a mistake, however, to see the task of radical behaviorism exclusively as a matter of explicating Skinner's writing. Consistent with Skinner's work, the task is to fully explore the ramifications of giving contingencies a central place in psychological theory, research, and practice.

Some writers (e.g., Hake, 1982; Skinner, 1969, p. 221, 1974, p. 7) have described radical behaviorism as a philosophy of the science of psychology. This description implies a distinction that radical behaviorists wish to make between the philosophy (radical behaviorism) and the science (operant psychology or behavior analysis). In discussing this distinction, Leigland (1984) observed that some work published in JEAB departs from the spirit of radical behaviorism, and conversely, that radical behaviorism implies new methodologies not found in the tradition of JEAB. Consistent with this, Hayes (1978) noted various levels of commitment to the operant enterprise. A commitment to operant methodology, techniques, and principles need not necessarily indicate a commitment to the philosophic perspective of radical behaviorism. In other words, people who contribute to JEAB and JABA do not necessarily follow the philosophy of radical behaviorism. Their commitment to operant psychology might be methodological, technological, and conceptual, but not philosophic. In short, radical behaviorism is the philosophy of psychology associated with research published in JEAB and JABA but not necessarily the philosophy of that research.

Day (1983) commented that describing radical behaviorism as a philosophy can be misleading, because radical behaviorism is more an exercise in psychology than in philosophy. It properly belongs to theoretical psychology, the branch of psychology that concerns itself with the broader metatheoretical aspects of psychological inquiry. Malagodi (1986) made the more radical suggestion, that radical behaviorism is a comprehensive theory of behavior, not merely a philosophy of the science of psychology. It integrates philosophic contributions to a science of behavior (read, *action*) with empirical contributions to that science. Radical behaviorism is best understood in this broader sense. It is, most centrally, an attempt to establish a contingency-oriented psychology. In pursuing this end, radical behaviorists engage in critiques of traditional psychology. As well, they engage in the work of developing an ongoing reformulation of psychology's subject matter, task, and method. Both aspects of radical behaviorism, the critique and the ongoing reformulation, require further discussion.

Criticisms of psychology offered by radical behaviorists have much in common with the criticisms offered by other writers. For example, radical behaviorists have criticized the traditional reliance upon crude measures of behavior, large numbers of subjects, episodic observation, and statistical analysis of group data in empirical research. They have also criticized the prevalence of premature theory without prior discovery of fruitful variables, the bodies of conflicting and inconsistent findings, the lack of unity and of cumulative progress, the persistence of a hooks-and-eye model of causality and of an organocentric model of psychological phenomena. Examples of these criticisms can be found in several of Skinner's books (e.g., 1953, 1969, 1972). The literature outside radical behaviorism offers similar criticisms (e.g., Carver, 1978; Coulter, 1982; DeLucca, 1979; Howard, 1986; Lichtenstein, 1980; Llewelyn & Kelly, 1980; Mishler, 1979; Pepitone, 1981; Sampson, 1983; Sarason, 1981; Sherif, 1979).

Radical behaviorism offers an ongoing reformulation of the subject matter, task, and method of psychology. This reformulation centers upon the concept of the contingency and the ramifications of this concept for how we conceive of the task and method of psychological inquiry. The concept of the contingency provides operant psychologists with a common outlook on a common domain, which opens the way to a unity not found elsewhere in psychology. It also places operant psychology in a research tradition different from that of nonoperant psychology. The emphasis on contingencies, and therefore on actions, puts radical behaviorism in the tradition of Dewey, Bentley, and Kantor, among others. These theorists insisted that human actions are the phenomena of psychological import. Radical behaviorists also insist that action is a subject matter in its own right, capable of description and explanation without resort to hypotheses about a biological or conceptual nervous system. Psychologies concerned with human action have always been a minority in psychology, as most psychologists are interested in action only as evidence for underlying biological or conceptual systems. In fact, most psychologists take the biological organism or the conceptual nervous system as the proper subject matter of psychology. Radical behaviorists explicitly reject this approach. They pursue a psychology of action and not a psychology of organisms and organocentric processes.

THE BEHAVIORISMS

The literature of psychology contains many statements hostile to behaviorism. These statements are puzzling. At least, they are puzzling if we accept means–end units as central to human action and if we accept human action as the proper domain of psychology. Is radical behaviorism included in the behaviorism rejected by many psychologists? The answers to this question are complex, in part because of the term *behaviorism* and its capacity to alienate and mislead. The term needs some discussion in order to clarify the relation of radical behaviorism and operant psychology to the rest of psychology.

The term *behaviorism* is problematic, because there is no one behaviorism. Many theorists have described themselves as behaviorists—Watson, Tolman, Hull, Hunter, and Skinner, among others. The variety of behaviorists is also evinced by a multitude of names that include *behaviorism: standard behaviorism, social behaviorism, paradigmatic behaviorism, purposive behaviorism, cognitive behaviorism, methodological behaviorism, subjective behaviorism, interbehaviorism, operant behaviorism,* and *eclectic behaviorism,* and others. The variety of terms suggests there is no one behaviorism and no single meaning for the word *behaviorism.* Consistent with this variety, critics have long warned against treating behaviorism in a global way. For example, Williams (1931) said that psychology has no one behaviorism. Harrell and Harrison (1938) said that the range of opinions called *behaviorism* could be behaviorisms only in name, otherwise, behaviorism would comprise contradictory opinions sampling the whole range of positions taken in psychology. Criticisms of behaviorism seem vacuous without mention of a specific behaviorism.

Despite the multiplicity of behaviorisms-by-name, the concept of behaviorism in psychology does have a core of meaning. Hocutt (1985) suggested that the commonality is in the commitment to making psychology a science. But that commitment would include all psychologists committed to a science of psychology, whether they identify themselves as behaviorists or not. An alternative strategy might restrict usage of the word *behaviorism* to the classical behaviorism espoused by Watson (e.g., 1913, 1919). Classical behaviorism was an attempt to make psychology an objective science by excluding introspection, a specialized form of self-report that psychologists had used as their primary research technique. Watson's behaviorism insisted that psychologists must rely on observation of publicly available events. As well, Watson's behaviorism was a stimulus–response psychology, which imposed the stimulus–response framework derived from the concept of the reflex on all psychological phenomena. The stimulus–response framework is discussed in detail in Chapter 13. For the moment, we can say that classical behaviorism was a stimulus–response psychology that insisted that publicly observable behavior constituted its only data base.

Radical behaviorism is not a stimulus–response behaviorism. As Day (1980) observed, it falls more within the tradition of the act psychologies. It has more in common with Dewey, Bentley, and Mead than with Watson, because it accepts action as a subject matter and rejects stimulus–response behaviorism. Consistent with this, Skinner has expressed doubt about the term *behaviorism*. He said that he calls himself a behaviorist but does not like the term (Skinner, in Evans, 1968, p. 24). Certainly, radical behaviorism rejects the stimulus–response framework and offers an alternative formulation of psychological phenomena inconsistent with the traditional framework it rejects. It also rejects the assumption of mechanistic causality and the exclusion of self-reports associated with stimulus–response psychology. In short, radical behaviorism departs from what most psychologists expect of a behaviorism.

It is regrettable that radical behaviorists did not heed McDougall's recommendation to restrict the term *behaviorism* to classical behaviorism. Adding the term *radical* does not help, because Watson's behaviorism was called *radical behaviorism* in the 1920s and 1930s (e.g., Calkins, 1921; Diserens, 1925; Harrell & Harrison, 1938; Jastrow, 1927; Miner, 1929). In this connection, Hineline (1980) suggested *radical functionalism* as an alternative to *radical behaviorism*. Another possibility is to speak of a contingency-oriented psychology and to restrict the word *behaviorism* to its original meaning of stimulus–response behaviorism. If radical behaviorists want other psychologists to listen to them, they might have to abandon the term *behaviorism* when referring to the psychology they espouse. The term *contingency-oriented psychology* states the kind of psychology in which radical behaviorists are interested. Alternatively, we could use the term *operant psychology* and define that term as meaning a contingency-oriented psychology. Using the term *psychology* might occasion objections from some radical behaviorists because the term has been taken to mean the study of mind in the sense of a conceptual nervous system. But that traditional interpretation depends on the mistaken belief that psychological terms such as *mind, memory, intelligence,* and the like, have to do with something other than behavior-in-context (i.e., action). If we understand that psychological phenomena consist of actions, then the term *psychology* is no longer abhorrent.

We have seen that the mainstream of psychology rejects behaviorism. At least, contributors to the psychological literature offer statements that denigrate behaviorism. Oddly enough, radical behaviorists also reject behaviorism, albeit behaviorism of a particular kind. Specifically, they contrast their approach to psychology with an approach they call *methodological behaviorism.* To a radical behaviorist, methodological behaviorism is the metatheoretical position held by the mainstream of psychology, which consists of psychologists who adhere to the generally accepted approach to psychological inquiry. This approach consists of a set of methodological and metatheoretical norms that radical behaviorists reject.

Some norms of methodological behaviorism concern research methods. For one thing, methodological behaviorism generally excludes reports of subjective experiences or private events and counts only reports of publicly observable events as acceptable data. That is, methodological behaviorism follows classical behaviorism in restricting relevant data to recorded observations of publicly observable behavior. Second, methodological behaviorism takes the scientistic view that scientific knowledge is superior to ordinary knowledge. This attitude permits psychologists to ignore ordinary knowledge and its proper contribution to the foundations of scientific psychology. Third, methodological behaviorism takes an empiricist approach to psychology which assumes that psychology's primary task is to collect data and that only data-collection will advance knowledge. An empiricist attitude affects how the difficulties bequeathed by ordinary knowledge are brought into the laboratory for investigation. In particular, ordinary language categories such as those designated by the terms *language, memory, learning,* and *perception* are accepted without analysis as the basis for empirical research. Fourth, methodological behaviorism is committed to traditional methods of experimental design and usually to techniques of statistical inference. It relies on groups of subjects, on averaged performances, and on statistical comparison of results.

Other norms of methodological behaviorism concern the nature of the subject matter of psychology. These assumptions are individualism, cognitivism, reductionism, and mechanism. In brief, individualism locates psychological phenomena inside the biological unit. Bentley (1941) and Dewey (1930), among others, rejected this location, and similar rejections continue to appear in the critical literature of modern psychology (e.g., Pepitone, 1981; Sampson, 1983; Sarason, 1981). Individualism permits cognitivism, which assumes that the phenomena of interest to academic psychology consist of a conceptual nervous system inside the organism. Individualism also permits biological reductionism, the belief that psychological phenomena are reducible to physiological, and specifically neurological, processes. Reductionism is a biological version of cognitivism. In turn, both cognitivism and reductionism are consistent with the mechanistic thinking that locates causes in the immediate antecedents of behavior. Cognitivism locates these causes in the conceptual nervous system, and reductionism locates them in the biological organism. This set of related assumptions about the nature of psychological phenomena are at the heart of the behaviorism that persists in the mainstream of academic psychology.

ISOLATION AND MISREPRESENTATION

Operant psychology is a minority position in the psychology departments where it is taught. This minority status is reflected in the title of a paper that Skinner presented to the Association for Behavior Analysis in 1981: "We happy few, but why so few?" It is also seen in Michael's (1980) comment that in the early years, operant psychologists were a minority group in academic settings. They were not part of the establishment. They acquired an interest in operant psychology through their own reading or through professors not part of the eclectic majority. This minority status has not changed.

Operant psychology is isolated from the rest of psychology. Operant and nonoperant psychologists seldom cite each other's work. Krantz (1972) reported some research relevant to this mutual isolation. He interviewed 35 senior operant psychologists, 60% of whom held editorial positions on JEAB, JABA, or both. Krantz found that most of his respondents saw some if not most nonoperant work as unworthy of citation. Krantz commented on JEAB's high rate of self-citation. He concluded that the mutual isolation of operant and nonoperant psychology resulted from differences in beliefs about the nature of psychology, which result in different methods, different attitudes toward explanation, and so forth. Thus, the differences between operant and nonoperant psychology are metatheoretical or at the level of our basic assumptions about psychology's subject matter, task, and method.

Other writers have commented on the isolation of operant psychology. Guttman (1977) noted that operant work is seldom referenced more than a few times each year in the *Journal of Experimental Psychology.* Greer (1982) commented that the major journals of the *American Educational Research Association* seldom notice philosophic and empirical developments in operant psychology relevant to education. Schoenfeld (1965) pointed out that social psychologists have largely ignored operant research and theory, and Winston (in Morris, et al., 1982) commented that operant research has had little influence in developmental psychology.

This isolation might indicate that operant psychology is becoming a separate discipline. Lemaine and his colleagues (Lemaine, MacLeod, Mulkay & Weingart, 1976) traced the emergence of other new disciplines and concluded that a low cross-citation rate is one indicator of such an emergence. Some writers have suggested that operant psychology should deliberately emerge as a separate discipline. Specifically, Skinner (1980, p. 71) said he has been thinking that operant psychologists should pursue this separation deliberately, and Fraley and Vargas (1986) offered the same conclusion. Seeking deliberate separation from mainstream psychology reflects the difficulties of pursuing a contingency-oriented psychology within the traditional context.

The difficulties of pursuing a contingency-oriented psychology arise in part because of the misconceptions that nonoperant psychologists hold about operant psychology. Some writers (e.g., Day, 1980; Goldiamond, 1974; Mapel, 1977) have indicated that discussions in the nonoperant literature contain many misunderstandings and misrepresentations of operant psychology. These misinterpretations evince a lack of scholarship. Concretely, there is a widespread belief that operant psychology takes movements rather than actions as its subject matter, that it denies private events, that it has no place for emotion, that it excludes self-awareness, that it insists upon the passive nature of human beings, that it holds mechanistic assumptions, and that it is a stimulus–response psychology, among other things. Mention of this lack of scholarship is scattered through the operant literature (e.g., Cooke, 1984; Harzem & Williams, 1983; Lowe & Higson, 1981; MacCorquodale, 1970; Todd & Morris, 1983).

The difficulties that operant psychologists face are aggravated by psychology textbooks that introduce students to operant psychology within the context of an eclectic approach. These textbooks present a selection of operant work under the headings of *Learning* or *Behavior Modification.* The selection fits the traditional concentration on data and cures. However, it omits the essence of operant psychology—the critique and the ongoing examination and reformulation of the basic issues of subject matter, task, and method. Indeed, textbook presentations of operant psychology are brief, selective, misleading, and sometimes false, a matter documented by

Cooke (1984) and by Todd and Morris (1983). The difficulties that face operant psychology are further aggravated by workshops for practitioners, which, as Greer (1982) noted, tend to avoid the philosophic and empirical complexities of operant research. Basic research and philosophic inquiry evoke impatience from those who want techniques that work. Consequently, workshops for educators, social workers, and other practitioners are not venues that welcome detailed and difficult conceptual argument. Practitioners *as* practitioners are quite rightly concerned with getting a job done and not with the theoretical justification of research. Even so, an impoverished form of a contingency-oriented psychology is too often presented to practitioners *as* behaviorism, and the contributions of radical behaviorism are missed.

RETREAT

Operant psychology has minority status in an academic discipline whose literature consistently ignores or misrepresents it. The minority status and the misrepresentations do not make it easy for operant research to flourish. In fact, many researchers have retreated from operant psychology over recent years. Hayes (1978) listed four aspects of this retreat: the drift of applied research toward a cure-help orientation, the theoretical emaciation of such research, the assimilation of basic research into general psychology, and the infighting of basic and applied researchers. Other writers (e.g., Cullen, 1981; Day, 1983; Ferster, 1978; Michael, 1980; Skinner, 1976, 1986) have similarly commented on the drift of basic research away from the initial aspirations associated with radical behaviorism. For example, Day (1983) acknowledged the drift toward the aims and research designs of traditional psychology, and Nevin (1980) commented that research published in JEAB is now less distinctive than it was once. Research published in JABA has also drifted from the spirit of radical behaviorism as many critics (e.g., Birnbrauer, 1979; Deitz, 1978; Michael, 1980; Pierce & Epling, 1980) have observed. The drift away from radical behaviorism illuminates Hayes' (1978) comment that people contributing to operant journals evince various levels of commitment to the operant enterprise. As things stand, a commitment to operant methodology, techniques, and principles need not necessarily also indicate a commitment to radical behaviorism. Indeed, some contributors to behavioral journals have never been radical behaviorists. For them, retreat is not the issue. The retreat from radical behaviorism, or, alternatively, the neglect of it, is understandable. The task of building a conceptually systematic psychology of action is hard work. It is easier to pursue the organocentric psychology that provides a ready-made methodology borrowed from elsewhere, that protects us from confronting the difficulties that a pristine science of action must deal with, that does not disturb our preconceptions about human beings, and that offers us greater professional recognition for our efforts.

In light of the retreat, the significance of a commitment to radical behaviorism needs some further discussion. This commitment is a commitment to a full exploration of the ramifications of a contingency-oriented psychology for how we proceed as researchers, theorists, and practitioners concerned with human conduct. The commitment is not merely to using operant methods, techniques, and principles. It is a commitment to changing how we think about psychological matters; specifically, a commitment to changing our discipline from a psychology of organocentric processes to a contextualist psychology of action. We need to understand radical behaviorism in the historical context implied by this latter commitment. In other words, we need to understand that the essential message of radical behaviorism is not something new in psychology. On the contrary, radical behaviorism belongs to a strand of thinking long present in our discipline, albeit a strand considered seriously by only a small minority of academic psychologists. That strand of thinking is seen in Dewey's (1930) insistence that psychology has no subject matter other than acts. It is also seen in McDougall's (1928) insistence that we need an intelligible psychology of action, a psychology that deals with the problems of conduct. We need to understand that radical behaviorists continue to pursue their work because psychologists have not met the challenge presented to them by past contributors to this minority position. Consistent with this, Skinner (1969, p. 267) said that once psychologists accept action as a subject matter in its own right, then radical behaviorism will be absorbed into psychology as a whole. Under these circumstances, radical behaviorism will die, not because it has failed, but because it has been successful. Radical behaviorism, or, more generally, the demand for a systematic psychology of action, will not die until we have such a psychology. At least, it will not die as long as some of us keep alive the minority tradition in psychology contributed to by Dewey, Bentley, McDougall, Kantor, Skinner, and others.

CONCLUSION

Radical behaviorists have not succeeded in communicating their insights to other psychologists. Part of the difficulty arises because radical behaviorism is an ongoing enterprise, and the problems it has taken on are far from solved. There is also difficulty with other psychologists who will not listen to complicated arguments when those arguments are presented by writers identified as behaviorists. Many psychologists see radical behaviorism as irrelevant, old-fashioned, and unworthy of serious consideration.

The difficulty arises largely because radical behaviorism violates most of the basic assumptions of traditional psychology. These violations stem from the insistence that there is nothing of psychological interest other than behavior-in-context (i.e., action). In this insistence, radical behaviorists depart from the traditional notion that action is important only as evidence for the psychological properties of the organism. A psychology that takes action as a subject matter in its own right confronts problems and issues very different from a psychology that takes action as evidence of its subject matter. As a result, the problems and issues of concern to radical behaviorists seem irrelevant and sometimes bizarre when considered from a mainstream perspective.

The central issue of contention between radical behaviorists and traditional psychologists is easily stated. Should psychologists accept action as a subject matter in its own right or, alternatively, continue to interpret action as evidence for organocentric processes and structures? Psychology as a whole needs scholarly philosophic work addressed to this issue. We should not underestimate the difficulty of the work required. Indeed, Ringen (1976) commented that such work will doubtless require something on the order of Galileo's critical analysis of Aristotelian physics and cosmology. The difficulties of this work, and particularly the difficulties of pursuing it in a hostile environment, do not justify a retreat from the challenge it presents. In this spirit, the remaining chapters continue to explore the general nature of action as a subject matter and the ramifications for psychology of fully accepting this subject matter.

CHAPTER 9

Organism and Person

INTRODUCTION

As traditionally understood, psychological phenomena are found either peripherally (i.e., in movements) or centrally (i.e., in neural or cognitive processes). These two locations are usually opposed, but they both give psychological phenomena a bodily location. This bodily location invites attempts to find physiological explanations of psychological phenomena. Contrary to this corporeal tradition, psychological phenomena are properly located in means–end units, some of which are transdermal in that they include bodily activities and extend beyond them. The present chapter develops the alternative position that psychological units are often transdermal. It also explores some of the consequences of this position for distinguishing psychology from physiology. The discussion should help to further clarify the general nature of the subject matter of psychology.

MOVEMENTS AND ACTS

Movements were discussed earlier in Chapter 6. In brief, they consist of motions of the body segments (legs, toes, hands, etc.) around the joints. Gross movement of the body as a whole through space depends on such motions of the body segments, and particularly of the limbs. Movement is the subject matter of *kinesiology* (e.g., Rasch & Burke, 1971), a science that contributes to physical education, sports medicine, and other such applied disciplines. Kinesiology has two branches, *kinematics* and *kinetics*. Kinematics describes bodily movements and determines how far and how fast the body moves, whereas kinetics asks what causes bodies to move. Both branches of kinesiology treat the body as a physical entity. They explain movements by referring to the muscular-skeletal system and to mechanical forces acting on the body. An example is an account by Morris (1977) of the human gait, which dealt with the mechanical behavior of the foot and ankle and with the walking cycle as the basic unit of gait.

Such an account deals with what we might call *skeletal behavior, physical behavior,* or *four-dimensional morphology.*

Psychology ignores kinesiology. Mention of this discipline seldom appears in psychology textbooks. Typically, the nervous system and the sensory systems receive more discussion than the motor systems of the body. Furthermore, psychologists seldom use the term *movement* in its technical sense of the motion of the body segments around the joints. Although movement is sometimes described as the gross motion of the body as a whole through space (e.g., Walker, 1942; Skinner, 1938, p. 6), the molecular details are seldom noted. More commonly, movement is equated with behavior and action and is not distinguished from them. Such usage does not take advantage of the kinesiological concept of movement. Instead, it introduces ambiguity by equating the words *behavior, movement,* and *conduct,* and by neglecting the distinction expressed by *movement* and *conduct.*

Acts are more than movements, whether of body segments moving around joints or of the body as a whole moving through space. We can derive this assertion from the concept of an action as a means–end unit, if only because many end results are outside the body and not of it in the way that movements are. But, apart from that, we know that actions are not movements, because of the discriminations we routinely make among different actions. We discriminate giving a lecture from rehearsing a lecture, writing an essay from writing a letter, watering the garden from hosing the driveway, and so on. We make these discriminations routinely and without conscious deliberation. Yet, the movements that such pairs of actions depend on can be indiscriminable. The movements that end in the garden being watered can be indiscriminable from the movements that end in the driveway being hosed, and so on. Our discriminations in these cases cannot depend on the movements alone, and, consequently, the units we discriminate among cannot be movements. Our discriminations depend on movements and their context seen together-at-once or as an undifferentiated whole. In discriminating watering the garden from hosing the driveway, we see the bodily movements and their occasion and results. We see the garden, the watering implement, and so forth, as much as we see the body's activities. The notion of "together-at-once" emphasizes that we do not see movements and context separately and then infer the action. Rather, the context is internal to the action, because without the context, the action would not be the action it is.

Consistent with this, some psychologists have argued that units of psychological interest belong to the behavior-context field and not exclusively to the organism. In this connection, Bentley (1941) distinguished intradermal from transdermal units. *Intradermal* (organismic or bodily) units (e.g., blood vessels, nerves, and glands) are located within the boundary made by the skin. *Transdermal* events run across the skin. An example is the act of a particular person voting on a particular occasion. This act is an event of organism-in-environment and is transdermal. Bentley noted that psychology wrongly localizes psychological phenomena intradermally. Dewey (1922/1957, pp. 14–17) rejected intradermal units on the same grounds. He noted that we attribute acts to persons and let this attribution implicitly locate acts in the body. Indeed, at first sight, where else can we find running, reading, sitting, and the like? Yet, many acts incorporate the body and its surroundings, a matter apparent in that even walking implicates the ground as much as the legs. Similarly, Walker (1942) said that earning a living, realizing an ambition, and the like, are not bodily movements. They are relations between movements and other variables. Kantor (e.g., 1947, pp. 139–140) also insisted that psychological events are not located solely in organisms but instead constitute field events that include extraorganismic factors. As a final example, Chein (1972, pp. 22–23) said that an act such as writing spreads over bodily and environmental events and through time. No study of bodily movements in isolation from their context will reveal an action.

LEVELS OF INTEGRATION

The principle of levels clarifies the distinction between movements and acts. The principle needs some general discussion before we consider how it applies to the distinction of interest.

The principle of levels has been discussed elsewhere (e.g., Bunge, 1973; Jessor, 1958; Novikoff, 1945a, 1945b). It treats natural phenomena as comprising a hierarchy of increasingly complex levels of integration. Such a hierarchy is illustrated by the following series: atoms, molecules, macromolecules, organelles (mitochondria, ribosomes, etc.), cells, tissues, organs, organ systems, and organisms. The lower levels (e.g., cells) participate in the higher levels, and the higher levels (e.g., organisms) depend on the lower levels.

The principle of levels relates to the concept of holism. Lower levels participate in higher levels by combining such that the lower levels become constituents of new organized wholes. Protons and electrons combine into atoms, atoms combine into molecules, molecules combine into cells, cells combine into organisms, and so on. Wholes at a lower level (e.g., cells at the cellular level) become constituents at a higher level (e.g., cells at the organismic level). A whole is more than the sum of its parts. It has unique properties we cannot predict from the combined properties of the lower levels that constitute it. For example, two gases combine and form a liquid. The properties of this liquid result from the combined properties of its constituent parts, but the liquid has properties that the constituent gases do not have: Water can put out a fire but its constituent gases cannot, and so on. Similarly, a triangle is a closed figure though its constituent lines and angles are not, and a melody affects a listener in a way that its constituent notes do not when heard separately.

The principle of levels implies that the new properties at each level are emergent properties at their own level. The principle also implies that each successive level is grounded in the lower levels that constitute it. For example, every biological level is grounded in lower biological levels and, ultimately, in the physical and chemical levels of integration. The physical level with laws that apply to the whole of the natural world is at the base of the natural hierarchy. These laws are valid at higher levels, but they do not explain the higher levels. For example, when considering protoplasm, we need to know the properties of the molecules that constitute the protoplasm, but we can describe protoplasm in terms without meaning at the level of molecules. That is, describing a higher level with laws appropriate to that higher level does not contradict or deny the laws of the lower levels. It only assumes that the higher levels have laws not found at the lower levels and that nature deserves investigation at all its levels.

ORGANISMS AND PERSONS

Bodily activities and acts constitute different levels of integration. Acts depend on bodily activities, just as other higher levels of integration depend on the lower levels that participate in them. In the domain of acts, we cannot have end results without bodily activity. Concretely expressed, we cannot drive home from work, get a cup of coffee, and so on, if our bodies do not hold postures and make movements. Bodily activities are no less required when we achieve our ends through symbolic contingencies. For example, when we gesture someone to stop or ask someone for a favor, our bodies move and hold various postures. In general, action presupposes bodily activities, and bodily activities are constituents of acts, as noted elsewhere (e.g., Guthrie, 1940; Guthrie & Edwards, 1949, p. 67; Harré, 1982). In other words, acts comprise a higher level of integration, a level that presupposes and depends on bodily activities but extends beyond them.

Furthermore, the principle of levels enables us to see a human being as a physical system, as a biological organism, and as a person. As Chein (1972, p. 7) pointed out, physical, biological, and psychological laws have concurrent relevance to human beings. As a physical body, a human being is a biomechanical entity, the movements and postures of which are subject to the principles of kinesiology. As a biological organism, a human being is subject to biological principles. For example, striking the patellar tendon has effects on the organism, as does presenting a bright light, or exposing the body to noxious chemicals. A human being is also a person. A person is an accumulation of acts grounded in the behavior (i.e., movements and postures) of a single organism. The principle of levels lets us accept that a human being is not just a physical system and, indeed, not just a biological system. As well, a human being is a psychological system that consists of an accumulation of acts with its underlying means–end structure.

As noted earlier, a human being enters the world as a biological organism (and as a physical body). An individual organism with sufficient morphological development acts on itself and on its surroundings. Once performance is maintained, modified, and suppressed by the contingencies implicit in this acting-upon-with-effects, we have a new level of organization. What we know of the structure of this level (i.e., the patterns in it) was summarized by Sidman (1986a, 1986b). To insist that this level is psychological does not deny the contribution of the laws of other levels to the specific episodes that constitute human lives. Moreover, it does not deny that variables from other levels (e.g., hormone levels, fatigue) are among the parameters of psychological laws. The present insistence is only that if psychologists wish to determine general principles of the kind we expect from a science, then they must follow the other sciences and abstract out a particular level of integration. Psychologists do not have to deal with everything, and they cannot take an omnibus subject matter if psychology is to become unequivocally a science. In short, the subject matter that psychologists properly deal with does not consist of human beings as multilevel entities, but rather of one particular level of integration in which human beings participate.

Talking about persons will offend psychologists who would rather talk about organisms. But, if some acts extend beyond the body, and if psychology takes acts as its subject matter, then psychology does not deal with organisms as such. Instead, it deals with accumulations of acts, and those accumulations seem to be what we mean by a person. At least, let us take *person* to represent the psychological level of integration just as we take *body* to represent the biomechanical level and *organism* to represent the biological level. The difficulty that most of us will have with this concept of a person reflects an intangibility that arises in part because acts are ephemeral and in part because accumulations of acts extend beyond momentary observations. To elaborate: We can point to some acts as they occur, but they do not persist for us to inspect as does, for example, the body. Furthermore, in dealing with accumulations of acts, we deal with phenomena that extend through time. In particular, what we observe now is the current manifestation of a temporally extended stream of events. This extension makes personhood intangible and enhances the appeal of the corporeal location of psychological phenomena. Adding to that appeal, some items have a bodily location (e.g., nail biting). Moreover, some items of conduct are private (daydreaming, performing mathematical calculations covertly, and the like), and some are inchoate (being about to turn right, feeling inclined to go, and so on). The salience to the individual of these private and inchoate acts, combined with psychology's rejection of the mundane events of daily life as scientifically uninteresting, leads us away from action and back to the organocentric mind. It leads us back to the organism and to the corporeal (or quasi-corporeal) domain that has fascinated psychologists for so long.

PSYCHOLOGY AND PHYSIOLOGY

Some psychologists (e.g., Lichtenstein, 1980; Woodworth, 1930) have said that the distinction between psychology and physiology is difficult to make. Going beyond that, other psychologists (e.g., Hebb, 1972, p. 16; Welford, 1976, p. 164; Williams, 1931) have suggested that the distinction cannot be made or that it is arbitrary. In general, psychologists do not sharply distinguish psychology from physiology. Some issues bearing on the distinction deserve review because they further illuminate the difficulties of specifying psychology's subject matter.

Some attempts to distinguish psychology from physiology have relied on the distinction between wholes and parts. For example, McDougall (1912, p. 85) suggested that physiology studies the activities of the organs (parts), and psychology studies the organism as a whole. Similarly, Woodworth (1930, p. 328) assigned the activities of the organism as a whole to psychology and the activities of cells and organs to physiology. Other psychologists (e.g., Hebb, 1972, p. 16; Williams, 1931) have made the same distinction. Consistent with this distinction, some psychologists (e.g., Hunter, 1919, p. 5; McDougall, 1912, p. 35; Tolman, 1958, p. 179) have said that psychology is about the behavior of the organism as a whole. From this perspective, behavior of psychological interest takes place in the whole organism and not in particular sensory, motor, or neural organs.

The concept of equifinality casts more light on the concept of the organism as a whole. Equifinality can involve different parts of the organism on different occasions, as when a rat presses a lever with its right paw on one occasion, with its left paw on another occasion, with its tail on another, and so on. Psychology deals with the whole organism in the sense that most acts do not require that the same body segments participate in the same way from one occasion to the next. As a result, equifinality better distinguishes psychology from physiology than does the concept of the whole organism. As Tolman (1932, pp. 17–19) pointed out, this latter concept derives from equifinality, which requires the mutual interconnection of the parts of the organism or, in other words, the whole organism.

The discussion suggests that an argument about the special domain of psychology can proceed like this. Put most simply, psychologists deal with the end results of bodily movements. Better, psychologists deal with end results and with equifinal classes, not with specific movements as such. Still better, psychologists properly deal with means–end units, and with bodily activities only as the equifinal bodily constituents of these means–end units.

BEHAVIOR

The word *behavior* conceals the distinction between movement and action. The word is ambiguous, such that some philosophers (Best, 1978, p. 85; Rayfield, 1970) have deliberately used it to cover movements and actions. Psychologists have used the word less deliberately, as noted by some critics (e.g., Coulter, 1982; Kitchener, 1977). Often, psychologists do not distinguish between behavior in the sense of movement and behavior in the sense of action. Certainly, the way psychologists use the term *behavior* suggests that the distinction between movement and action is unimportant to them.

As Schoenfeld (1976) remarked, psychologists do not honor their own definitions when talking about behavior. For example, Watson defined behavior as comprising muscle contractions and glandular secretions. But he also said that a person ignorant of the nervous system and the effectors could write a behaviorist account. Tolman (1932, pp. 6–7) commented on Watson's dalliance with two different concepts of behavior. He said that if behavior consists of muscular contractions and glandular secretions, then a person ignorant of neural and muscular events could not write a behaviorist account of anything. As another example, Skinner has sometimes treated behavior as bodily activity. For example, he said he would define behavior as the movement of an organism in space in relation either to its point of origin or to some other object (Skinner in Evans, 1968, p. 8). Elsewhere, Skinner (1953, p. 45) wrote that behavior is a primary characteristic of organisms and that we almost identify it with life. As another example, Skinner (1969, p. 173) described behavior as the physiology of an anatomy, and he spoke of the "skeletal behavior with which the individual operates upon his [or her] environment" (Skinner, 1957, p. 34). If read together with the claim that behavior is the subject matter of psychology, these comments wrongly imply that this subject matter consists of bodily activities. Contradicting that, other comments by Skinner suggest that the word *behavior* designates action. For example, Skinner (1975) identified the following items as single instances of behavior:

a pigeon picks up a stick to build a nest, a child a block to complete a tower, and a scientist a pen to write on paper. These examples are actions and suggest that the units of interest to Skinner are actions and not movements.

Equivocation concerning the meaning of the word *behavior* has encouraged the mistaken belief that radical behaviorism prescribes movements as the subject matter of psychology. This belief is often expressed with reference to behaviorism and not specifically to radical behaviorism. Inevitably, radical behaviorism is lumped in with behaviorism in general. Critics (e.g., Blanshard, 1965; Coulter, 1982; Kvale, 1976a; Midgley, 1978, p. 106; Rubinstein, 1977) who hold this belief speak of the behaviorist reduction of conduct to mechanical responses, of the reduction of motives to bodily movements, of the treatment of action as colorless movement, of the location of thoughts and feelings in nerves and muscles, of the muscular approach to mind, and of the narrowing of psychology's domain to movements and traces of movements. To such critics, behaviorism reduces psychological events to bodily events. From this perspective, the word *behavior,* as used by behaviorists, means movements or the use of energy to change the spatiotemporal coordinates of the body. Further, behaviorists are presumed (Blanshard, 1965) to translate psychological things into bodily things. Consequently, behaviorism is thought to advocate a corporeal location of psychological phenomena and a corporeal interpretation of psychological problems. This behaviorism is the behaviorism that psychology must abandon. It is far from the contingency-oriented psychology advocated by radical behaviorism.

Many writers (e.g., Deitz & Arrington, 1983; Ferster, 1973; Harzem & Williams, 1983; Kitchener, 1977; Lee, 1983; McCall, 1972) have denied that radical behaviorism prescribes movements as the subject matter of psychology. These writers have insisted that radical behaviorism prescribes the behavior of interest in daily life (i.e., acts) as the subject matter of psychology and not the motor behavior of interest to kinesiology. The phenomena of interest to psychology are more extensive than behavior in the sense of bodily activities. As noted by Goldiamond (1974, 1975a), one example is reading, where behavior change (i.e., establishing appropriate eye movements) is trivial compared to bringing speaking, previously occasioned otherwise, under the discriminative control of print. The psychologically significant changes are not in the behavior (i.e., movement) but in the contingencies and their discriminative effects (i.e., action). Ambiguities *can* be found in what radical behaviorists say about their subject matter. But we need to see that these ambiguities reflect the difficulties that psychology as a whole will face in ridding itself of its behavioristic preconceptions.

The word *behavior* confuses psychological thinking by leading us to see only one kind of phenomenon. This perception is seen in the distinction (e.g., Bermant & Alcock, 1973; Hinde, 1970, pp. 10–13; White, 1971, p. 12, p. 32) between movement-defined descriptions of behavior and consequence-defined descriptions. This latter distinction is between alternative descriptions of behavior and not between two levels of integration. Movement-defined descriptions concern matters of interest to kinesiology, whereas consequence-defined descriptions concern end results and equifinal classes. In other words, movement-defined descriptions deal with what the behavior of interest is, whereas consequence-defined descriptions deal with what the behavior does. Theorists who make this latter distinction see the two kinds of descriptions as descriptions of the one phenomenon (i.e., behavior), which, indeed, they are. From this perspective, we can easily see consequence-defined descriptions as mere stopgaps useful only until we can describe the behavior anatomically. But that notion does not see that psychology properly deals with actions and that actions are units that comprise equifinal classes and end results and not just the equifinal classes.

A similar difficulty arises in attempts to discriminate actions from happenings. This distinction has been discussed elsewhere (e.g., Meldon, 1970; Shwayder, 1965, p. 3, p. 33; Zuriff, 1975). The distinction between actions and happenings is not well-formulated. Still, we can distinguish clear examples of events that occur because a person is engaging in action (writing an essay, crossing a road, etc.) from clear examples of events that happen to a person (death of a spouse, phone call from a friend, etc.) or to a person's body (sneezing, disease, etc.). Bodily happenings include coughing, hiccoughing, and vomiting. Intuitively, we would not include these events as acts. Even so, the items we usually count as bodily happenings might on some occasions count as events a person engages in to effect an end result such as obtaining social attention or escaping from demands. The philosophic difficulty concerning the distinction seems to arise because attempts to explicate it start with behavior and try to discriminate one kind of behavior (i.e., actions) from another (i.e., happenings). The strategy tacitly assumes that actions are behaviors of a particular kind and that the problem is to say what kind. But the problem of which behaviors are actions and which are happenings is the wrong problem. Actions are identified by end results, and they are units that conjoin bodily activities and end results. Bodily activities can be bodily happenings, and they can be constituents of actions. Trying to determine which behaviors are actions overlooks conduct as a level of integration, which depends on bodily behavior but extends beyond it.

Failure to distinguish between movement and action arises in discussions concerning whether we can acquire new behavior. It is easy to suppose that behavior is like a species' anatomy and that there can be no new behavior without a new nervous system, musculature, and skeleton.

But this supposition implicitly accepts that the word *behavior* designates the bodily activities of holding postures and making movements. In that sense, there can be no new behavior. But there can be new behavior in the sense of new conduct. For example, when an English-speaking person learns to speak Spanish, there are no new movements, just new combinations of movements. There is new conduct—a new end (that of making oneself understood in a Spanish-speaking community) and the means to that end. To state the matter differently, we always act within the constraints of our inherited anatomy, such that new behavior in the psychological sense consists of combinations of movements of the effectors. But, as far as we know, new psychological units can be added to the *action* repertoire indefinitely, by building on the basic *movement* repertoire of the body. That is, we walk, run, skip, jump, and so on, and the same biological structure and motor patterns permits all of this. In fact, it seems that contingencies can elaborate recombinations of our motor repertoire almost endlessly.

Assertions (e.g., Hebb, 1974; Staddon & Simmelhag, 1971) that psychology is a biological science show a failure to distinguish between movements and acts. Suppose we read these assertions in conjunction with some other assertions. Consider Marr's (1984) comment that behavior is a biological property of organisms and Skinner's (1953, p. 45) statement that behavior is a primary characteristic of organisms. If behavior is the subject matter of psychology, and if behavior is a property of organisms, then psychology surely is a biological science. But the subject matter of psychology consists of means–end units, and these units are often transdermal. Stated more radically, our subject matter is not of the organism even if it requires the participation of an organism. We should assert that, in principle, psychology is an autonomous science that builds on but extends beyond a science of organisms.

REDUCTIONISM

Reductionism is a methodological norm of traditional psychology. Its persistence reflects the failure of psychologists to distinguish psychology from physiology and conduct from bodily activity. Reductionism needs some discussion because its persistent acceptance by many psychologists blocks the emergence of psychology as an autonomous science.

Reductionists assume that the sciences are ordered hierarchically, from physics through chemistry to the social sciences. Physics and chemistry, at the base of the hierarchy, deal with the lowest levels of integration. Biology is in the middle, and psychology and the social sciences are at the highest levels. Reductionists assume that we can translate the terms, concepts, and laws of higher-level disciplines (e.g., psychology) into the terms, concepts, and laws of lower-level disciplines (e.g., physiology). They also assume that the lower the level to which we reduce statements about higher-order levels, the more fundamental the explanation.

Reductionists in psychology assume that psychological units have physiological correlates. This assumption is seen in Bergmann's (1953) statement that everything of psychological interest has a physiological correlate. It is also seen in Woodworth's (1930) statement that "eating one's dinner" is a molar description of events that physiologists can describe more analytically. Physiologists would speak of sensory, motor, and neural processes but would still describe the same phenomenon that psychologists speak of as "eating one's dinner." In a similar vein, Jastrow (1927) noted that the psychology of the 1920s assumed that the life mental is a correlate of the life bodily, thus equating mental (psychological) and bodily (organismic) phenomena. In another early statement, Warren (1922) urged psychologists to understand memory, imagination, and thinking as adjustment phenomena of the central nervous system. This way of thinking locates psychological phenomena in the body and, more specifically, in the brain, and this brain dogma persists in modern psychology. Indeed, Russell, Mead, and Hayes (1954) spoke of "behavior and its 'organ' the nervous system" (p. 156). From this point of view, psychological descriptions set problems whose solution lies in physiological mechanisms. Exemplifying this attitude, Baerends (1984) said that concepts such as reinforcement and contingencies are transitory steps toward a description of the physiological mechanisms that underlie behavior. This attitude sees the study of human action as a stop-gap that will suffice until a physiological account becomes available.

Describing sensory, muscular, or neural processes tells us about sensory, muscular, and neural processes but nothing about conduct. Ignoring this reality and trying to reduce psychology to physiology is like trying to reduce the behavior of an organ to the behavior of its cells. As Eisenberg (1960) noted, the behavior of individual cells is altered through their participation in an organ, even though the cells are still subject to the laws of cellular chemistry. Similarly, the body that participates in conduct is subject to physiological laws, but conduct still needs description at its own level just as the organs of the body need description at their own level. Bodily involvement has no independent meaning psychologically because the body acquires its significance psychologically only as a constituent of conduct. Of course, without the body, there would be no conduct, and, in this sense, psychological facts are grounded in physiological facts. But conduct is comprehensible only in terms of its means–end structure, something for which the body and its parts are necessary but not sufficient.

Reductionists forget that behavior of psychological interest participates in equifinal classes, classes defined by end results rarely dependent on any fixed segment of the body. Take, for example, the action of writing. As Hunter (1932) remarked, this action is not intrinsic to a particular body segment. If I lose one hand, I might write with the other. If I lose both hands, I might use my feet, and if I lose my hands and my feet, I might write using my mouth. Motor involvement in psychological units can shift from one part of the body to another as circumstances warrant or demand. Apart from that, the same psychological unit can contain an almost infinite number of different bodily events. Skinner (1938, p. 37) commented on the indefinitely various motor constituents of the action of a rat pressing a lever. Jessor (1958) similarly noted that the same psychological unit can contain an almost infinite variety of different bodily events. Indeed, as Peters (1960, p. 18) insisted, the means–end character of conduct makes it impossible to stipulate in full detail what the behaviors that have a particular result *must* be. In consequence, the connection between the equifinal class of an action and the structure of the body is necessarily tenuous. Even so, the difficulty of listing every motor event that belongs to an equifinal class has not persuaded psychologists that reductionism is futile.

Instead of seeing that conduct is a subject matter in its own right, psychologists have wanted to interpret psychological phenomena in terms borrowed from physiology and physics. In doing this, they have assumed that psychological phenomena are already well described. But every successful example of reductionism in the other sciences has depended on the prior existence of a well-developed body of knowledge in the higher-order science. One example is the reduction of chemical knowledge to physical knowledge. The problem is that psychology has no well-developed body of knowledge, with the consequence that any attempt to reduce psychological phenomena to physiological or physical events *must* fail. Reductionism has blocked progress in psychology. It has retarded the development of psychology as an autonomous science with its own subject matter, techniques, and concepts. As long as psychologists can emphasize the physiology of behavior *and* say they are doing psychology, they will miss or miscontrue the means–end character of their subject matter.

Parrott (1983) pointed out that Skinner has been inconsistent about reductionism. In some places, he has asserted the autonomy of psychology. Elsewhere, Skinner (1974, p. 249) has said that psychological facts will be reducible to physiology and then to biochemistry, chemistry, physics, and subatomic physics. In addition, Skinner has described his psychology as a branch of biology (e.g., Skinner, 1969, p. 221, 1975). In an apparently contradicting statement, Skinner has argued for an autonomous science of psychology and for treating behavior (read, conduct) as a subject matter in its own right. He has argued for the advantages of investigating psychological phenomena at its own level (Skinner, 1938,

p. 429). He has also insisted (Skinner, 1972, p. 275) that behavior is part of the natural domain that we can study with scientifically acceptable methods and without reductive explanation. The essence of Skinner's position is a commitment to studying conduct at its own level. This position does not reject the multilevel reality out of which we abstract conduct for the purpose of psychological inquiry. Radical behaviorism does not assume an empty organism, and it does not reject physiological research. On the contrary, physiological and psychological research properly contribute to the same enterprise—the search for reliable knowledge. A commitment to an autonomous science of psychology is nothing more or less than a commitment to conduct as a subject matter in its own right.

AUTONOMY

Fascination with the organism blocks acceptance of an autonomous science of psychology. In this regard, Wessells (1982) said that cognitive psychologists are trying to reestablish the organism as the proper object of psychological inquiry. From the present perspective, a return to the organism, if a return at all, can only block progress. Certainly, the criticism has been made before that psychology has forgotten its subject matter and has become fascinated with the organism. The peculiar thing is that psychologists who are fascinated by the organism treat the organism as a black box filled with conceptual structures and processes. They deal with a conceptual organism and not with a biological organism. Means–end units are hard enough to see as such without the obfuscation that comes about through this organocentric reinterpretation of the events of conduct.

A psychology that takes persons as its subject matter would concern itself with persons and not with organisms. Sciences other than psychology concern themselves with the physical, biochemical, kinesiological, neural, and other properties of human beings. Psychology properly assumes these other properties and their investigation by other disciplines. Stated differently, psychologists *as* psychologists can ignore the biochemical, neurological, and other nonpsychological details of a human being. We can do that knowing that such details are complex. The same neglect of other levels happens in physics, as Ziman (1978, p. 84) explained. For example, in the kinetic theory of gases, atoms are treated as tiny spheres, even though we know they are more than that. It is a matter of the information required for the purpose at hand. Whitehead (1953, pp. 249–250) explained that each science abstracts out a level of integration and ignores all other levels for its own purpose. So, physics ignores the chemical composition of objects, chemistry ignores the biological involvement, and so on. Psychology should do the same with its particular level of integration. It should concentrate on the means–end structure of conduct and ignore the other levels of integration pertinent to understanding human beings. At least, it should do that for the purposes of developing psychological principles.

Psychology is not peculiar among the sciences in abstracting out a circumscribed domain. But many psychologists will feel uncomfortable with the proposal that psychology should deal only with the domain of action. This discomfort reflects the freedom from conceptual systematicity that the word *behavior* has permitted. The word has let psychologists include everything from physics to sociology under the rubric of psychology. Critics (e.g., Hunter 1932; Luchins & Luchins 1965, p. 35; MacLeod 1965) have commented on the conglomerate nature of psychology that has followed our collective failure to specify the domain that is peculiarly psychological. We can specify such a domain and subsequently narrow the scope of psychological inquiry without denying the multilevel nature of human life.

Accepting the principle of levels requires that we abstract out a domain for psychological inquiry, but it also reminds us that practical problems outside the laboratory usually involve more than one level of integration. One example is the field of scientific agriculture in which hardly any science is omitted—physics, biology, and chemistry. In fact, several writers have acknowledged the multilevelled nature of human problems. For example, Blurton-Jones (1976) commented that we need information from biochemistry through sociology to explain the simplest aspects of human development. Sarason (1981) noted that human misery arises from diverse sources and that psychology's understanding of the individual human being needs reexamining in this light. Manicas and Secord (1983) described human acts as involving physical, biological, psychological, and sociological systems. They said that multidisciplinary effort is required to explain behavior because of that. Parmelee (1924, p. 2) made the same point long ago. He said that the study of behavior is biological, psychological, and sociological. It cannot be exclusively claimed by biology, psychology, or sociology. Rather, it is a hybrid of these three sciences. In short, the multilevelled nature of human life has been amply acknowledged. The significance of this multiplicity of levels to the way we go about building a science of psychology has not become part of the common outlook shared by all psychologists.

CONCLUSION

Psychologists have long been fascinated with the body and its contents, both real and imagined. Given this corporeal orientation, many critics interpret behaviorism as offering a peripheral account of psychological matters. From this perspective, the opposition to behaviorism is seen to offer an account that emphasizes the central properties of the organism. In this latter account, categories borrowed from ordinary language are given a central location. Intelligence, memory, and the like, become properties of the organism, albeit in the first instance psychological rather than biological properties. The unspoken assumption that psychological categories have a bodily location reflects a conviction that psychology can become a science only by reducing psychological events to a lower level. However, attempting to achieve this reduction of psychology relies on wishful thinking and the smoke screen of scientism. As Bolles (1983) noted, most psychologists are unaware of the details of the motor coordinations of the body in holding postures and moving. Furthermore, the obstacle presented by equifinality to the task of obtaining the motor details for any particular action most often appears to be overlooked. Psychologists have skipped over the concrete particulars of action. In doing so, they have omitted the domain of action and with it the connection between psychological and physiological phenomena implicit in the concept of an action as a means–end unit.

Radical behaviorism departs from the majority view in offering a contextualist account of psychology's subject matter. Consequently, it follows a minority tradition espoused by Bentley, Dewey, and Kantor, among others. The corporeal tradition in psychology makes this contextualist alternative difficult to understand. This alternative does not deal with the psychological properties of the organism in a context. Rather, it insists that the subject matter of psychology is behavior-in-context. This insistence lets contextualists distinguish body from person, movement from action, and physiology from psychology. It also lets them reject reductionism. Certainly, we could reduce the various constituents of conduct (movements, end results) to their biological and physical properties. But we would have nothing psychological left; conduct is something more than movements and physical changes brought about by movements. Taking behavior-in-context as psychology's subject matter allows contextualists to insist that psychology is an autonomous science that deals with something other than the organism. Finally, contextualists can accept that psychology *as* psychology does not have to deal with everything. The problem of accounting for human lives is not exclusively the task of psychology.

CHAPTER 10

More on Persons

INTRODUCTION

The distinction between organisms and persons is difficult to accept. The difficulty arises in part because the psychological nouns and the verbs of consciousness obscure the events which constitute the concrete tier of conduct. Unless we see these concrete events (i.e., acts) and recognize their significance, we will not follow through with what our understanding of them implies for the general nature of psychological inquiry. The psychological nouns include *intelligence, personality, memory, imagination, curiosity, knowledge, motivation, belief, fear, shyness, expectations, anxiety,* and the like. The verbs of consciousness comprise the verbs of emotion (*fear, hope,* etc.), cognition (*know, think,* etc.), and intent (*want, intend,* etc.). Most psychologists take the categories designated by these nouns and verbs *as* psychological. Consistent with this, Shwayder (1965, p. 12) used the term *mentalistic language* when referring to such words, and Alston (1974) noted that cognitive-purposive theories are committed to using the concepts designated by them. Most psychologists seem to assume that the psychological nouns and the verbs of consciousness designate entities and processes inside the organism. This chapter presents the contrary argument, which explains how the psychological nouns and the verbs of consciousness designate broad classes of conduct (i.e., behavior-in-context). This chapter also discusses three consequences of the traditional assumption that mentalistic terms designate psychological properties of the organism. The intellectual consequences of this organocentric interpretation block our acceptance of the concept of a person as an accumulation of acts.

MENTALISTIC LANGUAGE

The psychological nouns present psychology with definitional problems. We find it hard to say what the psychological nouns mean. Attempts to provide nominal definitions for them have not been successful. Multiple, inconsistent definitions of *motivation, intelligence, language,* and other terms are commonplace.

Difficulties in providing nominal definitions for the psychological nouns seem unavoidable. In ordinary discourse, the psychological nouns gain their meanings from multiple contexts. Coulter (1979, p. 35) illustrated this multiplicity of contexts with the word *mind.* We speak of a person with an untrained mind, where we might mean that the person cannot perform certain tasks effectively. We speak of a person having a blank mind when the person cannot recall something for the moment. We ask what is going on in a person's mind when asking about undisclosed intentions, we say a person has lost his or her mind when the person is acting irrationally or violently, and so on. Indeed, expressions containing the word *mind* are many and diverse: "Mind your own business,'" "Don't mind me," "I have a mind of my own," "Mind your p's and q's," "Out of sight, out of mind," "I'm of two minds," and so on. Skinner (1974, pp. 68–69) also noted both the multiplicity of English idioms that contain the word *mind* and our capacity to paraphrase them with statements about how we act. Stating the matter in general terms, Deitz (1986) noted that we can paraphrase idioms that have psychological implications in such a way that we make statements about behavior-in-context.

Problems arise when we take psychological nouns out of context and offer nominal definitions for them. When we do that, we lose the context and have nothing to indicate what the words mean. We should deal with the psychological nouns in their contexts. In doing that, we would deal with expressions rather than with single words, and we would seek paraphrases rather than definitions. For example, we would deal with "don't mind me," "out of sight, out of mind," and the like, rather than with "mind," and we would paraphrase each expression ("carry on with what you're doing," "don't let me interrupt you," and so on). Some paraphrases would mention acts or kinds of acts, returning us to the events of conduct. For example, we might speak of someone expressing his affection. When asked, we can paraphrase this statement, often by mentioning particular acts. The acts we could describe as "expressing one's affection" are diverse. Buying flowers, hugging someone, doing the dishes for them, smiling, and any number of other acts might count in a particular context as expressing affection. Such acts in those contexts are treated by the verbal community as loosely connected, and, in that sense, "expressing one's affection" designates a broad class of acts. The term *affection,* which appears in various statements ("expressing affection," "withholding affection," "seeking affection," and so on), might be understood as designating a broader class.

Alternatively, we might choose to deal with the psychological nouns in isolation and transform them linguistically, so that they do not mislead us. We can convert nouns derived from adverbs or adjectives into adverbs or adjectives; for example, *intelligence* becomes *acting intelligently, stupid* becomes *acting stupidly, motivation* becomes *motivated behavior, mind* becomes *acting mindfully,* and so on. This transformation might lead us to consider a proposal by Schafer (1976) that adverbs in the verb-adverb format (e.g., "she spoke sarcastically," "he argued angrily") indicate various modes of acting. These modes of acting amount to certain additional behaviors. For example, when we perform acts angrily, we engage in additional behavior such as tensing our muscles, clenching our teeth, thinking of attack, and so on. When we perform acts happily, we perform collateral behavior such as smiling, laughing, and so on. Returning to the question of how we might treat the psychological nouns, it is worth noting that the tactic of translating nouns into adverbs or adjectives relates to how we derive psychological nouns in the first place, as several writers (e.g., Klopfer, 1973; Pear, 1983; Skinner, 1953, p. 202) have acknowledged. For example, *conscious,* an adjective that precedes the names of some acts, becomes transformed into the noun *consciousness.* More generally, we start with *intelligent, aggressive,* and so on, or with *angrily, sadly,* and so on, and end with *intelligence, aggression, anger, sadness,* and so on. The strategy of converting nouns into adjectives or adverbs reverses this practice.

Insisting that the psychological nouns designate classes of acts and modes of acting departs from tradition in psychology. As things stand, the psychological nouns are taken as designating properties of the person, with the person conceived of as a nonphysical surrogate of an organism. Estes (1975) stated this view explicitly: Memory is a property of the organism. It is not a property of the organism-environment system. This same view is implicit in Norman's (1980) representation of mainstream thinking in psychology. In that representation, memory, attention, and the like, are placed inside the organism between sensory input and motor output.

It is tempting to dismiss the psychological nouns along with this S-O-R psychology that treats *memory* and the like as designating intervening variables. In practice we cannot dismiss the psychological nouns by declaration, a matter noted by some writers (e.g., Brener, 1980; English, 1933). The problem is not the words themselves but rather our confusion about what they designate. As Miner (1929) pointed out long ago, we must not let the psychological nouns suggest ghostlike entities inside the body. Likewise, Bode (1922) insisted that we have to take *emotion, ambition,* and the like, as we find them and not insist that they represent mental or neural states inside the organism. The alternative view is that if we do take the psychological nouns as we find them, then we would realize that they represent action or behavior-in-context. This view has long been considered. Dewey (1930) and Ryle (1949/1966) argued in favor of it. Recent contributors to the literature of radical behaviorism (Deitz & Arrington, 1983, 1984) have discussed Wittgenstein's contribution to this strand of thinking. Other contributors to it include McKearney (1977), Malcolm (1970, 1971, 1978), and Schafer (1976).

If the psychological nouns do provide abbreviated ways of talking about acts, then we should not be surprised to find a means–end interpretation of some psychological nouns in the literature. Consistent with this expectation, Churchman and Ackoff (1947) related the concept of personality to the ends a person pursues and the means used to pursue them. Allport's (1936/1937) notion of teleonomic trends implied this means–end concept of personality. It directed investigators to group acts according to what the individual was trying to effect by engaging in them (avoiding responsibility, maintaining self-esteem, etc.). *Intelligence* is another psychological noun that has been given a means–end interpretation. Peters (1960, p. 13) commented that the concept of intelligence is inseparable from the concept of an action, because part of what we mean by *intelligence* is varying the means to an end. Edwards (1928) also commented that the concept of intelligence has to do with variability, flexibility, versatility, and plasticity. As another example, Skinner (in Evans, 1968, p. 11) suggested that emotion has to do with the disposition to engage in acts defined by certain kinds of consequences. Anger is a strong disposition to attack, fear a disposition to run away, and so on. Goldiamond (1968) made the same point about the language of morality. Terms such as *conscience, morality, altruism,* and *loyalty* have to do with a nonordinary, puzzling, or anomalous relation between acts and their consequences. For example, a soldier who chooses torture or death over betraying his or her colleagues is said to behave morally (Goldiamond, 1968). Other terms for which a means–end interpretation has been suggested include *habit* (Peters, 1960, pp. 45-46), *motivation* (e.g., Goldiamond, 1966), *inhibition, timidity,* and *caution* (Skinner, 1974, p. 63), and *bravery, courage,* and *audacity* (Skinner, 1974, p. 64).

Taking the psychological nouns as designators of means–end units might help us identify various networks of contingencies that shape and maintain human conduct. For example, identifying what is meant by the words *competition* and *cooperation* has encouraged the study of relevant contingencies; similarly with *trust, generosity,* and so on (e.g., Schmitt, 1984). Conversely, empirical work has helped us clarify some of these psychological categories. An example is Glenn's (1983) work on explicating the meaning of *denial, lying, obsessing,* and other terms that designate categories of verbal behavior relevant to clinical practice. Other examples include Layng and Adronis' (1984) work on hallucinations, Goldiamond's (e.g., 1974, 1984) work concerning what we mean by the term *abnormal behavior,* and Ferster's (1961, 1973) work on the concepts of autism and depression. We need mentalistic terms in systematic psychological inquiry because these terms summarize our experience of conduct by identifying broad classes of action. Rather than dismiss the psychological nouns or uncritically locate their referents inside the organism, it would be better to work at identifying the acts and contingencies that lead us to talk in these ways (Lee, 1986).

Let us turn briefly to the verbs of consciousness: *Remembering, knowing, believing,* and the like, differ from *running, writing, driving,* and other action categories in a way that is easy to notice but difficult to specify. We readily count the former terms as designating mental processes whereas we easily dismiss the latter terms as designating mere behavior. The verbs of consciousness also seem different from the psychological nouns, at least with respect to the possibility of translating them into action language. It makes little sense to transform the verbs of consciousness into adjectives (*remembering acts, knowing acts,* etc.) as we can with psychological nouns such as *consciousness, intelligence,* and the like (e.g., *conscious acts*). Still, *remembering, knowing,* and the like, seem to name classes of acts. Malcolm (1970, 1978) developed an argument for this interpretation. Suppose you put your keys in the kitchen drawer and later someone asks you where you put them. You might act in any one of several different ways in reply. You might point to the kitchen drawer, or you might imagine the past event of putting the keys in the drawer and then say where they are, or you might go to the drawer and retrieve the keys, and so on. You could refer to any of these different events as remembering where you put your keys. In this case, the word *remembering* would apply across diverse acts not connected by any essential thing. The same argument could be made for the words *forgetting, imagining, believing,* and so forth.

In conclusion, a contingency-oriented psychology does have a place for the psychological nouns and for the verbs of consciousness. It does not exclude them, as must be plain to anyone reading Skinner's books. However, a contingency-oriented psychology does argue with traditional psychology about how we should understand the psychological categories designated by these words. The traditional notion that they represent processes or entities separate from action and inside the organism is rejected. In contrast to this traditional assumption, a contingency-oriented psychology retains the psychological nouns *and* connects them, in principle, to the particulars of conduct. That is, we expect the psychological nouns and the verbs of consciousness to have empirical content in relation to the domain of acts and not in relation to the internal contents of the organism. Saying that much does little more than set the problem. Even so, the setting of that problem is itself not insignificant.

SOME CONSEQUENCES

Uncritical acceptance of the psychological nouns as the starting point for a scientific inquiry has had several intellectual consequences that need some discussion.

Jargon

Naivity about the psychological nouns has led to a morass of what we might call *nominal nonsense*. Consider, for example, the following statement by Guthrie (1959): "As psychologists, our chief concern is with the phenomenon of learning. This process is what we usually mean by the word 'mind.' The possession of a mind means the ability to learn" (p. 174). A statement by Brinker and Lewis (1982) provides another example of this nominal nonsense. They said that an infant's experience of a contingency produces the expectancy that the world can be controlled, which provides the motivation further to control the world, which in turn develops an interest in such control. Other examples include Averill's (1968) statement that frustration causes anger in bereavement and Harding's (1982) proposal that infants engaging in goal-directed behavior are acting with intention, which in turn organizes the behavior directed to the goal. Assertions such as "frustration causes anger," "intentions organize goal-directed behavior," and "motivation develops an interest" are great commonsense. However, they have no place in inquiry that is scientific (or protoscientific) because they are formally true rather than empirically testable.

Feyerabend's (1962, pp. 19-23, pp. 29-32, pp. 44-45) discussion about myths supports this interpretation. Myths are systems of concepts which, like scientific theories, offer interpretations of nature grounded in experience. The factual basis of theory is not what distinguishes theory from myth. First, a theory is fallible, whereas a myth is incorrigible. Thus, most people believe, albeit tacitly, that commonsense already embodies the truth. Second, a myth has logical necessity. Its constituent statements are interrelated so that the myth is preserved under every circumstance. A myth can cite many facts in its favor and can offer an explanation for every fact. For example, as Averill (1968) explained, any behavior of a bereaved person will be considered grieving if he or she was close to the deceased. If grieving is denied, then either the relationship was not close or the bereaved person is pathological. Appropriately, some critics (e.g., Shotter, 1980; Smedslund, 1978) have commented that psychological assertions framed with the psychological nouns state what is logically necessary given the ordinary language of conduct and the logical connections among its terms. These assertions are open only to tests of logical consistency. Their infallibility and the logical necessity of their conclusions precludes experimental criticism.

We should exercise caution in using the psychological nouns to formulate hypotheses and to interpret findings. Better, we should eschew assertions that do nothing more than pile one psychological noun upon another. Guthrie's (1959) discussion about the word *mind* exemplifies this practice, as does Brinker and Lewis' (1982) account of the contingency-shaped behavior of the human infant. The terms upon which the accounts are built do not have the empirical content we require of scientific terms. We cannot define the terms ostensively, and we cannot offer a compelling linkage between them and the terms we can define ostensively. At least, no such linkage is offered in the writings of psychologists who use the psychological nouns in the manner under discussion.

Purpose and Intention

Fascination with the psychological nouns has let psychologists overlook the primacy of contingency-shaped and contingency-governed behavior. This oversight arises from confusion about the concepts of intention and purpose. Acts that we can describe as intentional or purposeful need not necessarily be performed with intent or on purpose. But desire to depart from the perceived physicalism of behaviorism has encouraged some psychologists to insist that their proper domain consists of intentional behavior. This insistence does little to clarify the subject matter of psychology, and, more than that, it obscures progress made by radical behaviorists in distinguishing behavior governed by unanalyzed contingencies from behavior governed by contingency statements.

Contrary to what some critics (e.g., Boden, 1972, pp. 91–94; Reason, 1979) seem to believe, radical behaviorism does not exclude the concepts of intention and purpose. However, the way in which radical behaviorists include these concepts depends on a distinction that many psychologists do not make. The distinction, discussed earlier, is between contingency-shaped or contingency-governed behavior, on the one hand, and rule-governed behavior (i.e., behavior governed by statements of contingencies), on the other. Behavior guided by contingency-statements counts as intentional behavior or as behavior engaged in purposely. For example, we can say a person intends or expects his or her behavior to have a particular result when we are talking about behavior guided by contingency-statements. We should not talk about intention, expectations, purposes, and the like, when we are talking about behavior shaped or governed by contingencies and not guided by contingency statements (e.g., Skinner, 1969, p. 147). Of course, conduct always has a means–end structure, and so we easily transform the end results of behavior into intentions, purposes, and so on, and locate them as causes inside the organism. We then say that action is steered by intentions and the like, so perpetuating an organocentric psychology and obscuring both the means–end structure of conduct and the distinction between performances shaped by contingencies and performances guided by statements of contingencies.

Many statements made by psychologists conflate contingency-shaped behavior and rule-governed behavior. An example is Bruner's (1982) statement that intentions steer most of what we think of as human action. Bruner said that intention is present if a person persists toward a certain end, chooses among alternative means to that end, corrects what is done when necessary, and ceases the line of action when the end is reached. From an operant perspective, the items listed by Bruner occur in contingency-shaped behavior, which is "steered" by personal history and current ecology. To count the performance as intentional, we would have to show that the person could state the relevant contingency and that the statement entered into the control of the person's behavior. Another example of how we conflate contingency-governed behavior with rule-governed behavior is the term *goal-directed behavior*. This term is often used to name the kind of behavior of special concern to psychology, but the meaning of "goal," as an end result consciously aimed for, obscures the distinction of interest. Another example of how our terminology obscures the distinction of interest is the tradition of interpreting the shaping of talking as the child testing hypotheses about language. This tradition implies a rational process of stating the contingencies and then of using those statements to guide behavior. Lundh (1981) commented that the notion of subjects testing hypotheses in contexts that involve only contingency-governed behavior extends the meaning of the word *hypotheses* too far. Similarly, stating that a child knows the difference between *pup* and *cup* might mean either that the child responds differentially to the two words or that the child can talk about the difference or both.

The language we use makes it easy to think that all conduct is intentional, purposeful, or rational, in the sense that the person states the relevant contingencies and acts in accordance with those statements. As Skinner (1969, p. 147) pointed out, we see statements of contingencies (resolutions, plans, laws, proverbs, etc.) more easily than we see the contingencies themselves. Consequently, we overemphasize the contingency-statements and neglect the contingencies and their effects. In a similar mode, Braybrooke (1968) commented on this neglect of contingencies and contingency-governed performances. Illustrating the neglect of contingency-governed behavior is von Cranach's (1982) concept of an action as "goal-directed, planned, intended and conscious behavior" (p. 36). This statement excludes contingency-shaped and contingency-governed performances from the category of action. Doing so might amount to a wish to deal exclusively with goal-intended action and an intention to use the term *action* for the subject matter of interest. Alternatively, it might indicate the intentional exclusion of contingency-governed performances from the category of action. Such an exclusion overlooks the fact that contingencies are present in the domain of action irrespective of whether the performance of interest is guided by statements of contingencies or not. That is, contingencies, whether stated or not, are the primary matters of psychological interest. Contingencies provide the starting point from which we can work out the other details of psychological phenomena through both empirical and rational means. To insist that psychology must start with the concepts of intention and purpose is tacitly to oppose a physicalism that radical behaviorism has long since surpassed if, indeed, it ever espoused physicalism at all.

Psychocentrism

Fascination with the psychological nouns has allowed psychologists to treat psychological phenomena as though they are free of the social order. The traditional location of psychological phenomena organocentrically encourages a biological conception of a person, which in turn promotes the view that the biological individual is the only scientific reality for psychology. This view has been called *individualism* (Pepitone, 1981), *the homocentric view of human behavior* (Skinner, 1969, p. 9), and *the organocentric assumption* or *organocentrism* (Kantor, 1963). Individualism starts psychological inquiry in the wrong place—in the biological individual rather than in the contingencies. This traditional starting place is so ingrained that giving primacy to contingencies seems like something other than psychology. Indeed, Kallos and Lundgren (1975) said that studying a system of relations rather than the psychological processes within individuals would lead to concepts not derivable from psychology. That is, psychology is seen, tacitly, as a discipline concerned primarily with the biological individual and only secondarily, if at all, with the relations into which the individual enters with events in the world.

Many critics (e.g., Dewey, 1922/1957; Kvale, 1973; Mishler, 1979; Norman, 1980; Sarason, 1981; Sherif, 1979) have commented on psychologists' neglect of the social, economic, and political realities of human lives. For example, Dewey (1922, pp. 84–85, p. 94, p. 322) commented that psychologists have isolated individual human beings from their surroundings. Sherif (1979) said that psychologists do research knowing nothing about their subjects' personal history and current ecology. In addition, Kvale (1973) mentioned the methodological blindness shown by psychologists to the social and material world outside the laboratory. As implied by the earlier discussion about the transdermal concept of a person, these criticisms do not go far enough. Psychology cannot solve its problems by relating environmental variables to various properties of the organocentric person. Admitting the social order in that way does not escape the individualism that wrongly locates psychological phenomena exclusively in the organism. Psychology can escape the limitations of individualism only by realizing that its subject matter resides in the interpenetration of the organism with the contingencies of the culture. That is, the contingencies of the culture do not constitute the environment for the events that count as psychological. Rather, the contingencies are constituents or ingredients of those events.

The concept of a person as the interpenetration of organism and contingencies implicitly accepts a level of integration beyond the psychological. This level consists of the network of contingencies maintained by the members of a social group. As Skinner (1977, p. 203) has noted, these contingencies transcend any individual member of the group because they exist ahead of his or her birth and continue after his or her death. The individual member of such a group is an inventer, a carrier, and a transmitter of cultural practices. These cultural practices consist of sets of contingencies, such as those of preparing meals, building shelters, designing clothing, arranging for childcare, and transmitting knowledge. Cultural practices would have no existence apart from the behavior of individuals. Still, the culture as a whole exists before and persists beyond the lifetime of any particular individual. In that sense, the culture is a level of integration beyond the psychological; or beyond the cumulative interpenetration of an organism with the contingencies of the culture.

Accepting a cultural level of integration departs from the psychocentrism that dominates psychology. Psychocentrism is the belief that social science is reducible to psychology. This form of reductionism supposes that we can reduce cultural facts to statements about individual human beings. Thus, we can reduce statements about wars, languages, universities, families, elections, marriages, and so on, to statements about the psychologies (motivations, emotions, abilities, etc.) of individual human beings. More concretely, psychocentrism supposes, for example, that conflicts between groups can be explained in terms of misperceptions, prejudices, errors of judgment, and the like, within individual members of the groups. This assumption turns conflict between groups into a problem exclusively of individuals. It leads us to look for the solution to social problems exclusively within individuals and not also in the means–end structure that supports and constrains the behavior of individuals. Theorists who hold the psychocentric assumption see the social sciences as stopgaps justifiable only until we develop an adequate account of individual minds. In short, psychocentrism is a form of reductionism, subject to criticism on the same grounds as biological reductionism. Psychocentrism does not allow us to see that human beings participate in multiple levels of integration or that we need inquiry at each separate level.

Psychocentrism lets us think that we do not have to consider the social, economic, and political realities of people's lives. We *can* ignore those realities for the purposes of psychological inquiry, but only if we remove ourselves from the content (i.e., the actual events) of conduct. As we will see in Chapter 11, we can find psychological principles that are universals of conduct by studying the structure (i.e., the abstract patterns) of conduct. But, in itself, knowledge of structure tells us nothing about the reality of people's lives. In regard to the content of conduct, structural knowledge gives us only a skeleton of concepts and principles that can direct our observations. We need to combine that structural knowledge with knowledge of the actual content of conduct. In other words, we also need a detailed study of the actual contingencies of particular settings that give psychological significance to the behavior of individuals. As soon as we do that, we become involved in the social, economic, and political realities of people's lives.

We face a conceptual struggle in trying to accept that social, political, and economic realities are constituents or ingredients of persons. We can find a starting point for the task of explicating this notion in Churchman and Ackoff's (1947) suggestion that the term *personality* has to do with the ends a person pursues and with the means by which the person pursues those ends. This suggestion is profitably considered together with a comment by Parsons and Shils (1951). They believed that the values of a culture will define the personality types found in that culture because a culture with those values (read, *work requirements*) will not survive as it is without those personality types. As pointed out before, many, if not most, work requirements are supraindividual in that they exist ahead of and persist beyond the life of any particular human being. Still, the work requirements that a particular human being has met in the past and continues to meet now are internal to what we mean when we talk about the psychological (as opposed to the physiological) properties of that individual. The work requirements provide the conditional structure of the means–end units that constitute the individual's personality. With this formulation, the social, economic, and political realities of people's lives cannot be ignored in understanding psychological content, because those realities are the work requirements that are constitutive of a person.

CONCLUSION

By starting with the psychological nouns, psychologists have let their discipline acquire the appearance of a science without the substance. Anyone can formulate a hypothesis expressed in terms of the psychological nouns. For example, we might hypothesize that people who believe in their own worth will have successful careers. Thus, high levels of self-worth will be associated with career success. No philosophic or scientific sophistication is required to formulate such a hypothesis. The hypothesis arises without any recasting from the difficulties that ordinary knowledge presents. The only obstacle to testing the hypothesis is the need to learn the traditional research methodologies of psychology. That obstacle is overcome by taking courses in research methodology and, later, by taking advice from someone who specializes in the design of psychological experiments. The result is an immense literature of conflicting and inconsistent findings that overawes us until we leave research for practice, leave psychology for some other enterprise, or join in.

Those of us who leave know there is something lacking in academic psychology. But we find it difficult to pinpoint what the problem is. Part of the problem is undoubtedly that psychology did not start where the other sciences started—in a set of conceptualized particulars. More basic than that, psychologists do not seem to recognize that psychology should start in concrete particulars. Attempts to insist upon this starting point are typically denigrated as behaviorism. To make matters worse, acts are not distinguished clearly from movements of the body, and the resulting confusion permits psychologists to dismiss acts as well as movements as mere behavior. Of course, psychologists cannot avoid dealing with acts empirically. What else is there for psychologists to observe? Still psychological formulations are rarely expressed in the language of acts and contingencies. Instead, they are most often expressed with the more obscure language built upon the psychological nouns and the verbs of consciousness. Psychologists have been able to avoid their obligation to deal with particulars because a psychology based on this language has had a certain plausibility.

Psychologists have been studying acts and contingencies, without recognizing that subject matter as such. In consequence, work describing means–end phenomena is easy to find in the literature of psychology. The difficulty lies in the effort required to retrieve the actual events observed and to guess what the relevant contingencies might be. As Segal (1975) said, we can cull something useful from the work of other psychologists, albeit with much effort and patience. An example is Tulving's (1985) partitioning of memory into procedural, semantic, and episodic systems, which could be reinterpreted as three broad classes of contingency systems relevant to acts that occur appropriately and with respect to other events long since gone (c.f., Skinner, 1969, p. 4). Another example is Reason's (1979) description of slips of the tongue and other lapses, which could be reinterpreted at the level of means–end phenomena without reductionist or cognitive implications (c.f., Skinner, 1957, pp. 293–309).

A final example is MacKay's (1982) account of fluency and equipotentiality within equifinal classes. His work contributes to our understanding of actions. Conversely, the empirical and philosophic developments of a contingency-oriented psychology contribute to his work, particularly with respect to the distinction between movement and action and its implications for psychological description. Interpreting the work of other psychologists in terms of acts and contingencies is not a matter of reducing psychological formulations to the language of behavior. Rather, it is a matter of seeing and stating the acts and contingencies that other psychologists have studied. It is also a matter of using what can be culled from that previous work as the foundation for further work which does not obscure the contingencies with speculation about organocentric processes.

CHAPTER 11

Structure
and Content

INTRODUCTION

This chapter develops the argument (Lee, 1987) that conduct has a structure and that the structure of conduct is the proper object of research and theory in experimental psychology. Chapter 12 points out that psychological research also properly concerns the content of conduct. The two chapters should make it clear that the psychological domain has two tiers; one tier concrete and particular (i.e., content), the other abstract and general (i.e., structure). They should also make it clear that psychologists should investigate both these tiers and pursue both experimental and nonexperimental inquiry. Of course, contributors to the literature of psychology (e.g., Allport, 1962; Franck, 1982; Holt, 1962; Manicas & Secord, 1983) have long discussed this second issue. But, as Franck (1982) asserted, we still do not have a clear understanding of the relation between experimental and nonexperimental inquiry in psychology. These two chapters address this relation and the need for both kinds of inquiry. The present chapter starts with a discussion about the content of natural domains in general and of the psychological domain in particular. It then points out that structure is abstracted from the particulars that constitute the content of a domain. The chapter concludes with a discussion of several traditions that distract us from the structure of the psychological domain.

CONTENT

Content consists of concrete particulars that we can point to or touch in principle if not in practice. For example, the content of the physical domain consists of physical objects (rocks, trees, etc.) distributed in particular places at particular times. The content of a domain is concrete, actual, and particular.

The nonexperimental sciences deal with content. Parts of biology deal with what happened at particular times to particular groups of organisms in particular parts of the world, astronomy and parts of geology study the distribution of matter in particular places at particular times, and so forth. Inspection, sometimes aided by instruments of observation (microscopes, telescopes, etc.), is enough to uncover the content of a domain. That is, questions about content are not questions that properly occasion experimentation. In other words, nonexperimental science seeks to understand particulars *as* particulars. Unlike the experimental sciences, it does not treat particulars as incidental to the discovery of laws.

Describing the content of a domain is an endless task. We could study a single particular (a cathedral, a tree, etc.) forever and not exhaust everything we could know about it. Even one person's thumb presents a vast domain. It has many constituents, and many events occur in it in a single second. A comprehensive description of any particular would never end. Bunge (1967, p. 27) insisted that even if we could describe content comprehensively, our account would still be incomplete because it would omit the laws of the domain. In Feibleman's (1972b, p. 114) terms, observing and reasoning are not enough to provide an account of the natural world. We also need experimentation and the resulting knowledge of the patterns in the domain.

Investigations that do not use the experimental method count as scientific if they use structural knowledge to predict and explain the particulars they observe. Biologists spend much time inspecting particulars, but they use the principles of genetics and other experimental sciences in their explanations. Astronomers make assertions about particular planets, stars, and so forth, but they make these assertions with knowledge of physical and chemical structure. Similarly, meteorologists use the laws and theories of physics and other sciences to predict and explain particular droughts and other meteorological phenomena. As Bunge (1973) noted, these disciplines are descriptive and nomothetic. They differ from other historical disciplines (history, anthropology, etc.) in that they use the laws and theories of the experimental sciences to predict and explain the content of their domains.

The importance of nonexperimental science needs some emphasis. After all, complete knowledge of structure, even if attainable, would not provide complete knowledge of the world. We also need knowledge of the initial conditions under which laws operate. To explain: Considered through time, the content of a domain is a series of transient and historically cumulative states. The state of a domain at any one time depends on the preceeding states and on the effects of structural processes on those states. Developing this point, Bunge (1973) explained that segments of content depend on the joint working of laws and actual circumstances. For example, a falling stone is acted upon by gravity (structural process), but the time and place of falling and the condition of the stone (initial conditions) depend on the history of the matter in the stone. To explain the rock's falling requires knowledge of gravity and knowledge of the initial conditions under which gravity operates. In short, to account for an actual event, we need knowledge of structure and content.

CONTENT OF CONDUCT

A psychology of the content of conduct faces the same limitations as any discipline that concerns itself with the content of a domain. In principle, fully describing an act is impossible. We face the practical difficulty that acts are emphemeral, such that we cannot hold them still for inspection. Even if we capture an act cinematically so that we can observe the same instance repeatedly, a full description of the act eludes us. Apart from anything else, we face difficulties arising from the hierarchical organization of conduct. Acts might contain two or more acts at a lower level of description, and so on. For example, driving to work encompasses the action of stopping at every red light, and that action encompasses observing the traffic lights, and so on. McFall (1982) indicated that a complete description of an act would mention each level of organization that participates in the act. We also face difficulties in trying to describe the full collection of acts because it constitutes an immense and endlessly changing domain, the description of which would be never-ending and continually changing. Anyway, no amount of description would be complete in itself, because it would omit the laws of the domain. Only an experimental science of conduct can provide those laws. Without them, descriptions of the content of conduct will always be incomplete, and proferred explanations of conduct will not count as scientific explanations. In short, we need to isolate and formulate laws of conduct if we want to claim that we have a science of psychology.

Some critics (e.g., Baron, 1971; Gergen, 1973; Keniston, 1971; Luria, 1971) have denied that psychologists can find laws. They believe that psychologists can only describe what actually occurs in human conduct under particular conditions. The argument can be expressed in the terms of a contingency-oriented psychology. The conduct typical of a particular time and place presumably reflects the actual contingencies of that time and place. Given that, the generalizations we make about the content of conduct are also historically and culturally bound. They reflect the actual contingencies and the effects of those contingencies on performance. Even conduct that seems universal, such as the construction of shelters and the preparation of meals, presumably reflects the actual contingencies common to all times and places in human history. The historical and culturally bound nature of conduct seems to imply that we cannot find universal patterns in conduct, and thus, that the search for universals is misguided and that psychology cannot do experimental science.

The argument against an experimental science of psychology is not convincing. Other domains are no less vast and changing (i.e., historical) than the psychological domain, and yet we have sciences in those domains. Bunge (1973) explained that branches of physical science study the histories of various physical domains. For example, particle physics studies the metamorpheses of particles, molecular paleontology studies chemical evolution, historical geology studies the formation and evolution of rock layers, and cosmogony studies the origin and evolution of stars, star clusters, and other astronomical particulars. Conduct is no less available to experimental inquiry. The critics have reached their conclusions because they have missed the purpose of experimentation in science. It is to uncover the structure (i.e., classes, properties, relations) of the domain of interest. The diversity, transience, and vastness of the content of a domain are irrelevant to the success or failure of this pursuit. The critics have also reached their conclusions because they have missed the abstract nature of experimental science. We need to consider something of this aspect of science before we turn to the problem of selecting strategic abstractions for psychology.

STRUCTURAL ABSTRACTIONS

The experimental sciences concern themselves with the abstract entities that Whitehead (1953) called "universals," "eternal objects," and "transcendent entities." These classes, properties, and relations are abstract in that they transcend particulars and are comprehensible without reference to any single particular. Indeed, experimental science deals with particulars only as members of classes, as representatives of properties, and as instances of laws.

Classes were discussed earlier. They belong at the interface of experimental science and natural history. Classes count as abstractions even though we arrive at them through the inspection of the content of a domain and not through experimentation. Properties consist of elements, traits, or magnitudes abstracted from limited classes of particulars. They are not proper parts of particulars, such as the legs of chairs or the handles of doors, which are themselves particulars. Rather, the properties of interest are abstract dimensions, such as mass, force, and volume.

The process of selecting classes and properties is not arbitrary and is not decided on the grounds that the chosen classes and properties are those most easily agreed upon. Rather, the selection depends on what works in finding invariances in the laboratory. If experimental work based on certain classes and properties does not reveal invariances, then we must suspect that we have chosen the wrong classes and properties. The search amounts to a bootstraps operation. We find invariances when we find the right classes and properties, and finding the invariances indicates we have found the right classes and properties.

Finding invariances requires a prior commitment to the belief that we *can* find invariances in the domain of interest. Sidman (1960) referred to this commitment when he said that in the early stages of inquiry, we can do experiments "with no other hypothesis than the simple faith that order will emerge" (p. 16). Van Melsen (1961, p. 49) mentioned that a similar commitment to finding invariances was essential in getting physics started. Without a commitment to finding invariances, investigators could not have begun to uncover the structure of matter. Psychology needs this same commitment to finding the invariances in its domain.

The invariances that signal that we have abstracted the right classes and properties are formulated as laws. Laws consist of statements about invariant relations among properties abstracted from limited classes of the subject matter. They are conceptual reconstructions of patterns (Bunge, 1967, p. 27), of permanent, abstract relationships (Feibleman, 1972b, p. 233), or of interconnections among aspects of a natural whole (Van Melsen, 1961, p. 100). Examples include the physical laws $F = ma$ and $E = mc^2$.

Laws are central to what we mean by science. Feibleman (1972b, p. 4) insisted that science *is* the experimental search for the laws of nature. Alternatively, Bunge (1967, p. 15) stated that science is an enterprise that uses the experimental method for the purpose of finding laws. Certainly, no discipline will find laws unless it uses the experimental method. This method induces nature to reveal the system of interconnected abstractions that constitute its structure. The method has been described elsewhere (e.g., Feibleman, 1972b; Russell, 1938; Van Melsen, 1961).

Laws unify concrete particulars that seem disparate and unrelated to ordinary observation. For example, in Galilean science, the same law applies to the courses of stars, to the falling of stones, to the oscillation of a pendulum, to the rise and fall of tides, and so on. These diverse items of content have the same structure. This structure transcends any single particular, but is still tied to the field of particulars because the properties related in a law are abstracted from classes of particulars. That is, mass, accelaration, and so forth, are properties abstracted from classes of physical objects. Structural patterns are exemplified in every actual member of the relevant class of particulars. They count as universal patterns with respect to the class. That limitation considered, structural abstractions are timeless and changeless, even if our conclusions about what is permanent can change. In finding these universal patterns, experimental science finds unity in diversity.

Laws give a science a degree of unity, and they create new questions that the science counts as its problems. Through the pursuit of these questions, sciences develop theories that integrate two or more laws and predict new ones. A theory consists of a system of law statements; for example, Newton's theory of motion. A law, therefore, formulates a single relation, whereas a theory formulates two or more interconnected relations. Theory contrasts with metatheory, which consists of the conceptual framework used to guide the search for laws. Although theory is an advanced stage of science, earlier inquiry is not atheoretical in the naive sense of being purely observational. On the contrary, the beginnings of scientific inquiry in conceptualized particulars makes science simultaneously abstract and concrete from the outset. Van Melsen (1961, pp. 84–85) noted that this starting point means that nothing is conceptualized (classified) before it is first observed, and nothing is observed before it is conceptualized. In this way, science begins in an indissoluble blend of observation and abstraction, such that we gain nothing by trying to determine whether our starting point is concrete or abstract. In summary, theory, in the sense of metatheory, is present from the outset, even if theories, as conceptual integrations of two or more laws, are not present.

Classes, properties, and relations are abstract. They are not entities we can point to or touch. Of course, abstractions are not unique to science. Ordinary thought also has abstractions, as seen, for example, in the psychological categories of memory, cognition, and mind. But the abstractions of science are connected through deductive pathways to terms we can define ostensively. This demonstrable connection to particulars distinguishes the abstract entities of science from those of nonscience. Stated differently, science transcends particulars *and* stays connected to them. Abstractions that do not retain that connection are not abstractions of science. Moreover, as Feibleman (1944) explained, the abstractions of science are quantitative or structural. We start with limited classes of particulars and abstract out the elements common to the members of those classes. These common elements are either quantitative because they deal with number, or structural because they deal with relations among the parts of a whole. In short, science deals with abstractions but only with abstractions of a certain kind.

PSYCHOLOGICAL STRUCTURE

The rudiments of psychological structure consist of the class-particular structure that reflection about the general nature of conduct reveals to us. That is, psychological structure consists at base of the classification that gives us limited classes of particulars (acts). We can abstract from these limited classes, the means–end structure of conduct with its classes of variants, end results, and two-term contingencies. The contingencies are structural abstractions. They have to do with the relation between the two parts of an action — the class of variants and the end result. Our intuitive knowledge of means–end structure, combined with experimental and philosophic work, has let us develop the beginnings of a systematic account of the structure of conduct. This account not only directs us to look for two-term, three-term, through n-term contingencies, but also suggests a variety of experimental questions (Sidman, 1986a, 1986b).

We distinguish principles of psychological structure from the actual contingencies that have incremental or decremental effects under particular conditions. This distinction is not well understood. Exemplifying the confusion, Gergen (1973) rejected the notion that reinforcement and punishment are universals on the grounds that particular reinforcers do not remain stable over time. It is true that the actual end results to which our bodily effort is allocated vary historically and culturally. But we can accept this transience of actual contingencies without rejecting the principles of reinforcement and punishment at the same time. Actual contingencies of blame, praise, or social approval upon behavior have to do with the content of conduct. They have to do with the actual work requirements that people must satisfy to get anything done under particular social, political, economic, or interpersonal conditions. In contrast, reinforcement, punishment, and the other principles of operant behavior have to do with the abstract patterns we can find in the domain of conduct. They are exemplified by actualities but are not themselves actualities. Consequently, finding that an actual contingency is not universally present in human societies or that an actual contingency does not have a universal effect does not negate the principles of reinforcement and punishment. It shows only that some actual contingencies and the effects of some actual contingencies are not universal in human conduct.

By considering Flavell's (1972) developmental principles we can further clarify the distinction between content and structure. These principles state how later-developing items of conduct are linked to earlier-developing items. The principles *are* principles. They are abstract and structural (i.e., having to do with relations). Flavell's first principle is addition. This principle concerns the acquisition of two distinct items of conduct, A and B, which are potentially alternative means to an end. An example is drinking by raising a cup to the mouth (A) and drinking through a straw (B). Item A is acquired first, and B later. Once acquired, the items coexist and alternate, although each item may predominate over the other on particular occasions. The second principle of substitution deals with two distinct variants, A and B, where B is acquired after A. In this case, B gradually replaces A or, at least, B becomes the dominant variant. For example, asking for food replaces gesturing for food.

Flavell's third principle is modification. Item A develops and gradually becomes B. That is, this principle has to do with the continuity of two items or the emergence of one item out of another item. The fourth principle is inclusion. Although discrete items, A, B, and so forth, are separate acts initially, they become integrated into a larger whole. For example, a child who could previously push objects and grasp objects (two separate acts) now pushes aside a pillow to grasp an object behind it. Flavell's fifth principle is mediation. In this case, item A contributes to the acquisition of item B but does not become part of it. That is, item A is part of the history that brought about item B.

Flavell's (1972) principles are compatible with operant principles. The principle of addition has to do with adding variants to an operant class and thus with broadening such a class. The principle of substitution has to do with the selection by differential contingencies of one variant from a previously broadened operant class. The variant or variants not selected apparently remain available, as noted by Flavell and systematically formulated by Epstein (1985a) with his principle of resurgence. The principle of modification relates to the operant principles of shaping, fading, and leaning. An example is the shaping of audible talking from inaudible talking. The principle of inclusion has to do with the operant principles of chaining and of composition (Skinner 1957, pp. 335–340, pp. 344–352) or the interconnection of separate repertoires (Epstein 1985b). Finally, Goldiamond (Goldiamond, 1966; Goldiamond & Dyrud, 1966) has discussed mediation in terms of the concept of a behavioral curriculum. Flavell spoke of cognitive items, rather than of acts, and he did not deal explicitly with contingencies, so the compatibility will undoubtedly be resisted.

Still, Flavell's principles identify patterns of interest to operant psychologists: the broadening and narrowing of classes of variants; the gradual changes seen in shaping, fading, and leaning; the construction of larger units when previously-separate items combine; and the behavioral curricula that constitute the histories of complex repertoires. Like operant principles, Flavell's principles have to do with patterns and not with actual content. But, operant principles differ from Flavell's in dealing with patterns of contingencies-and-their-effects (e.g., differential reinforcement) and not with patterns that are the effects of contingencies (e.g., substitution). Stated otherwise, Flavell's principles omit the independent variables that a scientific account must include. Even so, they *are* principles and have to do with patterns and not with dated instances.

DISTRACTIONS

Most psychologists disregard or dismiss operant psychology and, in doing so, they neglect the structural knowledge summarized by Sidman (1986a, 1986b). This neglect reflects both a rejection of conduct as a subject matter and a competing interest in organocentric matters. It also reflects the isolation of operant psychology and the misconceptions about it. Other traditions in psychology also operate against acceptance of structural knowledge. Three of these traditions are considered in the following discussion which should help to clarify the concept of psychological structure.

Rejection of the Laboratory

Some psychologists have difficulty accepting that the laboratory is an appropriate place to pursue psychological research. Laboratories are seen as artificial and as incapable of sustaining the full richness of the conduct outside them. Furthermore, the laboratory study of conduct is rejected because it leaves behind the interpersonal, social, and other realities of human lives. The relevance of laboratory work to an understanding of conduct is questioned on these grounds which, in fact, turn out to be unconvincing.

The contrived nature of laboratory work is not unique to psychology. Laboratory experiments in physics are artificial and deal with phenomena that seem unlike what is found outside the laboratory. Indeed, Ziman (1978, pp. 166–167) noted that the conditions of observation and the phenomena observed in the physics laboratory almost caricature the actual content of the world. And yet no one would ask a physicist to study hydrodynamics in the largest rivers of the world or gravity by observing falling leaves. Moreover, no one would distinguish gravitational phenomena in the laboratory from such phenomena outside the laboratory. Likewise, Van Melsen (1961, pp. 270–271) noted that chemists make no intuitive distinction between compounds occurring naturally and compounds produced in the laboratory. They simply compel the processes of nature to take their course in the laboratory. These considerations suggest that the contrived nature of laboratory work provides no grounds for rejecting laboratory work in psychology.

Laboratory research is essential in psychology if we want to develop a body of scientific knowledge. We need laboratories to isolate variables and to identify invariant connections in our subject matter. At the same time, we can admit that laboratories do not support the full richness of conduct observed outside of them. Of course, the physics laboratory also does not support the full richness of the physical world. But then, laboratory work is not meant to deal with the richness of the concrete tier of the domain of interest. Rather, laboratory work has to do with the structural patterns we abstract from a domain. More completely, experimental science seeks knowledge of structure for two reasons: first, structure and not content extends beyond the reach of ordinary observation (i.e., is extraordinary) and, second, structure and not content contains replicable patterns (i.e., is reliable). The charge that laboratory work in psychology leaves behind the context of human lives neglects the abstract nature of experimental science. The charge also reflects psychology's neglect of nonexperimental work. In other words, the charge is a reaction to the attitude that Klein (1942) called "experimentalism." Experimentalists treat experimental work as psychology's totem and reject work of any other kind. In doing this, they forget that much of the scientific enterprise deals with particulars *as* particulars. As Manicas and Secord (1983) emphasized, psychologists must admit biographical and diagnostic work as part of their commitment. Admitting such work neither excludes laboratory work nor makes such work unnecessary. Thus, we do not have to reject laboratory research in order to admit field research as a legitimate and essential part of psychological inquiry.

Along with this defence of the laboratory, we can also insist that experimental work in psychology has an essential but limited contribution to the task of explaining the actual events of human lives. Consider the following: The world outside the laboratory is an open system containing a multitude of events in constant flux. The only exception is the domain of celestial mechanics, which is a closed system like a laboratory. Laws are found only in closed systems, and they hold only under special, usually idealized conditions. Cartwright (1980) noted that a law taken as a description of nature is false unless qualified by a statement of these conditions and irrelevant to actual events if so qualified. Each law describes what happens to a dependent variable when one independent variable is at work. However, the actual events that constitute the content of nature involve a multiplicity of these functional relations that independent variables enter into with dependent variables. More than that, actual events are products of many independent variables from many levels of integration interacting in complex ways under particular historical conditions. The implied limitation upon the scope of the laws of any single science has consequences for how we construe the task of psychology. Manicas and Secord (1983) argued that fully explaining the actual acts of a particular person requires structural knowledge from physics, chemistry, biology, psychology, and sociology, as well as historical information relating to the individual case. Consistent with this, Manicas and Secord rejected the traditional assumption that psychologists can fully explain actual episodes of human lives with principles derived from psychological research conducted in the laboratory. The rejection of the traditional assumption does not reject experimental psychology as such. However, it *does* limit the purpose and scope of this enterprise by implying that experimental psychology properly concerns itself exclusively with the structural patterns of the psychological level of integration.

Statistical Inference

Persuading psychologists to accept existing knowledge of psychological structure is also difficult because psychological research depends on a research methodology incompatible with operant methodology. Using this former methodology, psychologists compare the averages of groups of subjects whose behavior they observe for limited periods of time. The comparison is made to determine whether any difference between the groups was unlikely to occur by chance. If such a difference was unlikely, then the result is statistically significant. Editors of psychology journals typically insist on a statistically significant result before they will consider publication of a research report. But statistical significance only means that the result was unlikely to occur by chance. It does not mean that the result had practical or theoretical significance, and it does not mean that a functional relation was demonstrated.

The mainstream literature is replete with studies using this methodology. Replication of the kind that operant psychologists insist upon is rarely achieved in this literature. On the contrary, a morass of conflicting and inconsistent results is more commonly found. One example, as Sherif (1979) indicated, is research on differences in the behavior of boys and girls. Even when replication is achieved, it is replication of the central tendency for a group of subjects. A group average can conceal a range of possible outcomes. For example, finding that a group of boys was more aggressive than a group of girls could mean that more boys than girls acted aggressively or that some boys performed more aggressively than most boys and girls. Replication of such a finding does not indicate the number of subjects that the finding represents. It contains no information about whether the original finding would be reliable across a series of individual subjects. Psychologists using this traditional methodology based on group-statistical analyses of data seem to be testing a theory. But this appearance is illusory. Moreover, they seem to be contributing to knowledge, if their publication lists are anything to go by. But that impression is also illusory. As Meehl (1967) commented, inferential statistics have let psychologists generate long publication lists without adding anything to an enduring body of knowledge.

Traditional methodology provides a formula that psychologists continue to use regardless of its larger failures. In the end, the methodology gives psychologists a soft option. It is easier to produce a statistically significant result for the averaged performance of a group than to produce a result that a critical audience can replicate in the performance of an individual subject. A statistically significant result can be had by increasing the number of subjects. An invariant relation, on the other hand, requires much conceptual and empirical preliminary work. As long as psychologists can rely on analysis of variance and other inferential statistics, they will not need to examine their presuppositions about the nature of psychological phenomena and the nature of psychological inquiry. They can go on producing more data, under the guise of science.

Mainstream psychology has little commitment to the unhurried stance required by the self-corrective process of replication as it was discussed by Sidman (1960) and Johnston and Pennypacker (1980). As some critics (e.g., Elms, 1975; Gloye, Craig & Carp, 1957) have noted, more emphasis is given to making startling contributions than to adding small increments to a body of reliable knowledge. Sherif (1979) remarked that it does not matter to most psychologists that these large and original contributions have the durability of a marshmallow. Of course, some writers (e.g., Carver, 1978; Elms, 1975; Gloye, Craig & Carp, 1957; Lykken, 1968; Shulman, 1970; Thompson, 1974) have urged psychologists to place more emphasis on replication. In any nontrivial sense replication would require much recasting of psychology's subject matter, task, and method because replicable knowledge has a schematic character derived from its foundation in conceptualized particulars. Calls for more attention to replication in psychological research seldom acknowledge the need for this recasting. Without that recasting, it might seem that replication is impossible on the grounds that there can be no transhistorical invariants in conduct. The argument is implicit in the assertions noted earlier that conduct is historically bound and that therefore psychology can do history but not science. In this way, psychology's difficulties with replication arise from the assumption that a good result must hold for all human beings universally, regardless of social or historical context. This conclusion arises because psychologists have not distinguished between the content and the structure of their domain and because experimental work in psychology does not begin self-consciously with structural abstractions; that is, with abstractions drawn from limited classes of particulars. A good result in an experimental psychology of action is a result that holds universally for one or more classes of acts. Consequently, the transhistorical invariants in psychology are to be found in the structural properties *of* conduct.

Personal Categories

Persuading psychologists to accept our knowledge of psychological structure is also difficult because this knowledge rests on a classification that many psychologists dismiss as uninteresting. Psychological research gives prominence to categories such as retarded, schizophrenic, good speller, and so forth. These categories implicitly identify individual human beings as the particulars of interest and types of human beings as the classes. So, this child instances the category of retarded children, and so on. A psychology based on these categories is concerned that generalizations based on some members of a category apply to all members of the category, and it uses inferential statistics for that purpose. Interest in personal categories does much to perpetuate the use of inferential statistics. It also does much to obscure conduct as a subject matter. Who would find any interest in, let alone see, the mundane particulars of conduct when they can address their inquiries to socially relevant categories such as retarded or gifted? After all, funding and other support is more available for research concerning these categories than for research on the minutiae of the structure of the domain of acts. The pressure for premature application, long deplored by critics (e.g., Deitz, 1978; Harzem & Williams, 1983; Pratt, 1939, pp. x-xi, pp. 175-176, p. 179; Spence, 1956, pp. 19-24; Vitulli, 1971), is likely to be pressure concerning retardation, delinquency, and other such categories. That pressure reflects urgent human needs. But if we are to have a science of conduct, we must address the details of conduct undistracted by categories that have social relevance but that do not necessarily have strategic significance.

Acceptance of personal categories as psychology's basic classes encourages research based on the uncertain foundation of a weak system of classification. Consensus among independent observers about how to categorize persons is rare: One observer's learning disabled child is another's culturally disadvantaged child, and similarly with "hyperactive" and "energetic," "emotionally disturbed" and "normally disruptive," and so on. Much overlap occurs across categories, with similarities in conduct across different categories and differences within a single category. Apart from that, the particulars so categorized are human beings, and human beings participate in multiple levels of integration. Only a very ambitious, or, perhaps, misdirected discipline, would attempt to build scientific knowledge of such multilevel particulars.

Armed with a dubious system of classification, psychologists do research addressed to the category. For example, they attempt to isolate the nature of various categories, as in research investigating the factors that distinguish schizophrenics from nonschizophrenics. An interest in personal categories encourages research that seeks to correlate various factors (socioeconomic background, sex, emotional adjustment, laterality, etc.) with the category of interest. Causal implications easily appear in interpretations of this research, despite the gross analytic level and the dependence on correlations rather than on functional relations. In addition, acceptance of personal categories leads investigators to compare one category with another (e.g., culturally disadvantaged versus advantaged). These comparisons are made with serious intent, despite the dubious status of the categories. The comparisons lead to generalizations such as "girls read better than boys." Generalizations of this kind state what ordinary observers can discern even if they do not necessarily agree upon what they mean. That is, they are generalizations about content and not about structure. Because these generalizations describe actualities, they are historically and culturally tagged and always dependent on historical and cultural conditions. A psychology commited to research of the kind suggested by these descriptive generalizations is a psychology that barely sees the concrete particulars of conduct, if at all.

Personal categories draw attention away from the conduct or misconduct that leads to the categorization. For example, the category of dyslexia obscures the fact that some children have more difficulty than others in learning to read, write, and spell. Alternatively, the category obscures the possibility that some sets of contingencies have more difficulty than others in shaping these repertoires. As well as distracting attention from concrete particulars and from contingencies, personal categories encourage a context-free psychology. The categories are often taken to describe the whole person in all settings and under all conditions. That is, personal categories encourage what Kagan (1976) called a "pan-situational traitism" (p. 191). They enable us to talk about people without requiring that we specify any concrete detail of the acts of interest, the current context, and the personal history. That manner of talking might suffice in ordinary discourse, but it only obscures and misleads in a technical context.

CONCLUSION

The concrete particulars of psychological interest are dated acts and not individual human beings. Individual human beings are multilevelled systems that participate in the physical, biological, psychological, and anthropological levels of integration. Psychologists cannot take individual human beings as their particulars and produce scientific knowledge at the same time. Scientific knowledge is built by abstracting out a particular level of integration and by studying it in isolation from other levels. As understood here, the psychological level of integration consists of the acts that particular persons engage in at particular times and in particular places. At least, the content of the psychological domain consists of those dated particulars. The structure of the psychological domain consists of the network of classes and relations that constitutes the abstract tier of the domain of acts. We have made substantial progress in understanding psychological structure (Sidman, 1986a, 1986b). Without an acceptance of dated acts as concrete particulars, widespread acceptance of this structural knowledge seems unlikely.

A psychology of action does not find the structure of its subject matter inside the organism. In that respect, it differs from traditional psychology, which conceptualizes behavior amorphously as the output of the organism and looks for the organocentric structure that controls this output. Instead, psychological structure is found in the domain of acts that requires the organism as a participant but that stretches beyond the organism and through time. Psychological structure is of this temporally extended and often transdermal domain. That much is evident by considering the principles of reinforcement and punishment, if nothing else. Identifying an exemplar of reinforcement, for example, requires that we observe events through time. We have to observe instances of the contingency, the increment in the performance, and evidence that the increment occurred because of the contingency. Further, the events observed most often stretch across the boundaries of the organism. More complex levels of psychological structure require more extended observation. An example is in identifying the phenomena of stimulus equivalence at the level of the four-term contingency. To identify this phenomenon, we establish a conditional discrimination and subsequently test for identity, symmetry, and transitivity. The extension through time is considerable. In conclusion, the structure of the psychological domain consists of the patterns that underlie historically cumulative streams of acts grounded in the bodily activities of individual organisms. In brief, psychological structure is *in* conduct.

CHAPTER 12

Means-End
Interpretation

INTRODUCTION

We have seen that *experimental* psychology properly deals with the functional relations into which contingencies enter with performance and with the phenomena (e.g., conditioned reinforcement, stimulus equivalence) that emerge from these functional relations. We have also seen that science includes nonexperimental inquiry. The question that now arises concerns the general nature of *nonexperimental* inquiry in psychology.

EQUIFINALITY

The first question for nonexperimental inquiry in psychology is "What is this person doing?" The insistence on this question contradicts the traditional notion that our first question is "What causes this person to behave in this way?" But the question of "What is this person doing?" follows from the central place that equifinality has in psychological phenomena.

As a consequence of equifinality, acts that belong to the *same* equifinal class can look *different.* For example, "Could I have another piece of cake" and "That cake was really good" look different, but they might be equivalent ways of getting another piece of cake. If so, they count as members of the same unit of conduct, and they have the same psychological significance. This first consequence of equifinality has been noted in the psychological literature (e.g., Churchman & Ackoff, 1947; Ferster, 1973; Murray, 1938, p. 56).

Equifinality also has the consequence that acts that look the *same* can belong to *different* equifinal classses and so differ in their psychological significance. For example, I often walk down the stairs in the building I work in. Each instance of walking down the stairs looks the same as the next. But, on one occasion, walking down the stairs has the result that I go to the staffroom, on another occasion it has the result that I go to the library, and so on. What looks like walking down the stairs, then, is on one occasion going to the staffroom, on another occasion going to the library, and so forth. In this case, psychological significance changes with little or no change in appearances. Again, this consequence of equifinality has been noted (e.g., Best, 1978, p. 79; Murray, 1938, p. 56; Purton, 1978; Walker, 1942).

Equifinality makes the description of conduct uncertain, because an observer cannot be sure about the class membership of an act. Multiple interpretations are possible, and there might be a discrepancy between the action ascribed and the action performed. Suppose we see a person walking down the stairs this morning at 10:00 a.m. Just by observing that act, we cannot say with confidence what the person is doing. The person might be going to morning tea, going to the library, and so on. To say that the person is walking down the stairs is not wrong. However, it is probably incomplete, if only because walking down the stairs is rarely an act we perform for its own sake. To make matters worse, a second episode of walking down the stairs is not necessarily a second instance of the same action. Further, some other form, perhaps taking an elevator, can also be an alternative means to the same end. In sum, a unit of conduct might be one of two or more different means to a single end, and it might be one means to two or more different ends. This susceptibility of conduct to multiple interpretations has been noted before (e.g., Campbell, 1954; Hunter, 1932; Kvale, 1976a; Muenzinger, 1927; Walker, 1942). It makes "What is this person doing" (or "What act is this act?" or "What is the meaning of this act?") the first question we must ask in inquiry addressed to the content of a person's conduct. Muenzinger (1927) commented that our need to ask this question is perhaps what makes a systematic psychology necessary at all. If we could easily and accurately identify the purposive unities in our own conduct and in the conduct of others, then we might not need a science of psychology. Giving an account of what a person is doing would be straightforward and not an occasion for inquiry.

Equifinality and its implications do not have the central place in psychological theory that we might expect. On the contrary, psychology proceeds in ways that do not follow logically from equifinality. Muenzinger (1927) said that the problem of different psychological realities is well-known to ordinary thought and not unknown in psychology but still does not command the attention it deserves. More recently, Kvale (1976a) offered a comment of the same kind. Indeed, psychologists seem to assume that behavior is easily described and that psychology's problem is to provide explanations. In fact, psychological description is problematic. We might agree, for example, that one person gazes towards another, but this description omits the means–end structure that gives gazing its meanings, which doubtless are multiple. Stating the means–end structure is part of the task of psychological description. Also illustrating the neglect of equifinality, we readily assume that two modes of conduct are different because they look different or are the same because they look the same. As Tennant and his colleagues noted, we distinguish an impotent man from an agoraphobic woman because their problems look different. Yet, this distinction might conceal the psychological significance of the acts that led to the categorizations. For example, both sets of acts might have the critical result of gaining attention from the person's spouse (Tennant, Cullen & Hattersley, 1981). Likewise, we distinguish obese persons from phobic persons, although the problems these persons present might have the same psychological significance. For example, as Goldiamond (1974) noted, the relevant acts might gain social attention or reduce the demands of others or both. Carr and Durand (1985) presented a similar interpretation of the problems of children we categorize as retarded, autistic, or schizophrenic. In general, operating at this level of ideal types seems plausible because it is close to the difficulties that ordinary thought raises about conduct. But this decontextualized pigeonholing of people avoids the demands of our subject matter and produces knowledge claims that do more to legitimize social stereotypes than to illuminate the psychological significance of human acts.

INTERPRETATION

Uncertainty about what a person is doing makes interpretation the key strategy in seeking to understand the content of conduct. Interpretation can start with an action (i.e., a class of acts) and look for the contingencies in which the action is embedded. Having identified the action of interest, we ask about the critical results of that action. In other words, we ask what ends are achieved, what is done, or how the action is effective. In asking this question, we want to know how the action of interest makes a difference to the person's life. That is, what does the action produce or prevent that would not be produced or prevented otherwise? We can then ask about the alternative means that the person has available to achieve the particular end. In part, this question is about the person's psychological resources; in particular, whether alternative repertoires are available and in what strength. As well, the question is about the person's ecology; for example, whether the milieu permits alternative means to the particular end or instead demands a narrowly specified performance. We can also ask about the consequences of alternative actions. If the person did not act as she or he does, but in some other way, then what consequences would follow? These interpretative strategies explore the network of contingencies for the action of interest and for its alternatives. The strategies have been developed by Goldiamond (e.g., 1974, 1984).

As Skinner (1953, pp. 40–41, 1957, p. 450) pointed out, all interpretations are limited by the information available. Due to a lack of information, we cannot answer questions about Hitler's behavior with certainty, we cannot be confident about the contingencies under which Shakespeare worked, and so on. Our interpretations are also limited by the number and complexity of the contingencies. We may be able to identify only a salient few of the relevant contingencies. Interpretative difficulties also arise because some contingencies are hard to see. This difficulty is not apparent because we easily find examples of contingencies from daily life. Yet the ease with which we give examples does not mean that every contingency is obvious to ordinary observation. As Skinner (1957, p. 451; 1969, p. 13, p. 150; 1974, p. 126) remarked, it is likely that some contingencies are subtle and may go unsuspected, that others are short-lived, and that others are ineffable. In the end, an interpretation is always a plausible guess about the relevant contingencies. We can only gather information and continue to regard our interpretations as fallible and always open to improvement. Of course, the impossibility of a complete and rigorous account of the content of conduct is hard to accept, because we have long presumed that definitive answers are available. We need to face this limitation with equanimity. Certainly, we need to be determined to resist the pressure to present our interpretations as anything other than hypotheses.

AWARENESS: STATING THE CONTINGENCIES

The issue of awareness enters into the problem of psychological interpretation. It is one thing to say that an observer might ascribe an action to a person's conduct that is not the action performed. It is another thing to say that actors themselves might make these mistakes. The latter possibility implies the assumption that actors do not necessarily know what they are doing. This assumption might seem incompatible with a psychology that gives the end results of behavior a central place. But to insist that end results give behavior its psychological significance does not mean that persons are necessarily aware of what they are doing. That is, we distinguish doing from doing-with-awareness. At least, a contingency-oriented psychology makes this distinction. Of course, the distinction between doing and doing-with-awareness has been made before. An early example is Schoen's (1927) distinction between purposive behavior, behavior that produces an end, and purposeful behavior, behavior deliberately directed toward a forseen end. Ringen (1976) expressed the same distinction between goal-directed behavior and conscious, intentional, or rule-guided behavior. The account that a contingency-oriented psychology gives of the distinction has the advantage of explicitly acknowledging contingencies.

A contingency-oriented psychology is concerned with effective behavior; behavior that has effects or end results. Such behavior can be entirely the result of past contingencies. Effective behavior can be shaped and maintained by contingencies that remain unanalyzed in the sense that the individual does not and perhaps cannot state them. Contingency-oriented psychologists refer to behavior of this kind as "contingency-shaped behavior." Other theorists have called it "knowing-how" (e.g., Dewey, 1922/1957, pp. 167–168; Ryle 1949/1966, pp. 28–29) and "tacit knowing" (Polanyi, 1962). Skinner (1974, p. 132, 1980, p. 341) spoke of behavior of this kind as acting intuitively, unconsciously, or instinctively. Skinner (1974, p. 132) commented that this contingency-shaped behavior is behaving as the effect of past contingencies that the person has not stated or cannot, at present, state. The person might not know *what* he or she is doing (at least, not fully), or *how* he or she is doing it (again, at least not fully), or both. The behavior is nonetheless effective because it satisfies the contingencies that maintain it.

The occurence of conduct without awareness is apparently difficult for us to accept. Indeed, Koch (1975) mentioned the work of Polanyi (1962) as a departure from the philosophic tradition that identifies the knowable with the sayable. This tradition makes it difficult for us to see conduct as initially and, perhaps as basically, intuitive in being shaped and maintained by unanalyzed contingencies. In developing an argument against an overcommitment to rationality, Polanyi (1962) insisted that there are things we know how to do although we cannot provide a good account of how we do them. For example, we might keep a bicycle upright or stay afloat while swimming and yet we might be unable to say how we do it. As another example, we recognize familiar faces in greeting people we know, yet any description we give of a familiar face would equally fit many other faces. Ryle (1949/1966, p. 30) gave the example of the wit who can appreciate and construct jokes but who cannot necessarily offer any recipes for how he or she does it. In these examples, the person cannot say *how* he or she performs an act. But we could equally consider examples in which the person cannot give a complete account of *what* he or she is doing. Goldiamond (1974, 1975a, 1975b, 1984) has given many examples. In one case, a man who smoked excessively during meetings was not merely smoking, but also escaping from demands for short intervals by lighting up. This interpretation of what the man was doing was supported when smoking ceased once coffee breaks were introduced whenever proceedings became tense. These examples aside, we do not easily accept that effective behavior can occur without awareness of what is done, how it is done, or both. The occurrence of effective behavior without awareness is something we must argue for in psychology.

A contingency-oriented psychology gives a basic place to contingency-shaped behavior. Skinner (1974, p. 132) described contingency-shaped behavior as the starting point for psychological inquiry. In addition, a contingency-oriented psychology admits that we know about contingencies in the sense that we can state some of them. We state contingencies, more or less completely, in descriptions ("when I do this, that happens"), in the rules of games, in definitions ([in this verbal community], "A" means [will have the same effect on listeners and readers as] "B"), in statements of purpose, in directions ("Turn left at the next intersection, then right [to get to your desination]"), in appreciation messages (Clinard, 1985, pp. 9–12), in religious and governmental laws, in proverbs, maxims, and truisms (e.g., Skinner 1969, p. 40), in the recipes of the craft psychologies ("Do not regret past failures [if you want to make the best use of your time now]"), in scientific laws (e.g., Lee, 1985; Skinner, 1969, pp. 157, 254; 1974, pp. 8, 124, 235), in reasoning ("if I do A, X is likely to happen, but if I do B, I will give up the chance to get Y, so I will do A"), and so on. These contingency statements imply or state an end result and a means to that end result. The end result might be the effecting or preventing of a change, the meeting of a standard, or the clarification of a situation.

The distinction mentioned earlier between doing (knowing how) and stating contingencies (knowing *that, about,* or *of*) requires further discussion in this context. Stating contingencies while speaking or writing is a kind of acting, so the distinction of interest is better stated as between acting as such and acting that is also stating contingencies. This distinction has been noted before. For example, Bower (1975) distinguished knowledge of how to do things (i.e., knowhow) from knowledge that certain propositions are true. Dewey (1922, pp. 177–178) distinguished knowing-how from knowledge-of, knowledge-about, and knowledge that. Ryle (1949/1966, pp. 28–29) distinguished knowing-how from knowing-that. The distinction is between doing something or acting in the practical, intuitive sense and giving a verbal account of what is done or of what might be done. Once recorded, statements of contingencies become entities free of the behavior that produces them (speaking or writing). These statements can become part of our collective knowledge of the world and its workings or, better, of its work requirements.

Statements of contingencies can prompt us to act in practical ways. A clear example consists of the traffic laws, which, ideally, prompt beginning drivers to give way to the right, drive a safe distance behind the vehicle in front, and so on. Rules of games, advice, and directions provide other examples. Empirical work (e.g., Ayllon & Azrin, 1964; Baron, Kaufman & Stauber, 1969) indicates that without initial prompting by contingency statements, we might not act in the ways required by the current contingencies. Of course, we can also construct our own statements of contingencies and use these statements to prompt our own behavior. Statements of purpose, including New Year's resolutions, provide examples. Consistent with our ordinary experience of these matters, operant research indicates that subjects not provided with instructions about the relevant contingencies will state the apparent contingencies for themselves (see Baron & Galizio, 1983, and Lowe, 1979 for discussions). Statements of contingencies can guide behavior that extended exposure to the relevant contingencies might otherwise have to shape. For example, shaping of effective driving behavior through direct exposure to the contingencies maintained by the vehicle, by the road, and by other vehicles on the road would be arduous, lengthy, and dangerous. The instructions provided by a driving instructor state the salient contingencies and circumvent an extended shaping of effective behavior by the contingencies themselves. Of course, behavior prompted by contingency statements requires support by other contingencies if it is to persist. The ineffectiveness of New Year's resolutions should remind us that contingency statements often exert weak control over our behavior. Empirical studies (e.g., Lattal, 1969; Packard, 1970; Redd & Wheeler, 1973; Schutte & Hopkins, 1970) also remind us of this reality. Furthermore, the fluency that leads us to identify behavior as skilled requires the shaping effects of differential contingencies of reinforcement. Prompting alone is not enough, if only because statements of contingencies rarely capture the full complexity and subtlety of the contingencies of interest. Still, we need to note that statements of contingencies are useful, not only when we talk with each other and to ourselves about the workings of the world, but also when we want to prompt behavior that the relevant contingencies might then support and shape.

Statements of contingencies are also important in the repertoires of behavior that have to do with what we might describe as self-awareness. That is, we can state some of the contingencies that support our own behavior. To make such statements, we engage in self-observing and in self-describing. This is prompted by other members of the verbal community when they ask us what we are doing, why we are doing it, what we plan to do next, how likely we are to do it, what we think the consequences of acting that way will be, how we feel about what we are doing, and so on. Conversations that include questions of this kind presumably occasion self-observing and self-describing, with results sometimes useful to other persons in managing their conduct in relation to ours. As well, in managing our own conduct, we can ask ourselves questions that prompt us to observe and describe what we do, when we do it, how we do it, how we feel about it, some of the conditions that give rise to it, and so on. Such conversations, whether social or not, can occasion the acts of self-observing and self-describing with their products, which consist of the statements about ourselves that we regard as our self-awareness. Skinner (1957, pp. 138–146) discussed self-awareness from this perspective, and Zettle and Hayes (1982) provided a framework for the various semantic therapies consistent with this interpretation of self-awareness in terms of contingency statements.

Psychologists have traditionally excluded self-awareness from the phenomena of interest to them. Hilgard (1980) traced this exclusion to Watson and to behaviorism. McDougall (1928) rejected this exclusion and insisted that a sane behaviorism would use data gathered by independent observers and by self-observers. But his insistence had little effect on the subsequent history of psychology. Relevant to this, Klein (1942) said that the psychology of his time induced a phobia in its students concerning observation of their own mental processes. If the term *mental processes* is understood as meaning a person's conduct, whether public, private, or inchoate, then this phobia has let academic psychologists exclude and ignore one of the most interesting aspects of human conduct.

A psychology that recognizes the inaccessibility of the content of conduct to laboratory research would give self-observing and self-reporting an essential place in its investigations of content. As implied earlier, we can properly bring only problems of psychological structure or problems of psychological technology into the laboratory. To find out about the actual content of conduct, we have to observe conduct as it is outside the laboratory. Goldiamond (1975b) pointed out that independent observers and self-observers have different vantage points on the content of conduct. As Goldiamond (1974) commented, if anything, self observers have an advantage. They have more contact with their own conduct than anyone else, and, given skills of observation and interpretation and the same information, they can interpret their own conduct just as an independent observer can. Consistent with this, Chase and Wylie (1985) commented that the persons best fitted to provide a fine-grain analysis of the contingencies of given settings are those with extended exposure to those settings. Concretely, teachers can provide accounts of classroom contingencies and their effects on performance (see Cullinan & Strickland, 1986), clinicians can provide accounts of clinical settings (see Ferster & Simons, 1966), and so on.

Most psychologists will not be enthusiastic about using self-reports in research. Reflecting this general lack of enthusiasm about self-reports, radical behaviorists (e.g., Day, 1980; Goldiamond, 1975b; Lowe & Horne, 1985) have had to defend the use of self-reports in their research. They would nonetheless agree with Shimoff (1986) that we must exercise caution in using data derived from self-reports. A constructive approach to the problem of using these data would recognize that skills of observing and reporting often have to be taught (Ferster, 1972; Glenn, 1983). Moreover, a constructive approach would recognize that the veracity of self-reports depends on the contingencies that operate on self-reporting, as indicated by studies of correspondence between verbal and nonverbal behavior (see Karlan & Rusch, 1982). In short, we can adopt a technical stance in relation to self-observing and self-reporting and investigate them rather than dismiss them apriori on the basis of scientistic preconceptions about how psychology should proceed.

The exclusion of self-reports is too often for the sake of a methodological purity that serves to keep many academic psychologists away from human lives as they are actually lived. This methodological purity stems in part from failing to realize that we need a nonexperimental psychology (i.e., a psychology of the actual content of conduct) as much as we need an experimental psychology (i.e., a psychology of structure). The exclusion of self-reports also serves to protect academic psychologists from the challenge of developing techniques to enhance our skills (i.e., skilled actions) of self-observing and self-reporting. Several writers (e.g., English, 1933; Neuringer, 1981, 1984; Sanford, 1965; Scriven, 1964) have pointed out that we would do better to start academic psychology in practical problems, a starting point consistent with the histories of the other experimental sciences (e.g., Beer, 1965; Kranzberg, 1968). For psychology, one of these practical problems is to develop techniques which will sharpen our skills of self-observing and self-reporting. A starting point for investigators who want to accept this challenge can be found in the work of Ferster (1972), Glenn (1983), and Skinner (1957, pp. 130–146, pp. 313–330).

NONEXPERIMENTAL PSYCHOLOGY

Some writers (e.g., Bass, 1974; Day, 1969) have insisted that psychologists would gain much from giving more attention to the actual content of human conduct. In this connection, Jastrow (1927) spoke of a natural history of the mind. Academic psychology has given little attention to questions of natural history because of the experimentalist attitude that denigrates the methods and products of natural history. As some critics (e.g., Gergen, 1978; Klein, 1942; Peele, 1981) have noted, many psychologists have seen the experiment, albeit a dubious form of the experiment, as the only valid source of psychological knowledge. Of course, the investigation of content complements rather than competes with experimental work. We need a natural history of conduct in the same way that astronomy, geology, and other descriptive sciences provide a natural history of matter. In particular, we need a natural history of conduct that will use what we know about the structure of conduct to interpret the content of conduct.

Outside academic psychology we already know much about the content of human conduct. Assertions of ignorance about it ignore the abundant knowledge available from daily experience, literature, the psychological crafts, newspapers, plays, history, and so on. Rejecting these sources of information depends on some self-congratulatory criterion of what is valued as a science. If we are engaged in psychological inquiry, rather than in scientism, why not get information from every source? If we do not, we limit the information available to us and distort the conclusions we make. As Lott (1985) noted, for example, feminist research based on letters, journals, and other such records of women's lives has revealed much at variance with what outside observers have reported. Disregarding such information has its sources in the peculiar history of psychology. That history has let psychologists regard only organocentric processes as psychological and only the products of traditional research methodologies as legitimate knowledge. In the process, we have missed preexisting knowledge of conduct as a legitimate and useful contribution to psychological knowledge. Skinner (1957, p. 11) admitted such knowledge when he said that the facts available for psychological interpretation are the facts available to any well-educated person. They are the events of conduct observed in daily life and the events reported in newspapers, in the publications of the social sciences and other disciplines, and elsewhere. They are not the products of laboratory research, which, after all, properly concern problems of psychological structure and not problems of content.

Scientific work addressed to the content of conduct need not become a free-for-all that accepts all manner of speculation. On the contrary, we need to use the principles of psychological structure to interpret our descriptions. At the least, such an interpretation will use the rudimentary knowledge of structure that we can extract from ordinary knowledge ahead of experimental inquiry. At best, it will also use the structural knowledge that we have extracted from experimental work. As some writers (e.g., Michael, 1980; Poppen, 1982) have acknowledged, the complexity of this latter task should not be underestimated. Poppen (1982) illustrated the complexity by discussing the scalloped performances noted by Weisberg and Waldrop (1972) for the passage of bills through the U.S. Congress and by other investigators for the study behavior of students (Mawhinney, Bostow, Laws, Blumenfeld & Hopkins, 1971). Poppen identified the following variables as possibly relevant to the scalloped performance: the periodic availability of the consequential event, the availability of a clock or a calendar to permit a temporal discrimination, explicit instructions about the temporal requirements, and a limited hold on the consequential event. We need to accept that the content of conduct involves a multiplicity of interacting variables and that interpretation is not a simple matter. The sheer number of variables will prompt critics to reject attempts to interpret content with the principles of psychological structure. But Goldiamond (1974, 1975a, 1975b, 1984) has demonstrated the feasibility of such interpretations as the bases for solving practical problems. In any case, investigations of the content of other domains achieve interpretations with practical significance despite the difficulties that arise for them from working in open systems. We need to develop the art of psychological interpretation in the midst of complexity, and we need to transmit this art to our students.

Interpreting conduct in terms of contingencies might seem new. As well, we might seem ignorant of the contingencies that operate outside the laboratory. But our interpretative knowledge could be more advanced than we think. At least, it might be more comprehensive than we think, even if it is more rudimentary than we would like. Contingencies are identified in many fields outside academic psychology and, indeed, outside academia. An example is the feminist and gay literatures, which identify many contingencies that women and gays participate in behaviorally. Another example is seen in Holt's (1969, 1970) work, which alludes to many of the contingencies maintained by our education system. Much of our reasoning in daily life is about contingencies. For example, newspaper reports about the hijackings of 1985 listed the contingencies taken into account by governmental agents in deciding on effective action. In addition, proverbs state contingencies. Skinner (e.g., 1969, p. 140) has provided examples: "Procrastination is the thief of time" suggests a contingency between putting off work now and being unpleasantly busy later and "A knife that cuts never fails to get knicks" suggests that effective behavior is likely also to have costs, and so on. Skinner (1969, p. 140) noted that proverbs seem to state subtle contingencies that have persisted as reasonably stable aspects of human experience over an extended period of time. We can also find contingency statements in the traffic laws, in the rules of games, and so on. In short, talking about conduct in terms of contingencies is not new. It is something we do routinely, most often without recognizing it as such. Indeed, it is part of our knowing-how to talk about conduct, even if the concept of a contingency is not yet a consensual part of our systematic knowledge of conduct.

CRAFT PSYCHOLOGIES

Included in our collective knowledge of conduct we find the statements of the craft psychologies. The craft psychologies include the psychologies contained in books on how to engage in conversation (e.g., McKay, Davis & Fanning, 1983), on how to cope with difficult people (e.g., Bramson, 1981), on how to think (e.g., DeBono, 1985), on how to write (e.g., King, 1978), on how to deal with burn-out (e.g., Freudenberger, 1985), and so on. For the most part, these psychologies arise outside academic psychology in the domain of practice, and they are usually dismissed by academics as "popular psychologies" that are unworthy of serious attention.

However, these bodies of advice do count as psychologies in that they deal with aspects of conduct. At least, from the perspective of a psychology of action, they count as psychologies.

The craft psychologies count as crafts because they have arisen through trial-and-error experience; specifically, of what seems to work in particular domains of conduct. Other crafts have included techniques of animal and plant breeding and prescientific industrial techniques such as cheesemaking, tanning, and fermentation. Crafts differ from applied sciences, which as Feibleman (1972a) explained, are literally basic-sciences applied. Unlike the techniques of the applied sciences, craft techniques exist ahead of the relevant basic sciences. They arise through trial-and-error experience, perhaps accumulated over generations, of what works in a particular domain, and they are transmitted by demonstration, apprenticeship, and verbal instruction based on recipes or rules of thumb. Craftspersons are concerned with developing and sometimes with formulating concrete techniques that get things made and done for human benefit and profit. In the psychological domain, this concern is with techniques of self-management that help us engage successfully in studying, thinking, public speaking, managing our time, conversing, handling criticism, setting goals, and other tasks of daily life.

Statements of the craft psychologies take the form of recipes: "If you want to achieve X, then you should do Y." The critical *components* of these recipes are the end result and the strategy or strategies (i.e., means) that might effect the result. The critical *issue* is whether the strategy will work under the actual work requirements of daily life. Self-experimentation, as described by Neuringer (1981, 1984), is one technique we might use in empirical work based on the recipes of the craft psychologies. In self-experimentation in this context, investigators would test the advice of the craft psychologies by following it systematically themselves and noting the results. They might also develop a training procedure, perhaps following the three-stage training model described by Ladd and Mize (1983), to teach nonspecialists to engage in self-experimentation. Briefly stated, the training procedure might begin with (a), textual instruction, resulting in subjects talking fluently about the relevant contingencies. Johnson and Chase's (1981) model for textual instruction might be useful in this regard. Following textual instruction, the subjects would engage in (b), supervised practice in contrived settings and, later, in (c), self-experimentation in ordinary (i.e., noncontrived) settings. This procedure is consistent with the strategy mentioned earlier of using self-reports to obtain information about the contingencies of particular domains. It suggests a method for checking and refining the recipes of the craft psychologies, for teaching the recipes and the strategies that the recipes describe, and for exploring the actual contingencies of daily life and their effects on how we perform and on how we feel.

We readily count the recipes of the craft psychologies as advice. But the possibility that they also serve to illuminate the local content of conduct will seem less plausible. And yet, these recipes do illuminate, in the sense of guiding observers to see the domains of criticism, of time management, and so forth, or to see these domains more clearly than before and in more detail. Stated differently, they guide observers to see the contingencies that constitute the work requirements of these domains or, in other words, the ways in which those domains currently work. An example is DeBono's (1986) advice about strategies for achieving success in the eyes of the world. The advice might prompt acts conducive to success. It also serves to illuminate something of the actual content of human conduct. Another example is Bramson's (1981) book on dealing with people who habitually act in difficult ways. Based on observation and on action research in business contexts, this book describes effective strategies for identifying and coping with difficult people. It also illuminates much about this aspect of interpersonal conduct. Descriptions of conduct expressed in the form of advice have merit that generally goes unnoticed. We want precise advice that points to the actual events of interest, and we want comprehensive advice that covers many of those events. As well, we want accurate advice that deals with the kinds of events that actually occur. Similarly, when seeking a description of conduct for cognitive rather than for pragmatic purposes, we want an accurate, precise, and comprehensive account. The craft psychologies have much to recommend them in this respect. From the perspective of a psychology of action, then, the recipes of the craft psychologies contribute knowledge of the actual (historical and local) contingencies of conduct as much as they give advice about how to achieve success in the tasks of daily life.

Most psychologists will probably dismiss the notion that we should value the craft psychologies as psychologies. This dismissal will arise in part from the presumption that psychology is properly about organocentric phenomena. It will also arise in part from the attitude held by many psychologists about the relation between research and practice. Bass (1974) described this attitude as the science-to-application approach, and Potter (1982) called it "the ideology of application." This attitude puts research ahead of practice, and it ignores or denies the potential contribution of practice to research. Relevant to this, Bass (1974) commented that psychologists are like the scientists of Ancient Greece in disdaining psychological technology and in placing too much emphasis on theory. He suggested that psychologists have tried to imitate the theoretical aspects of physics without developing the essential technology. Consistent with these comments, some writers (e.g., Bass, 1974; Beer, 1965; Kranzberg,

1968; Ziman, 1976, pp. 8–35) have noted the contribution of craft to science and, indeed, the convergence of craft and speculation in the early stages of experimental science. Contrary to this, psychology did not emerge out of craft. Bode (1922) commented that psychology grew out of theological and philosophical speculation, and Holt (1962) noted that Fechner and Wundt started with problems far removed from what ordinary people think of as problems of psychology. Agreeing with this view, Luchins and Luchins (1965, pp. 375–376) said that psychology did not begin with folk wisdom or with the behavioral technologies and their rules of thumb, but with the scholarly speculation of traditional philosophy. Blinkered by these origins and by a persistent commitment to organocentrism, most psychologists will find it difficult to accept that the craft psychologies contribute to psychological knowledge.

The importance of the craft psychologies to a psychology of action can be emphasized by considering another criticism of academic psychology as it is currently pursued. Many critics (e.g., Barlow, 1981; Gaylord-Ross, 1979; Kvale, 1976b; Roberts & Russell, 1975; Sprinthal, 1975) have commented that psychological research has had little impact on practice. For example, Barlow (1981) observed that clinical psychologists are not greatly influenced by clinical research, and Sprinthal (1975) noted that educators see research as contributing little or nothing to the actual problems of teaching. In general, as Goldiamond and his colleagues (Goldiamond, Dyrud & Miller, 1965) pointed out, practitioners who have completed their degree work in academic psychology seldom maintain any pretense of a relation between practice and research. The paradox is that the meager impact of academic psychology on practice occurs alongside abundant knowledge about conduct that has arisen outside academic psychology and that is typically excluded from it. We do not have to wait for applications derived from laboratory psychology to effect significant improvements in human conduct. What we need is to develop effective training programs to teach the recipes and the strategies already available. To do that successfully, we need the agencies that control the relevant resources (money, personnel, etc.) to arrange the contingencies under which such work will flourish. We also need agencies and institutions to provide the work requirements that will maintain the personal and interpersonal skills that are taught. To say that is to imply agreement with Wiener's (1972) insistence that sometimes problems of conduct are political rather than technological problems. Sometimes they might have more to do with a lack of resources to implement the technology than with a lack of technology as such. Similarly, our apparent lack of a psychological technology, however primitive, might have more to do with how we currently conceive of psychology than with the nature of the psychological knowledge actually available to us from all sources.

In the academic context, we need to recognize that we already have extensive practical knowledge about the work-requirements of particular task domains. As explained before, this knowledge is available in the recipes of the craft psychologies. Departing from the orthodox view about these recipes, Campbell (1975) indicated that these "recipes for living" have emerged from generations of social history. He implied that we in academic psychology should give them more credence than we do. More than that, we should include these recipes as part of the nonexperimental branch of a science of psychology. Duckworth (1981) has already suggested this on different grounds. Certainly, knowledge of this kind, which is practical, concrete, and relevant to daily life, is the knowledge most people expect to encounter when they enter a university to earn a psychology degree. We should not dismiss this expectation as a reflection of ignorance. On the contrary, perhaps we should interpret the expectation as reflecting preconceptions based on the ordinary psychological knowledge bequeathed to us by past generations in ordinary language, in the psychological crafts, and in literature. Beginning students of psychology have to be taught the scientistic criteria that blind many academic psychologists to the psychological knowledge already available outside academia. They do not accept these criteria as a matter of course. Perhaps we should seriously consider the expectation of our beginning students that academic psychology will be practical, concrete, and relevant. We can fulfil that expectation by presenting the recipes of the craft psychologies as tentative (i.e., fallible) statements of the actual contingencies that constitute the concrete tasks of daily life. That practical and relevant presentation of the concept of the contingency would naturally lead to a presentation of what we know about the structure of conduct.

CONCLUSION

This discussion suggests a psychology that departs markedly from the psychology presented in the introductory textbooks of academic psychology. That established psychology is laboratory-based, often takes animals as its subjects, and shows little direct interest in the mundane particulars of human conduct. The psychology of the content of conduct espoused here depends on investigators observing and interpreting events outside the laboratory. It is a local psychology, a psychology of the contingencies that operate under particular historical conditions in particular domains of action. In addition, it is a psychology committed to illuminating the work requirements of various domains and the costs and benefits of various acts for each of the participants in these domains. Most of all, it is a psychology that builds directly and explicitly on our ordinary and specialized experience of the way in which these various domains actually work.

This psychology of content is inevitably local and historical. As Koch (1975) suggested on different grounds, a psychology of content will consist more of psychological studies than of psychology in the narrow sense. That is, it will be pursued in various contexts, including schools of education, law, and business, and in departments of psychology. After all, the content of conduct is vast, and this vastness extends across several disciplines just as the content of the physical world extends across more than one discipline (astronomy, geology, etc.).

The present discussion also seems to depart markedly from the contents of the *Journal of the Experimental Analysis of Behavior,* where many contingency-oriented psychologists publish their experimental research. The contents of that journal suggest a laboratory science concerned with the minutiae of the structure of conduct. Of course, operant psychologists (e.g., Baron & Perone, 1982; Buskist, 1983; Hake, 1982; Harzem & Williams, 1983; Lowe, 1979) are increasingly interested in extending their research program to human social and verbal behavior. Even so, at face value, this extension does not contradict the apparent gap between the experimental research and the task of interpreting human conduct as it occurs outside the laboratory. Human operant research is still conducted in the laboratory and is still concerned with structural problems. Of course, the gap is in fact only apparent, for the laboratory work and the interpretative work share a common framework and reflect a common commitment. The framework is provided in its most rudimentary form by the concept of the two-term contingency, understood as formulating the work requirements found wherever human beings expend effort with results. The commitment is to action as a subject matter in its own right, as a particular level of integration that we can abstract out and study independently of other levels in which human beings participate. Knowledge about the structural patterns in the psychological level of integration is the unique contribution of an experimental science of psychology. This experimental science departs from a psychology of the content of conduct in dealing with structure and not with content. Still, it shares the same commitment to action as a natural domain that has abstract and concrete tiers and that invites both experimental and nonexperimental inquiry.

CHAPTER 13

Stimulus-Response Psychology

INTRODUCTION

A psychology of action will seem uncontroversial to the nonspecialist. It seems plain that in conducting our lives we pursue ends and vary the means to those ends, whether consciously or not. A psychology of means and ends needs defense in academic psychology. This defense is necessary because psychology is based on a concept borrowed inappropriately by psychologists from physiology. That concept—the concept of the reflex— has given us a conceptual framework that obscures conduct. The present chapter discusses the concept of the reflex and some of its consequences for how we think about our subject matter and task.

STIMULUS-RESPONSE PSYCHOLOGIES

The concept of the reflex originated in the work of Descartes and was elaborated by physiologists, particularly in the 19th century. As Schoenfeld (1972) noted, the concept has two senses. First, it designates a relation between a physical stimulus and a muscular or glandular response. An example is the pupillary reflex in which a bright light elicits pupillary constriction. Second, the concept of the reflex sometimes designates the bodily counterpart of a stimulus–response relation. Known as the "reflex arc," this latter sense of the concept is a convenient fiction with no accepted anatomical or physiological definition (Efron, 1966). The present discussion concerns the concept of the reflex only in the sense of a stimulus–response relation.

Stimulus–response psychologies are psychologies based on the concept of the reflex. They identify psychology's task as a matter of finding stimulus–response connections. Watson's (1919, p. 10) statement of stimulus–response psychology directed psychologists to look for stimuli, responses, and relations between them, just as the concept of the reflex directs us to look for stimuli, responses, and relations between them. Stimulus–response psychologies lead us to expect that given a stimulus, we

151

might predict the response, and that given a response, we might retrodict the stimulus. These psychologies organize psychological knowledge around the concept of the reflex. They see love, hope, intelligence, memory, and the like, as stimulus–response units. According to some critics (e.g., Dashiell, 1949; McDougall, 1928; Skinner, 1973; von Bertalanffy, 1951), this formulation treats acts and feelings as mechanical responses to stimuli, and it treats persons as robots or penny-in-the-slot machines.

S-O-R Psychology

Stimulus–response psychology did not work in its unelaborated form, because human behavior, as it occurs in conduct, is more variable and less stimulus-bound than stimulus–response psychology supposes. In dealing with these difficulties, psychologists elaborated the stimulus–response model, by adding the organism as a third variable intervening between stimuli and responses. As Skinner (1969, pp. 3–28) explained, they developed a S–O–R psychology which allowed the basic stimulus–response model to persist.

The concept of the intervening variable is associated with modern forms of S–O–R psychology. This concept gives theoretical status to the practice of locating psychological entities inside the organism, in a conceptual nervous system. An example is Kimble's (1967) statement that reinforced practice (independent variable) produces learning (intervening variable), which produces a relatively permanent change in behavior (dependent variable). It is also evident in a statement by Woodworth (1958): "You meet an old acquaintance and speak to him. He hesitates for a moment and then smiles and calls you by name. The intervening variable here is recognition" (p. 26). That is, your presence (stimulus) occasions recognition (intervening variable), which in turn produces the greeting (response). Purpose, expectation, memory, and other psychological categories are similarly located between stimuli (input) and responses (output). This strategy indicates that the S–O–R model has no difficulty with the psychological nouns, the problematic nature of which was discussed earlier. S–O–R psychology accepts the psychological nouns without question and gives them organocentric referents between sensory input and motor output. This practice follows the tradition of bifurcating a human being into a physical body and a nonphysical mind. In this tradition, the physical body of a human being behaves, and the nonphysical mind, located between sensory input and motor output, directs the behavior of the body. The notion of an intervening variable gives scientistic expression to this ordinary notion.

Cognitivism

S–O–R psychology persists in cognitivism, the metatheoretical position that dominates modern psychology. This claim will seem implausible at first sight, because cognitivism is ostensibly a departure from behaviorism and thus, for most of us, a departure from stimulus–response psychology.

Norman (1980) described the cognitive position in the following way. Sensory transducers feed information about the environment to central processing structures, which consist of perceptual systems, motor systems, memory systems, and so on. They analyze and interpret information from the environment and feed it to response systems that control movements of the body. Thus, the cognitive model links sensory input to motor output via the mediation of central structures and processes. The nature of these central (or cognitive) structures and processes needs some clarification.

Cognitive processes do not consist of conscious experiences accessible only to the actor. We easily think otherwise because we imagine that cognitivism deals with the mind and because we often equate "mind" with private experiences. As Ryle (1949/1966, p. 28) noted, we think of our minds as places where we engage in daydreaming and other such activities that we alone can know directly. When cognitivists talk about cognitive processes, they are not talking about private events accessible only to whoever is acting. Nor are they talking about unconscious experiences, as Gopnik (1984) and Mischel (1976) noted. Moreover, cognitive processes are not behavioral entities. On the contrary, cognitivists dismiss behavior as a surface phenomenon, as an index or manifestation of organocentric phenomena. A statement by Uttal (1973, p. 3) exemplifies this dismissal. He said that behavior is not the subject matter of psychology. Rather, it provides an approach to the subject matter that consists of consciousness, memory, and the like. Similarly, Chomsky (1968, p. 58) dismissed behavior as evidence for the mental structures that properly concern psychology. Likewise, Estes (1975) said that behavior is an index for the information-processing activities of real interest of psychology. A difficulty exists in interpreting what cognitivists mean by the term *behavior* in statements such as these, because the concept of behavior in psychology is amorphous, undeveloped, and equivocal. But, if *behavior* means acts, then these dismissals of behavior make clear that cognitive processes do not consist of acts such as spelling a word, completing a crossword puzzle, or finding an entry in a dictionary.

Cognitive processes are theoretical entities. They include semantic networks, schemas, scripts, cognitive maps, mental representations, and plans. As described by Fodor (1981), these theoretical entities are meant to represent internal structures and processes that intervene between sensory input and motor output, and they are thought to explain bodily movements and speech sounds. As Fodor and his colleagues (Fodor, Bever & Garrett, 1974, p. xi) insisted, behavior is meant to result from the complex interaction of cognitive structures. Norman (1981) offered the example that we might attribute an action sequence, such as walking to a restaurant, to a schema, conceived of as a memory unit that appropriate conditions activate. Abelson (1981) gave the example of a script, as a cognitive structure that organizes a person's comprehension of stereo-typed event sequences. Coulter (1982) commented, that these cognitive structures constitute a middle ground juxtaposed between action, on the one hand, and the nervous system, on the other. In Skinner's (1977) terms, they are surrogates of the contingencies that we would do better to deal with directly and explicitly *as* contingencies. Ades (1981) remarked that cognitive psychology is characterized by its concern with less-than-natural phenomena. Cognitive psychologists *are* concerned with natural phenomena; specifically, with acts. The problem is that they construe acts as evidence for a cognitive middle ground and that they insist that this less-than-natural middle ground is the proper subject matter of psychology. Anyone reading Abelson's (1981) paper, for example, would surely be forgiven for supposing that the discussion is about the transdermal, historically cumulative domain of acts and not literally about the internal machinery of the organism.

A comment by Bates and her colleagues (Bates, Bretheron, Beeghly-Smith & McNew, 1982) casts some light on the sources of cognitivism. They said that cognitivism has incorporated the ideas espoused by Tolman. As Skinner (1969, p. 28) noted, Tolman only seemed to surpass stimulus-response psychology. In fact, Tolman (1932, p. 418) insisted that behavior is a stimulus-response phenomenon and that stimuli, responses, and the determinants of responses are all that psychologists have to study. Although Tolman explicitly rejected the notion that behavior is an aggregation of reflexes, he still retained the stimulus-response framework. As Koffka (1933) acknowledged, Tolman insisted that psychology was an autonomous science, yet, contrary to the spirit of autonomy, he claimed that psychological events correspond exactly to the physiological events they depend on. In short, Tolman's psychology was an unsuccessful attempt to escape the blinkers of S-R thinking imposed by the concept of the reflex.

Some writers (e.g., Ades, 1981; Hamlyn, 1981; Rachlin, 1977; Skinner, 1969, pp. 25-28, 1977) have criticized cognitivism, on the grounds that it elaborates the S-O-R framework that psychology should abandon. Cognitivists will deny that cognitivism is a stimulus-response psychology. Certainly, they make that denial implicit when they denigrate stimulus-response psychology. In addition, Tyler (1970) explicitly denied the stimulus-response status of cognitivism. He admitted that the shift from *stimulus* and *response* to *input* and *output* seems like no more than a linguistic matter. However, he insisted that the shift is more significant than that impression suggests because it opens the way to the recognition that a complex internal program controls the input-output sequence. That is, the counterargument is that cognitivism does not concentrate on sensory input and motor output but instead on central systems that link sensory input and motor output. This new emphasis on central systems retains the basic stimulus-response model. If cognitivists do not retain the stimulus-response model, what reason do they have to talk about sensory input and motor output, and why do they seek to isolate central systems assumed to link sensory and motor events?

Interactionism

Interactionism might seem to have replaced S-O-R psychology. Interactionism is a metatheoretical position long present in psychology (see Ekehammer, 1974), which directs us to look for the determinants of behavior in both organismic and environmental variables. This position contrasts with the alternatives that emphasize either organism or environment. Fischer (1980) said that most psychologists now believe they must consider both organism and environment in developing psychological theories. Going further, we can interpret interactionism as a statement about psychology's subject matter; it consists of the organism-environment interaction. Vale and Vale (1969) implied this interpretation when they said that the interaction might be the appropriate locus for psychological inquiry. Consistent with this, Turvey and Carello (1981) interpreted the term *cognition* as meaning the coordination of organism and environment. This emphasis on organism-environment interaction suggests a departure from an organocentric psychology. However, in practice, most psychologists give lip service to interactionism and concentrate their theoretical efforts on central processes. Norman (1980) pointed this out in his criticism of cognitive psychology.

When considered carefully, interactionism only serves to conceal and perpetuate S-O-R psychology. It takes behavior (read, output of the body) as psychology's problem and admits organocentric and environmental causes. Psychological phenomena, such as traits and personality, are then located inside the organism and are endowed with causal properties in relation to behavior. This persistence of S-O-R psychology is apparent in a discussion by Hunt (1975) about the model represented by the formula $B = f(P, E)$. In this formula, "B" represents the dependent variable (behavior), "P" represents the person, and "E" represents the independent variable (environment). Hunt gave the concrete example of learning (B) as a joint function of the kind of student (P) and the method of teaching (E). He said we could equally use the model with the symbols "S," "O," and "R," representing *stimulus, organism,* and *response.* This statement expresses the S–O–R psychology implicit in the B = f (P, E) model. As well, it points to the conceptual inexactitudes (*learning, kind of student, method of teaching*) that pass for scientific variables when psychologists begin their conceptual and empirical arguments somewhere other than in the particulars of conduct.

BEYOND STIMULUS-RESPONSE PSYCHOLOGY

Stimulus–response psychology has long had critics. In an early critique, Dewey (1896) warned psychologists against adopting the reflex as their basic unit. Other theorists (e.g., Bode, 1922; Goldstein, 1951; McDougall, 1928; Russell, 1938, pp. 9–13; Skinner, 1969, pp. 3–28; Sloane, 1945) have echoed Dewey's warning or contributed their own. At the base of these criticisms was the insistence that we must abandon stimulus-response psychology because it does not fit psychological phenomena.

Stimulus–response psychology is inappropriate because it fits reflexes which are outside the domain of psychology. At least, they are outside the domain of psychology if that domain consists of means-end units. McDougall (1912, pp. 51–54) excluded reflexes on the grounds that reflexive behavior does not have the properties that interest psychologists. In other words, reflexive behavior does not have the goal-oriented character of psychological behavior, the motor variability of that behavior, and so on. Other theorists (e.g., Chein, 1972, p. 77; Lundh, 1981) have excluded reflexes from psychology on similar grounds. If reflexes are outside the domain of psychology, why try to impose a model derived from the concept of the reflex on conduct?

Looking at the same issue from a different perspective, stimulus-response psychology is inappropriate because acts are not stimulus-response units. Seeing acts through the conceptual spectacles of stimulus-response psychology conceals the means–end nature of conduct and misdirects inquiry. First of all, stimulus–response psychology directs us to look for stimulus-response units rather than for means (classes of variants) and ends. It does not indicate any possibility that the past, present, and future results of behavior have something to do with how people conduct themselves. Second, stimulus-response psychology ignores the observation that we name acts for the results of behavior, and it ignores the implications that this aspect of ordinary psychology has for scientific psychology. That is, it ignores the possibility that the results of behavior properly have an explicit and central place in psychological formulations.

Moreover, stimulus-response psychology treats units of behavior as punctate events, whereas the behavioral units that properly interest psychologists are classes of variants, the members of which might look very different from each other. Certainly, stimulus–response psychology does not prepare us to look for equifinal classes and for the consequences of equifinality for how we interpret conduct. Furthermore, stimulus–response psychology misleads us about the effect of the current situation upon behavior. It leads us to look for a stimulus for every episode of behavior. This mode of thinking is so automatic that we find it hard to think of acts as merely occuring. Instead, we assume that an act must be a reaction to current stimuli, and we look for those stimuli. The notion that current stimuli cause us to act leaves no place for the possibility that the current situation only increases or decreases our disposition to act in particular ways.

Most of all, the S–O–R psychologies give no place to contingencies. This neglect of contingencies has long been criticized more or less directly. For example, McDougall (1928) said that much experimental work in psychology has been unproductive because experimenters have neglected the purposive nature of conduct. In other words, they have neglected the contingencies. Likewise, Burgess (1968) commented that contingencies are always present in experimental settings, such that the results of experiments not dealing explicitly with contingencies are necessarily artificial and misleading. Critics (e.g., Pierce & Epling, 1980; Sidman, 1986a; Skinner, 1977) have noted the neglect of contingencies in special education, social psychology, cognitive psychology, and in other branches of psychological inquiry. This neglect doubtless reflects the continuing domination of psychological thought by S–O–R psychology. S–O–R psychology directs our attention to the presumed psychological properties of the organism which are meant to mediate the environmental and genetic influences on motor output. As some critics (e.g., Malcolm, 1970; Ryle, 1949/1966, p. 50, p. 162) have insisted, in accepting this model of psychological phenomena, psychologists have made the mistake of looking *behind* behavior instead of *beyond* it. As well, they have made the mistake of classifying contingencies as environmental variables and as a consequence they have missed the potential that the concept of the contingency has for clarifying the means–end nature of psychology's subject matter.

The way in which the concept of the contingency emerged historically has alienated psychologists from it. Doubtless they associate it with the behaviorism they reject and, with the behavior modification that they often regard as contributing nothing to psychological theory. For whatever reason, psychologists typically ignore contingencies, the functional relations they enter into, and the emergent phenomena associated with these relations. They regard a contingency-oriented psychology as trivial at best, and in the process they ignore a body of well-replicated findings. From this perspective, it is easy to reject the concept of the contingency on the grounds that it constrains our hypothesis. But, of course a contingency orientation constrains our hypotheses. It pressures us to look at acts *as* acts and thus as events embedded in a system of overlapping and interlocking contingencies. Constraining our thinking is one function of a conceptual framework. Such a framework ties our work to a common outlook on a common domain and permits us to contribute to a cumulative body of knowledge. Investigators concerned with contributing to such a body of knowledge do not fear constraints upon their formulations and methodology. Still, the cognitive objection to a contingency orientation probably arises less because of these constraints as such and more because investigators who pursue a contingency-oriented psychology desist from making hypotheses about processes presumed to intervene between sensory input and motor output. They desist because they do not embrace the S-O-R psychology which makes hypotheses about central causal processes seem interesting.

With its commitment to contingencies, radical behaviorism plainly does not advocate a stimulus–response psychology. However, psychologists (e.g., Alston, 1974; Dember, 1974; Fodor, 1981) mistakenly equate radical behaviorism with the stimulus–response behaviorism of Watson and Hull and with Pavlov's classical conditioning. These critics see radical behaviorism as an impoverished stimulus–response psychology. As an example, Fodor (1981) said that Skinner developed Watson's proposal for a stimulus–response psychology and that he prescribed psychology's task as the cataloguing of relations between stimuli and responses. As another example, Dember (1974) spoke of Skinner's (1957) putative attempt to apply stimulus–response psychology to language. Radical behaviorists and others (e.g., Day, 1980; Hineline, 1980; Mapel, 1977; Richelle, 1976) have acknowledged and rejected these misconceptions. Radical behaviorism is not a stimulus–response psychology. On the contrary, radical behaviorism explicitly rejects this traditional framework (e.g., Skinner, 1969, pp. 3–28, 1973; 1977).

The belief that radical behaviorism is a stimulus–response psychology arises in part from a lack of scholarship. Mainstream psychologists depend on their own literature when they discuss radical behaviorism. This results in the misrepresentation of radical behaviorism noted elsewhere (e.g., Cooke, 1984; Todd & Morris, 1983). In particular, Day (1980) pointed out that mainstream psychologists see Skinner's work as contributing to learning theory. They teach it within the context of an eclectic psychology without acknowledging its philosophic complexities. In the process, mainstream psychologists assimilate the empirical work as a contribution to the traditional stimulus–response framework and ignore the philosophic work initiated by Skinner as irrelevant to the real business of psychology.

Despite assertions to the contrary in its literature, outmoded terminology and usage gives the impression that radical behaviorism is a stimulus–response psychology. Radical behaviorism seems like a stimulus–response psychology because radical behaviorists continue to use the terms *stimulus* and *response*. These terms entered the language of radical behaviorism because Skinner talked about his early work as if it involved the study of reflexes. Contradicting the implications of this early terminology, Schoenfeld (1976) expressed doubt that Skinner's research paradigm descended from a reflex ancestor at all. Consistent with this, Skinner soon dropped *reflex* and used *operant* to emphasize the spontaneous (i.e., nonelicited) nature of the behavior of interest. The term operant was meant to emphasize the acting of organisms upon their environments with effects. Furthermore, Skinner introduced the term *discriminative stimulus* to distinguish the first term of a three-term contingency from an eliciting stimulus. In addition, Skinner (in Evans, 1968, pp. 20–21) has expressed his dissatisfaction with the term *response* on the grounds that it does not capture the fluidity of operant behavior. Even so, persistence of the terms *stimulus* and *response* in operant psychology, however much they have been qualified and redefined, gives the impression to outsiders that this psychology is a stimulus–response behaviorism.

In fact, the terms *stimulus* and *response* have been widely criticized (e.g., Guthrie, 1959; Hamlyn, 1981; Henle, 1976; Jessor, 1958; Schoenfeld, 1972, 1976; Tolman, 1959) for both their ambiguity and their capacity to mislead. Like *behavior, response* designates diverse events, including salivation, lever pressing, writing a novel, getting married, and cardiac rate changes. Similarly, *response* is ambiguous between movement and act, such that we can easily define *response* as meaning movement and yet use the language of acts when talking about these units. There is also the disadvantage that the word ordinarily connotes a reaction to something. This connotation has lead critics to believe that psychologists assume that conduct is a passive reaction to stimuli. *Response* suffers the further disadvantage of suggesting a punctate event, whereas behavior of psychological interest consists of classes of variants. *Stimulus* is also problematic, if only because it ordinarily connotes something that impels a reaction. The term leads us to debate where the stimulus for a particular response is. That is, talking about stimuli and responses leads us into stimulus–response thinking whether we notice that consequence or not.

The terms *stimulus* and *response* bring difficulties to psychology that cannot be answered by finding better ways to define them. Rather, we must eliminate them from our technical vocabulary. Their origin in reflexology leads us to think in terms of stimulus input and motor output and from there to other notions that further misconstrue psychological phenomena. Psychologists have no reason to use the terms *stimulus* and *response* aside from the historical accident that led to the adoption of these terms. We need not be constrained by our history. More concretely, we can talk about means–end phenomena without using the terms *stimulus* and *response*. A printed page can be a printed page instead of a textual stimulus, a question can be a question instead of a verbal stimulus, and so forth. Similarly, writing can be writing instead of a writing response, talking can be talking instead of a linguistic response, and so on. This change would not only eliminate much empty jargon, but would also help us eliminate stimulus-response psychology from our thinking. And it would tie our formulations more closely to our subject matter.

CAUSALITY

Contiguous Causality

Stimulus–response psychologies impose an assumption of contiguous causality on psychological thinking. Causality of this kind has also been called "push-pull," "hooks-and-eye," or "mechanistic." It is the causal mode favored by commonsense. As Horton (1967) explained, commonsense abhors action-at-a-distance and looks for causes in conditions adjacent in time and space to the phenomenon of interest. In commonsense terms, causes should be linked to effects as hooks and eyes are linked to each other. If a contiguous cause cannot be found, then commonsense bridges the gap between the actual events with hypothetical mediating events. In short, contiguous causality links cause and effect directly, or alternatively, indirectly with a causal chain that bridges the gap. The assumption of contiguous causality is easy to grasp, has great appeal to Western thought, and is strongly defended. Indeed, it seems impossible to conceive of causality in any other way.

S–R psychologies assume contiguous causality. An unelaborated S–R psychology sees a human being as an entity moved about by motor organs operating in response to physical stimuli impinging on the sense organs. As noted earlier, investigators working within this unelaborated stimulus-response framework could not find convincing causes adjacent to the behavior. Rather than discard stimulus–response psychology, psychologists added organocentric variables. These variables are the adjustment processes of early S–O–R psychology (e.g., Warren, 1922), the intervening variables of Tolman's psychology, and currently, the information-processing structures of cognitive psychology. They let psychology borrow the Western concept of a person that locates psychological phenomena centrally and endows them with causal powers in relation to behavior. By introducing these organocentric variables, psychologists retained the assumption of contiguous causality. The putative causes were still contiguous with behavior, but they were now inside the organism rather than outside where an unelaborated stimulus–response psychology had placed them.

Mechanistic explanations that rely on the assumption of contiguous causality are the norm in psychology. Approaches that give the status of an intervening variable to memory, intelligence, and other such categories, accept mechanistic thinking. They propose or imply a cause present at the same time, in the immediate situation, and intervening between sensory input and motor output. Personal categories, such as retarded and schizophrenic, also let us adopt a hooks-and-eye causality. We too often speak as if membership in the category is an organocentric quality that explains behavior. Explanations that attribute conduct to biological causes follow the same reasoning. As King (1978) noted, reductionism lets us attribute conduct and misconduct to biological causes. It also lets us pursue the brain dogma that treats attending, remembering, and other psychological entities as functions of the brain. This reductionist strategy places a current cause materially, albeit hypothetically, in the situation of interest. In this respect, reductionism is a material version of cognitivism and is no less mechanistic.

Action-at-a-Distance

The concept of action-at-a-distance is an alternative to contiguous causality. This concept admits spatial and temporal gaps between the independent and dependent variables of a functional relation. At least, it admits such gaps within the single level of integration that a particular science abstracts out and studies. Stated otherwise, the concept of action-at-a-distance does not direct us to look for hooks-and-eyes connections in our subject matter. Instead, it directs us to look only for invariant connections and to accept that these connections might extend across temporal and spatial gaps without mediation at the particular level of integration. Some writers (e.g., Oppenheimer, 1956; Rachlin, 1977) have indicated that physics advanced when physicists realized that physical forces can act at a distance and that causes need not be linked to their effects through a chain of mediators. Psychologists need to accept that conditions relevant to psychological events can also act at a distance.

The concept of action-at-a-distance relates well to the concept of a person as an accumulation of acts. An accumulation of acts extends through time and across the boundaries of the organism. Therefore, such an accumulation is historically cumulative and transdermal. The significance of transdermality was discussed earlier in relation to the notion that persons are entities that encompass organismic and extraorganismic events. The significance of the historically cumulative nature of a person's conduct requires discussion here. When we consider a momentary segment of conduct, we miss the historical context of that segment. But without knowing something of the past, we cannot understand current performance. Without considering the past, we do not describe the extension through time that *is* the person. Skinner (in Cohen, 1977) admitted that a complete or extensive mapping of the past is not possible. But, through the recognition of the importance of history, we direct our inferences to history and particularly to the means–end structure of past conduct. Consequently, we see that current acts realize dispositions established by past contingencies. That insight reduces the sense of impossibility we have when watching a skilled performer. The sense of impossibility arises because we see the performance out of its historical context.

Psychologists neglect personal history. They take an ahistorical strategy, focussing on hypothetical structures inside the organism and thus in the current situation. Consistent with this neglect, Phillips and Orton (1983) noted that *history* is not a term frequently used by psychologists. Also consistent with the neglect of personal history, episodic research predominates in psychology. Psychologists who engage in such research look at selected parts of conduct over limited periods of time, often a few minutes. This research seldom approaches psychological hypotheses by building a history and by studying the effects of this history on subsequent performance. Even when a personal history is built, psychologists seldom attribute the results to the history. Instead they attribute performance to psychological categories such as knowledge, intention, and so forth, with these categories formulated as intervening variables. An account in terms of historical and current contingencies does not interest most psychologists. This lack of interest arises because most psychologists see organismic structures and not means–end structures as the phenomenon of interest to them. The result is that personal history is neglected both conceptually and methodologically.

Accepting action-at-a-distance requires that we accept temporal gaps only at the psychological level of integration and not across all levels. Accepting this, Skinner (e.g., 1972, pp. 269–270, 1984a, 1984b) insisted that the temporal gap between past contingencies and current performance at the psychological level is mediated by the physiology of the organism. Presumably, past contingencies change the organism so that it behaves differently now. Describing this physiological mediation of the effects of past contingencies is properly the task of the physiologist. At the psychological level, it is enough to say that a person had some past experience and now behaves in a different way as a result. In a real sense, he or she is a different person (a different accumulation of acts or of means–end units). In other words, psychology *as* psychology does not have to account for changes in the organism. Those changes are properly part of a physiological account. Indeed, anyone not indoctrinated in the myth of the corporeal person would not expect to find any mention of muscles, neurons, and the like, in a psychological account. To insist that psychology is not physiology is to insist that psychology's task is to describe and explain conduct at the level of conduct. To accept that task, psychologists will have to distinguish action from movement, and they will have to accept that their subject matter does not consist of the internal machinery, real or imagined, that makes the body move.

Cognitive psychologists use a storage model to mediate between past experience and present conduct. For example, MacKay (1982) suggested that our environmental goals are encoded (i.e., stored) in long-term memory. This assumption leads us to the question of how such entities are stored in the brain (e.g., Connolly, 1977). This concept of storage is appealing, but it has no meaning when applied to the biological organism. After all, if we heat an egg, we say the egg was cooked (i.e., has changed). Branch (1977) noted that we do not say the egg has stored the information that it was heated. Only the conceptual organism stores information, and the conceptual organism persists only to link past contingencies and their cumulative effects with current performance. But that temporal gap does not need a conceptual organism to mediate it. It is mediated by the biological organism which psychology should presuppose.

We do not need to infer copies, representations, and the like, to mediate between past experience and current performance. Instead, we can describe the past experiences and note that they have changed our disposition to act. For example, a person who avoids flying might have had his or her disposition to fly changed by the past experiences of an earache during a descent, reports of hijacking, and so forth. Internal representations of these events are surrogates of past events that we would be better to deal with directly. These surrogates serve to reassure theorists who cannot tolerate action-at-a-distance. They also serve to perpetuate the concept of an intervening variable to the detriment of psychological knowledge. Moreover, they spare psychologists the conceptual and methodological challenge of dealing directly and explicitly with conduct as a subject matter in its own right.

Variation and Selection

A contingency-oriented psychology accepts action-at-a-distance. In doing so, it rejects contiguous causality and favors variation and selection as a causal mode.

Variation is implicit in the concept of a class of variants. The concept formulates the ordinary observation that there is more than one means to an end; that we can vary how we achieve a particular end result from one occasion to the next. The concept of variation is consistent with field observations of variants; for example, in talking (e.g., Foppa, 1978), in babbling (Elbers, 1982), and in spelling (e.g., Beers, Beers & Grant, 1977). Likewise, the concept of variation relates to laboratory studies that have described variation and have investigated the conditions that increase and decrease the extent of it (e.g., Antonitis, 1951; Muenzinger, 1928; Vogel & Annau, 1973; Schwartz, 1982). Related to this, some early studies attempted to determine whether variation is random or reflects the functional organization of repertoire. These studies were reviewed by Russell (1938, pp. 146–148) and by Dashiell (1949, pp. 406–408). They seem related to Epstein's (1985a) work on extinction-induced resurgence, the appearance of previously successful variants when one or more members of the same equifinal class is no longer successful.

The variation available at any one time depends in part on the extent to which past contingencies have added variants to an equifinal class. The extent to which a person might engage in the variants available in turn might depend on the relative costs and benefits of doing so (e.g., Goldiamond, 1974, 1975a, 1975b, 1984). Consequently, past contingencies contribute to the amount and kind of variation available, and current contingencies have a selective function with respect to current variation. In other words, current contingencies select from the variants available, a process seen directly in the studies of differential reinforcement mentioned above. In these studies, a subset of a pool of variants produces the critical result, and members of that subset are selected by the contingency. (This selective function should make it clear that contingencies do not have the eliciting function of stimuli. On the contrary, the effects of contingencies on performance are delayed rather than immediate, and they have to do with the strengthening or weakening of variants rather than with the eliciting of behavior.)

With few exceptions, mainstream psychology has not considered variation and selection as a causal mode. Warren (1930) argued for it, but, apart from Skinner (e.g., 1973, 1981), Campbell (e.g., 1956, 1975) and Staddon (e.g., Staddon, 1973; Staddon & Simmelhag, 1971) are the only clear exceptions to this neglect. The predisposition to look for mechanistic explanations makes variation and selection seem irrelevant and nonscientific to most psychologists. Apart from anything else, variation and selection requires that we accept action-at-a-distance. After all, the cumulative effects of contingencies are apparent only after a delay. That delay makes variation and selection unpalatable to psychologists who want a current cause. Moreover, the process of selection is not easy to see, particularly outside the laboratory. Contingencies themselves are not easy to see. In addition, the past contingencies that shaped the current repertoire are not present in the current setting. In other words, selection by contingencies is a process extended in time beyond any momentary observation of conduct. To accept selection as a causal mode requires that we recognize psychology's subject matter has extension in time. A psychology that insists upon current causes and values the results of experiments based on episodic observation is unlikely to accept this temporal extension of psychological phenomena, let alone accept the challenge of formulating it.

CONCLUSION

Psychological thought has been reflexological through the 20th century. It has been dominated by the stimulus–response model borrowed from physiology. Bolles (1983) reminded us that this model has let psychologists think that explaining human behavior presents no problem. Consistent with that, McDougall (1928) said that stimulus–response psychology attracted psychologists who disliked difficult problems and preferred fictitious solutions. In accepting the S–O–R model, psychologists could avoid philosophic work and plunge immediately into data collecting. Psychologists only needed to look for stimuli, responses, and the relations between stimuli and responses. They could build conceptually on what physiology already knew about reflexes, and they did not have to confront a subject matter with special properties of its own. Later, they had only to elaborate the central processes that the Western concept of a person presupposed, and again they did not engage in sustained philosophic work to scrutinize their basic assumptions. At least, they did not engage in such work with a consensual outcome that directed psychological inquiry away from the stimulus–response model. By retaining the stimulus–response framework in the modified form of a S–O–R psychology, psychologists also uncritically accepted the Western concept of a person. They accepted the notion that a person (i.e., an entity of psychological interest) is a nonphysical surrogate of a human body.

Stimulus-response psychology is the essence of behaviorism. Indeed, Mursell (1922) described the stimulus–response formulation as the bedrock of behaviorism. Consistent with this, McDougall (1928) described behaviorism as a mechanistic psychology. These early statements are consistent with modern notions of what *behaviorism* means. In this sense, radical behaviorists can say they are not behaviorists or, alternatively, that the name *behaviorism* is inappropriate for their enterprise. In contrast, although cognitivists overtly reject stimulus–response behaviorism, the psychology they espouse suggests they tacitly accept the stimulus–response model.

A minority of psychologists has long rejected stimulus–response behaviorism. For example, Bode (1922) rejected the domination of psy-.

chological thought by reflexology. He urged psychologists to accept the challenge of developing an autonomous science that confronts purposive behavior as a subject matter. As another example, McDougall (1928) rejected mechanistic thinking as an elaborate academic fiction that ignores the most basic and obvious facts about human conduct. To McDougall, those facts centered around the pursuance of ends and the occurrence of variants. Later critics (e.g., Gauld & Shotter, 1977; Hamlyn, 1981; Russell, 1938; Skinner, 1969, 1981) have offered similar objections to a mechanistic stimulus–response psychology. Despite these criticisms, stimulus–response thinking persists in psychology. It is possible that this mode of thinking persists because we have not found a better framework. But it is also possible that stimulus–response thinking persists because many influential psychologists have not accepted the arguments of the critics or have not recognized the relevance of the arguments to the psychology they espouse.

Radical behaviorists are among the critics of stimulus–response psychology, but their contribution to an alternative psychology of action goes unnoticed because it is too quickly dismissed as behaviorism. Relevant to this, Joynson (1980) noted that critics of psychology agree on two matters. First, they reject the mechanistic presuppositions of traditional psychology. And, second, they insist that psychologists must develop new concepts and methods appropriate to persons as purposive beings. Likewise, radical behaviorists are engaged in developing a critique and reformulation of psychology that rejects the mechanistic formulation and accepts the means–end nature of conduct. Other critics of psychology will continue to dismiss the contributions of radical behaviorists only to the detriment of progress in psychology as a whole. That progress depends on psychologists developing alternatives to the various intellectual and methodological consequences of S–O–R psychology.

CHAPTER 14

Final Comments

Let us use the term *means-end hypothesis* to refer to the hypothesis that the means-end unit is the basic unit in psychological inquiry. The importance of the means-end hypothesis is hard to overemphasize. Relevant to this, Feynman and his colleagues (Feynman, Leighton & Sands, 1963, p. 1-2) asked what one sentence in physics contains the most information in the fewest words. They said that the required sentence is the atomic hypothesis that all physical things are made of atoms. They also said that, given some imagination and thought, this one sentence contains an enormous amount of information. Scriven (1956) expressed doubt that any such hypothesis could be found in psychology. Specifically, he said it seems unlikely that psychologists will find anything as simple and as important as the hypothesis of universal gravitation. But the means-end hypothesis has the required simplicity. Given some imagination and thought, this hypothesis contains much information about the general nature of psychological phenomena.

There are three kinds of evidence that suggest that the means-end hypothesis is a strategic hypothesis. First, treating contingencies (i.e., conditional means-end units) as independent variables has allowed us to produce a body of well-replicated findings in the laboratory. In connection with this laboratory work, we can talk about n-term contingencies, the functional relations that contingencies enter into with behavior, and the phenomena that emerge from these functional relations, as summarized by Sidman (1986a, 1986b). Second, the means-end hypothesis lets us clarify many persistent doubts about the direction taken by psychology. As shown in this book, the hypothesis helps to clarify doubts about individualism, reductionism, psychocentrism, and other matters of concern to critics. Third, the means-end hypothesis implies much about the general nature of psychological phenomena and about the general nature of psychological inquiry. These implications include the distinctions between organism and person, between content and structure, and between contiguous causality and action-at-a-distance.

Whether the means–end hypothesis is in fact a strategic hypothesis can only be decided in the long run. Affirmation of strategic status will depend on the continuing development of a body of well-replicated findings, on the further clarification of the philosophic problems of psychology, and, indeed, on the capacity of the means–end hypothesis to let us integrate otherwise disparate findings. Ziman (1971) commented that this latter task of intellectual synthesis is extremely important in science as a whole. The challenge to develop an intellectual synthesis in psychology will not be met if psychologists scrutinize the means–end hypothesis in its rudimentary form, find it lacking, and dismiss it as inadequate. As Sidman (1986b) pointed out, for too long psychologists have engaged in the scientific malpractice of ignoring or rejecting what is known already on the grounds that it does not account for everything. In this connection, it is worth emphasizing that the means–end hypothesis is not a completed dogma that invites agreement or disagreement. Rather, it is a working hypothesis where the empirical and conceptual ramifications need to be more fully explored. The fact that much remains to be done should invite those of us who sense the incomplete nature of what we have achieved to follow through the ramifications of the hypothesis, patiently and in detail. To accept this invitation, we must desist from the academic luxury of developing clever but destructive arguments that add nothing to the task of building a systematic body of psychological knowledge. The more psychologists who accept the present invitation the better; long-term evaluation of the means–end hypothesis will depend on the constructive effort of a large number of psychologists over an extended interval of time.

It would be naive to expect that psychologists will welcome the proposal that the means–end hypothesis has strategic status. Apart from anything else, many psychologists will reject this proposal because they believe that the concept of the contingency (as a conditional means–end unit) is too pedestrian. Psychologists have become used to dealing with memory, learning, perception, and the like, as categories that designate entities and processes with presumed existence apart from action. In contrast, the concept of the contingency formulates the mundane work requirements that human beings must satisfy to get anything done, made, or achieved in the world. The concept constrains us to deal empirically and conceptually with human effectiveness and lack of effectiveness and with the reactivity and nonreactivity of human contexts. It constrains us to deal with personal histories and current ecologies, and with the details of how structural principles operate within particular accumulations of acts. These matters will seem too concrete and too closely tied to practice for psychologists concerned with the organocentric person.

But the onus is on psychologists who pursue this organocentric psychology to show, in detail, why psychology should not take its starting point in concrete and practical concerns. It will not suffice in this connection to defend a more abstract starting point on the grounds that other sciences deal with abstractions. Dealing with abstractions as such is not the issue. A psychology of action also deals with abstractions, but it finds its abstractions in its subject matter, the concrete tier of which consists of dated acts as they accumulate through time. By starting self-consciously in acts, a psychology of action departs from traditional psychology, which starts in memory, learning, and the like, and insists that these categories designate processes and entities inside the organism. In turn these are meant to explain behavior construed amorphously as the activities of the organism. Investigators who wish to pursue this organocentric psychology should develop a detailed defense of their starting point. If that defense could be built, which seems unlikely, it might illuminate why our culture continues to support and fund research that tacitly promises to make the organocentric person more intelligible to us. The concept of the organocentric person is far removed from the concrete realities (i.e., acts and work requirements) of daily life, which our culture should call upon psychologists to address. Theorists who purport that their psychological formulations are scientific must tie those formulations unequivocally to these concrete realities of daily life and of practice. Our responsibility as academic psychologists is to make these realities more intelligible than they are already ahead of specialized inquiry. To do that, we must rid ourselves of the scientistic pretensions that will not let us admit that scientific psychology is properly grounded in the strategic concepts of ordinary psychological knowledge.

The proposal that the concept of the contingency has strategic significance will also seem unacceptable because many psychologists mistakenly interpret the concept very narrowly. They equate contingencies exclusively with contrived contingencies, and they overlook the vast number of contingencies with end results closely bound to the behavior that produces them. We need to insist that the concept of the contingency formulates the work requirements that are inevitable and ubiquitous in the domain of conduct. We also need to insist that psychologists must deal directly and explicitly with the domain that comprises these work requirements together with the cumulative effects that work requirements have on performance. Most of all, we need to insist that psychologists who do not confront this subject matter are doing something other than psychology or at least are confronting something other than the subject matter that ordinary knowledge bequeaths to a science of psychology.

Finally, the means–end hypothesis will seem unacceptable to many psychologists because it is not an empirical hypothesis. No one can design and conduct a crucial experiment, in Platt's (1964) sense, that might increase our collective confidence in the means–end hypothesis. Therefore, many psychologists will insist that the hypothesis is uninteresting. Relevant to this, Mohr (1977, p. 66) pointed out that most scientific theories consist of theoretical principles, comparable to axioms, and of empirical laws, testable by experiment. The foundations of a science consist of the theoretical principles. As some writers (e.g., Bunge, 1959, p. 47; Gladin, 1961) have commented, we select foundations for their logical fertility, not for their empirical testability. Martin (1945) observed that psychologists have neglected the foundational concepts that could provide the background for their empirical work. Perhaps this neglect arises just because these foundations are axiomatic and not empirical. The antiphilosophic stance taken by many psychologists would account for the widespread lack of interest in the foundational concepts of psychology. Yet, these foundational concepts cannot be separated from empirical matters, because foundational concepts properly guide the development of empirical hypothesis and serve as the basis for integrating the results of empirical work. To ignore our foundational concepts is to condemn academic psychology to the status of a data-collecting enterprise that will probably continue to obscure the essential nature of human conduct.

No one should underestimate the amount of effort required to make the conceptual shift from an organocentric psychology to a psychology of action. Doubtless the change required is of the same order as the Darwinian revolution in biology. In this respect, aspects of the history of biology and psychology are remarkably similar. As noted by Mayr (1972), abundant evidence in favor of evolution was available by 1830, but most scientists continued to support creationism. The slow acceptance of evolutionary concepts did not occur because of lack of evidence. It occurred because evolutionary concepts required biologists to accept a new metascientific credo. That credo involved the development and clarification of many concepts over an extended period of time. Acceptance of the means–end hypothesis in psychology will be of the same order. It will require much work by many investigators over a long period of time, and it will require and produce a fundamental change in the way psychologists conceive of their subject matter and task.

The means–end hypothesis requires that psychologists move beyond behaviorism in how they think about psychology's subject matter and task. In response to this requirement, most psychologists will assert that they are not behaviorists and that the requirement does not apply to them. Certainly, it is difficult say what behaviorism is. Even so, there is a case for saying that behaviorism is a stimulus–response psychology or, better, a S–O–R psychology that accepts individualism, reductionism, and mechanistic causality. Pepitone (1981) included individualism, reductionism, and mechanistic thinking among the norms of contemporary psychology. To that extent, contemporary psychology is behaviorist, despite the stated rejection of behaviorism by many psychologists. It is a psychology that locates psychological phenomena in the body (rather than in a historically cumulative and transdermal field), that takes its primary dichotomy as between organism and environment (instead of between means and ends), that looks for explanations of the content of action in organismic and environmental variables (rather than in statements of structural principles and of the conditions under which the principles operate in the particular case), and that expects its functional variables to have contiguity with the phenomena of interest (rather than to operate at a temporal distance). Individualism and the other norms of psychology do not follow from the hypothesis that the subject matter of psychology consists of actions and that actions are means–end units. Instead, these norms were imported into psychology along with the stimulus–response framework borrowed from physiology. If psychologists could accept that acts are psychological particulars and that contingencies provide the basic structure of the domain of acts, they might see acts and contingencies where now they see individual human beings, their contents (real and imagined), and their environments. In other words, psychologists might see that they should base psychology on the dichotomies of means and ends and of past and present rather than on the dichotomy of organism and environment. In doing so, they might begin to extricate psychology from the blinkers of behaviorism.

Critics might further object to the argument presented in this book by denying that it accurately represents Skinnerian psychology. This objection misses the point. In the end, what counts is the development of a systematic psychology of the structure and content of action. If work initiated by Skinner illuminates the nature of action, then it contributes to a psychology of action. Certainly, Skinner has done more than any other psychologist to develop the ramifications of a contingency-oriented psychology, and his work deserves careful study and explication. But, if some parts of radical behaviorism do not contribute to a psychology of action, then we should feel free to abandon them. In doing that, we accept the spirit of radical behaviorism, which is to explore the general nature of the subject matter, task, and method of a science of psychology with a commitment to behavior (read, "action") as a subject matter in its own right. In the process, we should look for contributions to a psychology of action, and we should not feel obliged to adopt the contributions of any particular writer in their entirety. Equally, we should not reject contributions to a psychology of action because we reject the context in which they are found.

We need to build a conceptually systematic psychology of action, and we need to scrutinize all potential contributions to this task. We have too long engaged in academic battle with each other over the interpretation of what turns out to be an ill-specified domain. Our domain is not made up of behavior, in some amorphous sense of the activities of organisms, and it is not made up of the contents of the organocentric person. At its core, our domain consists of acts and of the work requirements or contingencies that constitute the conditional structure of the domain of acts. It is time we abandoned the sophistry of the pseudoscience that intellectual history has bequeathed to us in academic psychology. It is time we concentrated our energies constructively and collectively on the challenge of building a science of human action.

REFERENCES

Abelson, R. P. (1981). Psychological status of the script concept. *American Psychologist, 36,* 715–729.

Ades, T. (1981). Time for a purge. *Cognition, 10,* 7–15.

Allport, D. A. (1975). The state of cognitive psychology. *Quarterly Journal of Experimental Psychology, 27,* 141–152.

Allport, F. H. (1936–1937). Teleonomic description in the study of personality. *Character and Personality, 5,* 202–214.

Allport, G. W. (1962). The general and the unique in psychological science. *Journal of Personality, 30,* 405–422.

Ayllon, T., & Azrin, N. H. (1964). Reinforcement and instructions with mental patients. *Journal of the Experimental Analysis of Behavior, 7,* 327–331.

Alston, W. P. (1974). Conceptual prolegomena to a psychological theory of intentional action. In S. C. Brown (Ed.), *Philosophy of psychology* (pp. 71–101). London: Macmillan.

Angell, J. R. (1913). Behavior as a category of psychology. *Psychological Review, 20,* 255–270.

Antonitis, J. J. (1951). Response variability in the white rat during conditioning, extinction, and reconditioning. *Journal of Experimental Psychology, 42,* 273–281.

Ausubel, D. P. (1968). Is there a discipline of educational psychology? *Educational Psychologist, 5,* 1; 4; 8–9.

Averill, J. R. (1968). Grief: Its nature and significance. *Psychological Bulletin, 70,* 721–748.

Baerends, G. P. (1984). Ontogenetic or phylogenetic—Another afterpain of the fallacious Cartesian dichotomy. *Behavioral and Brain Sciences, 7,* 679–680.

Balz, A. G. A. (1940). Concerning the subject-matter of psychology. *Psychological Review, 47,* 322–337.

Bandura, A. (1974). Behavior theory and the models of man. *American Psychologist, 29,* 859–869.

Bandura, A. (1977). Self-efficacy: Toward a unifying theory of behavioral change. *Psychological Review, 84,* 191–215.

Bandura, A. (1982). Self-efficacy mechanisms in human agency. *American Psychologist, 37,* 122–147.

Barlow, D. H. (1981). On the relation of clinical research to clinical practice: Current issues, new directions. *Journal of Consulting and Clinical Psychology, 49,* 147–155.

173

Baron, A., & Galizio, M. (1983). Instructional control of human operant behavior. *The Psychological Record, 33,* 495–520.

Baron, A., Kaufman, A., & Stauber, K. A. (1969). Effects of instructions and reinforcement feedback on human operant behavior maintained by fixed-interval reinforcement. *Journal of the Experimental Analysis of Behavior, 12,* 701–712.

Baron, A., & Perone, M. (1982). The place of the human subject in the operant laboratory. *The Behavior Analyst, 5,* 143–158.

Baron, J. (1971). Is experimental psychology relevant? *American Psychologist, 26,* 713–716.

Bass, B. M. (1974). The substance and the shadow. *American Psychologist, 29,* 870–886.

Bates, E., Bretheron, I., Beeghly-Smith, M., & McNew, S. (1982). Social bases of language development: A reassessment. *Advances in Child Development and Behavior, 16,* 7–75.

Beer, J. J. (1965). The historical relations of science and technology: Introduction. *Technology and Culture, 6,* 547–552.

Beers, J. W., Beers, C. S., & Grant, K. (1977). The logic behind children's spelling. *Elementary School Journal, 77,* 238–242.

Beidel, D. C., & Turner, S. M. (1986). A critique of the theoretical bases of cognitive-behavioral theories and therapy. *Clinical Psychology Review, 6,* 177–197.

Bentley, A. F. (1941). The behavioral superfice. *Psychological Review, 48,* 39–59.

Bergmann, G. (1953). Theoretical psychology. *Annual Review of Psychology, 4,* 435–458.

Bermant, G., & Alcock, J. (1973). Perspectives on animal behavior. In G. Bermant (Ed.), *Perspectives on animal behavior* (pp. 1–47). Glenview, IL: Scott, Foresman.

Bernard, C. (1957). *An introduction to the study of experimental medicine.* (H. C. Greene, Trans.). New York: Dover Publications. (Original work published 1957)

Best, D. (1978). *Philosophy and human movement.* London: Allen & Unwin.

Bethlehem, D. (1984). Two cultures in psychology. *Bulletin of the British Psychological Society, 37,* 113–115.

Bijou, S. W. (1971). Environment and intelligence: A behavioral analysis. In R. Cancro (Ed.), *Intelligence: Genetic and environmental influences* (pp. 221–239). New York: Grune & Stratton.

Birnbrauer, J. S. (1979). Applied behavior analysis, service and the acquisition of knowledge. *The Behavior Analyst, 2,* 15–21.

Blanshard, B. (1965). Critical reflections on behaviorism. *Proceedings of the American Philosophical Society, 109,* 22–28.

Blurton-Jones, N. G. (1976). Growing points in human ethology: Another link between ethology and the social sciences? In P. P. G. Bateson & R. A. Hinde (Eds.), *Growing points in ethology* (pp. 427–450). Cambridge: Cambridge University Press.

Bode, B. H. (1922). What is psychology? *Psychological Review, 29,* 250–258.

Boden, M. A. (1972). *Purposive explanation in psychology.* Cambridge, MA: Harvard University Press.

Bolles, R. C. (1983). The explanation of behavior. *The Psychological Record, 33,* 31–48.

Bower, G. H. (1975). Cognitive psychology: An introduction. In W. K. Estes (Ed.), *Handbook of learning and cognitive processes: Vol. 1. Introduction to concepts and issues* (pp. 25–80). Hillsdale, NJ: Lawrence Erlbaum Associates.

Bramson, R. M. (1981). *Coping with difficult people.* New York: Ballantine.

Branch, M. N. (1977). On the role of "memory" in the analysis of behavior. *Journal of the Experimental Analysis of Behavior, 28,* 171–179.

Branch, M. N., & Malagodi, E. F. (1980) Where have all the behaviorists gone? *The Behavior Analyst, 3,* 31–38.

Brand, M. (1970). Introduction. In M. Brand (Ed.), *The nature of human action* (pp. 3–21). Glenview, IL: Scott, Foresman.

Brand, M. (1971). The language of not doing. *American Philosophical Quarterly, 8,* 45–53.

Braybrooke, D. (1968). Taking liberties with the concept of rules. *The Monist, 52,* 329–358.

Brener, J. M. (1980). Energy, information and man. In A. J. Chapman & D. M. Jones (Eds.), *Models of man* (pp. 87–97). Leicester, England: British Psychological Society.

Brinker, R. P., & Lewis, M. (1982). Making the world work with microcomputers: A learning prosthesis for handicapped infants. *Exceptional Children, 49,* 163–170.

Brown, A. L. (1982). Learning how to learn from reading. In J. A. Langer & M. T. Smith-Burke (Eds.), *Reader meets author/Bridging the gap* (pp. 26–54). Newark, DE: International Reading Association.

Brown, L., Branston, M. B., Hamre-Nietupski, S., Pumpian, I., Certo, N., & Gruenewald, L. (1979). A strategy for developing chronological-age-appropriate and functional curricular content for severely handicapped adolescents and young adults. *Journal of Special Education, 13,* 81–90.

Bruner, J. S. (1972). Nature and uses of immaturity. *American Psychologist, 27,* 687–708.

Bruner, J. S. (1973). Organization of early skilled action. *Child Development, 44,* 1–11.

Bruner, J. S. (1982). The organization of action and the nature of adult-infant transaction. In M. von Cranach & R. Harré (Eds.), *The analysis of action* (pp. 313–327). Cambridge: Cambridge University Press.

Brunswik, E. (1943). Organismic achievement and environmental probability. *Psychological Review, 50,* 255–272.

Bunge, M. (1959). *Metascientific inquiries.* Springfield, IL: Charles C. Thomas.

Bunge, M. (1967). *Scientific research: Vol. 1. The search for system.* New York: Springer-Verlag.

Bunge, M. (1973). *Method, model and matter.* Dordrecht, Holland and Boston: D. Reidel.

Burgess, I. S. (1972). Psychology and Kuhn's concept of paradigm. *Journal of Behavioral Science, 1,* 193–200.

Burgess, R. L. (1968). Communication networks: An experimental reevaluation. *Journal of Experimental Social Psychology, 4,* 324–337.

Burgess, R. L., & Akers, R. L. (1966). Are operant principles tautological? *Psychological Record, 16,* 305–312.

Burnham, J. C. (1968). On the origins of behaviorism. *Journal of the History of the Behavioral Sciences, 4,* 143–151.

Buskist, W. F. (1983). Introduction. *Psychological Record, 33,* 451–456.

Buskist, W. F., & Miller, H. L. (1982a). The analysis of human operant behavior: A brief census of the literature: 1958–1981. *The Behavior Analyst, 5,* 137–141.

Buskist, W. F., & Miller, H. L. (1982b). The study of human operant behavior, 1958–1981: A topical bibliography. *Psychological Record, 32,* 249–268.

Cairns, R. B., & Valsiner, J. (1984). Child psychology. *Annual Review of Psychology, 35,* 553–577.

Calkins, M. W. (1921). The truly psychological behaviorism. *Psychological Review, 28,* 1–18.

Campbell, D. T. (1954). Operational delineation of "What is learned" via the transposition experiment. *Psychological Review, 61,* 167–174.

Campbell, D. T. (1956). Perception as substitute trial and error. *Psychological Review, 63,* 330–342.

Campbell, D. T. (1975). On the conflicts between biological and social evolution and between psychology and moral tradition. *American Psychologist, 30,* 1103–1126.

Cantril, H., Ames, A., Jr., Hastorf, A. H., & Ittelson, W. H. (1949). Psychology and scientific research. II. Scientific inquiry and scientific method. *Science, 110,* 491–497.

Carr, E. G., & Durand, V. M. (1985). The social-communicative basis of severe behavior problems in children. In S. Reiss & R. R. Bootzin (Eds.), *Theoretical issues in behavior therapy* (pp. 219–254). Orlando, FL: Academic Press.

Cartwright, D. (1979). Contemporary social psychology in historical perspective. *Social Psychology Quarterly, 42,* 82–93.

Cartwright, N. (1980). The truth doesn't explain much. *American Philosophical Quarterly, 17,* 159–163.

Carver, R. P. (1978). The case against statistical significance testing. *Harvard Educational Review, 48,* 378–399.

Catania, A. C. (1973a). The concept of the operant in the analysis of behavior. *Behaviorism, 1,* 103–116.

Catania, A. C. (1973b). The nature of learning. In J. A. Nevin & G. S. Reynolds (Eds.), *The study of behavior: Learning, motivation, emotion, and instinct* (pp. 30–68). Glenview, IL: Scott, Foresman.

Catania, A. C. (1973c). The psychologies of structure, function and development. *American Psychologist, 28,* 434–443.

Chase, P. N., & Wylie, R. G. (1985). Doctoral training in behavior analysis: Training generalized problem-solving skills. *The Behavior Analyst, 8,* 159–176.

Chein, I. (1972). *The science of behavior and the image of man.* London: Tavistock.

Chiszar, D., & Carpen, K. (1980). Origin and synthesis. *American Psychologist, 35,* 958-962.

Chomsky, N. (1959). Review of *Verbal Behavior* by B. F. Skinner. *Language, 35,* 26-58.

Chomsky, N. (1968). *Language and mind.* New York: Harcourt, Brace & World.

Churchman, C. W., & Ackoff, R. L. (1947). An experimental measure of personality. *Philosophy of Science, 14,* 304-332.

Clinard, H. H. (1985). *Winning ways to succeed with people.* Houston: Gulf.

Cohen, D. (1977). *Psychologists on psychology.* New York: Taplinger.

Cohen, M. R. (1949). *Studies in Philosophy and Science.* New York: Frederick Ungar.

Connolly, K. (1977). The nature of motor skill development. *Journal of Human Movement Studies, 3,* 128-143.

Cooke, N. L. (1984). Misrepresentations of the behavioral model in preservice teacher education textbooks. In W. L. Heward, T. E. Heron, D. S. Hill, & J. Trap-Porter (Eds.), *Focus on behavior analysis in education* (pp. 197-217). Columbus, OH: Merrill.

Cooper, J. O., Heron, T. E., & Heward, W. L. (1987). *Applied behavior analysis.* Columbus, OH: Merrill.

Coulter, J. (1979). *The social construction of mind: Studies in ethnomethodology and linguistic philosophy.* Totowa, NJ: Rowman & Littlefield.

Coulter, J. (1982). Theoretical problems of cognitive science. *Inquiry, 25,* 3-26.

Cullen, C. (1981). The flight to the laboratory. *The Behavior Analyst, 4,* 81-83.

Cullinan, B. E., & Strickland, D. S. (1986). The early years: Language, literature and literacy in classroom research. *The Reading Teacher, 39,* 798-806.

Curtis, B. (1985). Wittgenstein and philosophy for children. *Journal of Philosophy for Children, 5,* 10-19.

Dashiell, J. F. (1949). *Fundamentals of general psychology* (3rd ed.). London: Pitman.

Davis, L. H. (1979). *Theory of action.* Englewood Cliffs, NJ: Prentice Hall.

Davis, R. C. (1953). Physical psychology. *Psychological Review, 60,* 7-14.

Day, W. F. (1969). Radical behaviorism in reconciliation with phenomenology. *Journal of the Experimental Analysis of Behavior, 12,* 315-328.

Day, W. (1976). Contemporary behaviorism and the concept of intention. In J. K. Cole & W. J. Arnold (Eds.), *Nebraska Symposium on Motivation* (Vol. 23, pp. 65-131). Lincoln: University of Nebraska Press.

Day, W. (1980). The historical antecedents of contemporary behaviorism. In R. W. Rieber & K. Salzinger (Eds.), *Psychology: Theoretical-historical perspectives* (pp. 203-262). New York: Academic Press.

Day, W. (1983). On the difference between radical and methodological behaviorism. *Behaviorism, 11,* 89-102.

De Bono, E. (1985). *De Bono's thinking course.* London: Ariel Books.

De Bono, E. (1986). *Tactics: The art and science of success.* London: Fontana.

Deitz, S. M. (1978). Current status of applied behavior analysis: Science versus technology. *American Psychologist, 33,* 805-814.

Deitz, S. M. (1982). Defining applied behavior analysis: An historical analogy. *The Behavior Analyst, 5,* 53-64.

Deitz, S. M. (1983). Two correct definitions of "applied." *The Behavior Analyst,* *6.* 105–106.

Deitz, S. M. (1986). Understanding cognitive language: The mental idioms in children's talk. *The Behavior Analyst, 9,* 161–166.

Deitz, S. M., & Arrington, R. L. (1983). Factors confusing language use in the analysis of behavior. *Behaviorism, 11,* 117–132.

Deitz, S. M., & Arrington, R. L. (1984). Wittgenstein's language-games and the call to cognition. *Behaviorism, 12,* 1–14.

DeLucca, J. (1979). Science and social scientists. *Methodology and Science, 12,* 55–67.

Dember, W. N. (1974). Motivation and the cognitive revolution. *American Psychologist, 29,* 161–168.

Dewey, J. (1896). The reflex arc concept in psychology. *Psychological Review, 3,* 357–370.

Dewey, J. (1930). Conduct and experience. In C. Murchison (Ed.), *Psychologies of 1930* (pp. 408–422). Worcester, MA: Clark University Press.

Dewey, J. (1957). *Human nature and conduct.* New York: The Modern Library. (Original work published 1922)

Diserens, C. M. (1925). Psychological objectivism. *Psychological Review, 32,* 121–152.

Duckworth, D. H. (1981). Toward a psychological science that can be applied. *Bulletin of the British Psychological Society, 34,* 237–240.

Edwards, A. S. (1928). Intelligence as the capacity for variability or versatility of response. *Psychological Review, 35,* 198–210.

Efron, R. (1966). The conditioned reflex: A meaningless concept. *Perspectives in Biology and Medicine, 9,* 488–514.

Eisenberg, L. (1960). Conceptual problems in relating brain and behavior. *American Journal of Orthopsychiatry, 30,* 37–48.

Ekehammar, B. (1974). Interactionism in personality from a historical perspective. *Psychological Bulletin, 81,* 1026–1048.

Elbers, L. (1982). Operating principles in repetitive babbling: A cognitive continuity approach. *Cognition, 12,* 45–63.

Elms, A. C. (1975). The crisis of confidence in social psychology. *American Psychologist, 30,* 967–976.

English, H. B. (1933). The ghostly tradition and the descriptive categories of psychology. *Psychological Review, 40,* 498–513.

Epstein, R. (1977). A listing of the published works of B. F. Skinner, with notes and comments. *Behaviorism, 5,* 99–110.

Epstein, R. (1985a). Extinction-induced resurgence: Preliminary investigations and possible applications. *The Psychological Record, 35,* 143–153.

Epstein, R. (1985b). The spontaneous interconnection of three repertoires. *The Psychological Record, 35,* 131–141.

Estes, W. K. (1975). The state of the field: General problems and issues of theory and metatheory. In W. K. Estes (Ed.), *Handbook of learning and cognitive processes: Vol. 1. Introduction to concepts and issues* (pp. 1–24). Hillsdale, NJ: Lawrence Erlbaum Associates.

Evans, R. I. (1968). *B. F. Skinner. The man and his ideas.* New York: Dutton.

Farr, R. M. (1978). On the varieties of social psychology: An essay on the relationships between psychology and other social sciences. *Social Science Information, 17,* 503–525.

Farrell, B. A. (1978). The progress of psychology. *British Journal of Psychology, 69,* 1–8.

Feibleman, J. K. (1944). The mythology of science. *Philosophy of Science, 11,* 117–121.

Feibleman, J. K. (1972a). Pure science, applied science, and technology: An attempt at definitions. In C. Mitcham & R. Mackey (Eds.), *Philosophy and technology: Readings in the philosophical problems of technology* (pp. 33–41). New York: Free Press.

Feibleman, J. K. (1972b). *Scientific method.* The Hague: Martinus Nijhoff.

Feigl, H. (1959). Philosophical embarrassments of psychology. *American Psychologist, 14,* 115–128.

Ferster, C. B. (1961). Positive reinforcement and behavioral deficits of autistic children. *Child Development, 32,* 437–456.

Ferster, C. B. (1972). An experimental analysis of clinical phenomena. *The Psychological Record, 22,* 1–16.

Ferster, C. B. (1973). A functional analysis of depression. *American Psychologist, 28,* 857–870.

Ferster, C. B. (1978). Is operant conditioning getting bored with behavior? *Journal of the Experimental Analysis of Behavior, 29,* 347–349.

Ferster, C. B. (1979). A laboratory model of psychotherapy: The boundary between clinical practice and experimental psychology. In P-O Sjödén, S. Bates, & W. S. Dockens, III (Eds.), *Trends in behavior therapy* (pp. 23–38). New York: Academic Press.

Ferster, C. B., & Culbertson, S. A. (1982). *Behavior principles* (3rd ed.). Englewood Cliffs, NJ: Prentice Hall.

Ferster, C. B., & Simons, J. (1966). Behavior therapy with children. *The Psychological Record, 16,* 65–71.

Feyerabend, P. K. (1962). *Knowledge without foundations.* Oberlin, OH: Oberlin.

Feynman, R. P., Leighton, R. B., & Sands, M. (1963). *The Feynman lectures on physics.* Reading, MA: Addison-Wesley.

Fischer, K. W. (1980). A theory of cognitive development: The control and construction of hierarchies of skills. *Psychological Review, 87,* 477–531.

Fiske, D. W. (1979). Two worlds of psychological phenomena. *American Psychologist, 34,* 733–739.

Flavell, J. H. (1972). An analysis of cognitive-development sequences. *Genetic Psychology Monographs, 86,* 279–350.

Fodor, J. A. (1981). The mind-body problem. *Scientific American, 244,* 124–132.

Fodor, J. A., Bever, T. G., & Garrett, M. F. (1974). *The psychology of language.* New York: McGraw-Hill.

Foppa, K. (1978). Language acquisition: A human ethological problem. *Social Science Information, 17,* 93–105.

Fraley, L. E., & Vargas, E. A. (1986). Separate disciplines: The study of behavior and the study of the psyche. *The Behavior Analyst, 9,* 47–59.

Franck, I. (1982). Psychology as a science: Resolving the idiographic-nomothetic controversy. *Journal for the Theory of Social Behavior, 12,* 1–20.

Freudenberger, H. J. (1985). *Burn out.* London: Arrow Books.

From, F. (1960). Perception of human action. In H. P. David & J. C. Brengelmann (Eds.), *Perspectives in personality research* (pp. 161–174). London: Crosby Lockwood & Son.

Furnham, A. (1983). Social psychology as common sense. *Bulletin of the British Psychological Society, 36,* 105–109.

Gauld, A. & Shotter, J. (1977). *Human action and its psychological investigation.* London: Routledge & Kegan Paul.

Gaylord-Ross, R. J. (1979). Mental retardation research, ecological validity, and the delivery of longitudinal education programs. *Journal of Special Education, 13,* 69–80.

Geertz, C. (1975). On the nature of anthropological understanding. *American Scientist, 63,* 47–53.

Gergen, K. J. (1973). Social psychology as history. *Journal of Personality and Social Psychology, 26,* 309–320.

Gergen, K. J. (1978). Experimentation in social psychology: A reappraisal. *European Journal of Social Psychology, 8,* 507–527.

Giorgi, A. (1976). Phenomenology and the foundations of psychology. In J. K. Cole & W. J. Arnold (Eds.), *Nebraska Symposium on Motivation* (Vol. 23, pp. 281–348). Lincoln: University of Nebraska Press.

Giorgi, A. (1984). The "unfinished business" of psychology. In D. P. Rogers (Ed.), *Foundations of psychology: Some personal views* (pp. 18–34). New York: Praeger.

Giorgi, A. (1985). Theoretical plurality and unity in psychology. *The Psychological Record, 35,* 177–181.

Givón, T. (1979). *On understanding grammar.* New York: Academic Press.

Gladin, L. L. (1961). Toward a unified psychology. *The Psychological Record, 11,* 405–421.

Glass, G. V., & Kliegl, R. M. (1983). An apology for research integration in the study of psychotherapy. *Journal of Consulting and Clinical Psychology, 51,* 28–41.

Glenn, S. S. (1983). Maladaptive functional relations in client verbal behavior. *The Behavior Analyst, 6,* 47–56.

Gloye, E., Craig, E., & Carp, F. (1957). On replication. *Psychological Reports, 3,* 299.

Goldiamond, I. (1966). Self-control procedures in personal behavior problems. In R. Ulrich, T. Stachnik, & J. Mabry (Eds.), *Control of human behavior* (pp. 115–127). Glenview, IL: Scott, Foresman.

Goldiamond, I. (1968). Moral behavior: A functional analysis. *Psychology Today, 2,* 31–34, 70.

Goldiamond, I. (1974). Toward a constructional approach to social problems. *Behaviorism, 2,* 1–84.

Goldiamond, I. (1975a). Alternative sets as a framework for behavioral formulations and research. *Behaviorism, 3,* 49–86.

Goldiamond, I. (1975b). Insider-outside problems: A constructional approach. *Rehabilitation Psychology, 22,* 103–116.

Goldiamond, I. (1984). Training parent trainers and ethicists in nonlinear analysis of behavior. In R. F. Dangel & R. A. Polster (Eds.), *Parent training: Foundations of research and practice* (pp. 504–546). New York: Guilford.

Goldiamond, I., Atkinson, C. J., & Bilger, R. C. (1962). Stabilization of behavior and prolonged exposure to delayed auditory feedback. *Science, 135,* 437–438.

Goldiamond, I., Dyrud, J. E. (1966). Reading as operant behavior. In J. Money & G. Schiffman (Eds.), *The disabled reader* (pp. 93–115). Baltimore: John Hopkins.

Goldiamond, I., Dyrud, J. E., & Miller, M. D. (1965). Practice as research in professional psychology. *Canadian Psychologist, 6,* 110–128.

Goldstein, K. (1951). *Human nature in the light of psychopathology.* Cambridge, MA: Harvard University Press.

Gopnik, A. (1984). In search of a theory of learning. *Behavioral and Brain Sciences, 7,* 627–628.

Greer, R. D. (1982). Countercontrols for the American Educational Research Association. *The Behavior Analyst, 5,* 65–76.

Guthrie, E. R. (1959). Association by contiguity. In S. Koch (Ed.), *Psychology: A study of a science: Vol. 2. General systematic formulations, learning, and special processes* (pp. 158–195). New York: McGraw-Hill.

Guthrie, E. R., & Edwards, A. L. (1949). *Psychology: A first course in human behavior.* New York: Harper.

Guttman, N. (1977). On Skinner and Hull: A reminiscence and projection. *American Psychologist, 32,* 321–328.

Hadfield, J. A. (1964). *Psychology and morals.* London: Methuen. (Original work published 1923)

Hake, D. F. (1982). The basic-applied continuum and the possible evolution of human operant social and verbal research. *The Behavior Analyst, 5,* 21–28.

Hamlyn, D. W. (1953). Behavior. *Philosophy, 28,* 132–145.

Hamlyn, D. W. (1981). Cognitive systems, 'folk psychology,' and knowledge. *Cognition, 10,* 115–118.

Harding, C. G. (1982). Development of the intention to communicate. *Human Development, 25,* 140–151.

Hargreaves, D. M. (1980). Common-sense models of action. In A. J. Chapman & D. M. Jones (Eds.), *Models of man* (pp. 215–225). Leicester, England: British Psychological Society.

Harré, R. (1982). Theoretical preliminaries to the study of action. In M. von Cranach & R. Harré (Eds.), *The analysis of action* (pp. 5–33). Cambridge: Cambridge University Press.

Harrell, W., & Harrison, R. (1938). The rise and fall of behaviorism. *Journal of General Psychology, 18,* 367–421.

Harris, M. (1977). *Cannibals and kings: The origins of cultures.* New York: Random House.

Harris, M. (1981). *American now: The anthropology of a changing culture*. New York: Simon & Schuster.

Harzem, P. (1984). Experimental analysis of individual differences and personality. *Journal of the Experimental Analysis of Behavior, 42*, 385–395.

Harzem, P., & Williams, R. A. (1983). On searching for a science of human behavior. *The Psychological Record, 33*, 565–574.

Hayes, S. C. (1978). Theory and technology in behavior analysis. *The Behavior Analyst, 1*, 25–33.

Hebb, D. O. (1949). *The organization of behavior*. New York: Wiley.

Hebb, D. O. (1972). *Textbook of psychology* (3rd ed.). Philadelphia: W. B. Saunders.

Hebb, D. O. (1974). What psychology is about. *American Psychologist, 29*, 71–79.

Heinen, J. R. K., & Stafford, K. R. (1979). Inherent predispositions and the study of human behavior. *The Psychological Record, 29*, 165–174.

Henle, M. (1976). Why study the history of psychology? *Annals of the New York Academy of Sciences, 270*, 14–20.

Higgins, J. R., & Spaeth, R. K. (1972). Relationship between consistency of movement and environmental condition. *Quest, 17*, 61–69.

Hilgard, E. R. (1980). Consciousness in contemporary psychology. *Annual Review of Psychology, 31*, 1–26.

Hinde, R. A. (1970). *Animal behavior: A synthesis of ethology and comparative psychology* (2nd ed.). Tokyo: McGraw-Hill Kogakusha.

Hineline, P. N. (1980). The language of behavior analysis: Its community, its functions, and its limitations. *Behaviorism, 8*, 67–86.

Hineline, P. N. (1984). Aversive control: A separate domain? *Journal of the Experimental Analysis of Behavior, 42*, 495–509.

Hitt, W. D. (1969). Two models of man. *American Psychologist, 24*, 651–658.

Hocutt, M. (1985). The truth in behaviorism: A review of G. E. Zuriff, *Behaviorism: A conceptual reconstruction. Behaviorism, 13*, 77–82.

Holt, J. (1969). *How children fail*. Middlesex, England: Penguin Books. (Original work published 1965)

Holt, J. (1970). *How children learn*. Middlesex, England: Penguin Books. (Original work published 1967)

Holt, R. R. (1962). Individuality and generalization in the psychology of personality. *Journal of Personality, 30*, 377–404.

Honig, W. K., & Staddon, J. E. R. (Eds.). (1977). *Handbook of operant behavior*. Englewood Cliffs, NJ: Prentice Hall.

Horton, R. (1967). African traditional thought and western science. *Africa, 37*, 50–71; 155–187.

Howard, G. S. (1986). *Dare we develop a human science?* Notre Dame, IN: Academic Publications.

Howarth, C. I. (1980). The structure of effective psychology: Man as a problem-solver. In A. J. Chapman & D. M. Jones (Eds.), *Models of man* (p. 143–160). Leicester, England: British Psychological Society.

Hudson, L. (1975). *Human beings.* London: Jonathan Cape.

Hunt, D. E. (1975). Person-environment interaction: A challenge found wanting before it was tried. *Review of Educational Research, 45,* 209–230.

Hunt, J. McV. (1969). The impact and limitations of the giant of developmental psychology. In D. Elkind & J. H. Flavell (Eds.), *Studies in cognitive development: Essays in honor of Jean Piaget* (pp. 3–66). New York: University Press.

Hunter, W. S. (1919). *General psychology.* Chicago, IL: University of Chicago Press.

Hunter, W. S. (1932). The psychological study of behavior. *Psychological Review, 39,* 1–24.

Hutten, E. H. (1956). *The language of modern physics.* London: Allen & Unwin.

James, W. (1961). *Psychology: The briefer course* (G. Allport, Ed.). New York: World Publishing. (Original work published 1892)

Jastrow, J. (1927). The reconstruction of psychology. *Psychological Review, 34,* 169–195.

Jessor, R. (1958). The problem of reductionism in psychology. *Psychological Review, 65,* 170–178.

Johnson, K. R., & Chase, P. N. (1981). Behavior analysis in instructional design: A functional typology of verbal tasks. *The Behavior Analyst, 4,* 103–121.

Johnston, J. M., & Pennypacker, H. S. (1980). *Strategies and tactics of human behavioral research.* Hillsdale, NJ: Lawrence Erlbaum Associates.

Joynson, R. B. (1974). *Psychology and common sense.* London: Routledge & Kegan Paul.

Joynson, R. B. (1980). Models of man: 1879–1979. In A. J. Chapman & D. M. Jones (Eds.), *Models of man* (pp. 1–12). Leicester: British Psychological Society.

Kagan, J. (1976). Emergent themes in human development. *American Scientist, 64,* 186–196.

Kallos, D., & Lundgren, U. P. (1975). Educational psychology: Its scope and limits. *British Journal of Educational Psychology, 45,* 111–121.

Kann, R. (1983). The method of repeated readings: Expanding the neurological impress method for use with disabled readers. *Journal of Learning Disabilities, 16,* 90–92.

Kantor, J. R. (1947). *Problems of physiological psychology.* Bloomington, IN: Principia Press.

Kantor, J. R. (1969). Scientific psychology and specious philosophy. *The Psychological Record, 19,* 15–27.

Karlan, G. R., & Rusch, F. R. (1982). Correspondence between saying and doing: Some thoughts on defining correspondence and future directions for application. *Journal of Applied Behavior Analysis, 15,* 151–162.

Keenan, M. (1986). Second-order schedules. *The Psychological Record, 36,* 407–417.

Keller, F. S., & Schoenfeld, W. N. (1950). *Principles of psychology.* New York: Appleton-Century-Crofts.

Kendall, F. P., & McCreary, E. K. (1983). *Muscles: Testing and function* (3rd ed.). Baltimore/London: Williams & Wilkins.

Kendall, P. C., & Lerner, R. M., & Craighead, W. E. (1984). Human development and intervention in childhood psychopathology. *Child Development, 55,* 71-82.

Keniston, K. (1971). Psychological development and historical change. *Journal of Interdisciplinary History, 2,* 330-345.

Kimble, G. A. (1967). The definition of learning and some useful distinctions. In G. A. Kimble (Ed.), *Foundations of conditioning and learning* (pp. 82-99). New York: Appleton-Century-Crofts.

Kimble, G. A., & Perlmutter, L. C. (1970). The problem of volition. *Psychological Review, 77,* 361-384.

King, L. M. (1978). Social and cultural influences on psychopathology. *Annual Review of Psychology, 29,* 405-433.

Kitchener, R. F. (1977). Behavior and behaviorism. *Behaviorism, 5,* 11-71.

Klein, D. B. (1942). Psychology's progress and the armchair taboo. *Psychological Review, 49,* 226-234.

Klopfer, P. H. (1973). Evolution and behavior. In G. Bermant (Ed.), *Perspectives on animal behavior* (pp. 48-71). Glenview, IL: Scott, Foresman.

Koch, S. (1951). Theoretical psychology, 1950: An overview. *Psychological Review, 58,* 295-301.

Koch, S. (1959). Epilogue. In S. Koch (Ed.), *Psychology: A study of a science* (Vol. 3, pp. 729-788). New York: McGraw Hill.

Koch, S. (1971). Reflections on the state of psychology. *Social Research, 38,* 669-709.

Koch, S. (1973). Theory and experiment in psychology. *Social Research, 40,* 691-707.

Koch, S. (1974). Psychology as science. In S. C. Brown (Ed.), *Philosophy of psychology* (pp. 3-39). London & Basingstoke: Macmillan.

Koch, S. (1975). Language communities, search cells, and the psychological studies. In W. J. Arnold (Ed.), *Nebraska Symposium on Motivation* (Vol. 23, pp. 477-559). Lincoln: University of Nebraska Press.

Koch, S. (1978). In M. Wertheimer (Ed.), Psychology and the future (pp. 637-639). *American Psychologist, 33,* 631-647.

Koch, S. (1981). The nature and limits of psychological knowledge. *American Psychologist, 36,* 257-269.

Koestler, A. (1978). *Janus: A summing up.* London: Hutchinson.

Koffka, K. (1933). Review of E. C. Tolman's *Purposive behavior in animals and men. Psychological Bulletin, 30,* 440-451.

Krantz, D. L. (1972). Schools and systems: The mutual isolation of operant and nonoperant psychology as a case study. *Journal of the History of the Behavioral Sciences, 8,* 86-102.

Kranzberg, M. (1968). The disunity of science-technology. *American Scientist, 56,* 21-34.

Kvale, S. (1973). The technological paradigm of psychological research. *Journal of Phenomenological Psychology, 3,* 143-159.

Kvale, S. (1976a). Meanings as data and human technology. *Scandinavian Journal of Psychology, 17,* 171-180.

Kvale, S. (1976b). The psychology of learning as ideology and technology. *Behaviorism, 4,* 97–116.

Kvale, S., & Grenness, C. E. (1967). Skinner and Sartre: Towards a radical phenomenology of behavior? *Review of Existential Psychology and Psychiatry, 7,* 128–150.

Ladd, G. W., & Mize, J. (1983). A cognitive-social learning model of social-skill training. *Psychological Review, 90,* 127–157.

Lakein, A. (1973). *How to get control of your time and your life.* New York: Signet.

Langford, G. (1971). *Human action.* New York: Doubleday.

Lashley, K. S., & Ball, J. (1929). Spinal conduction and kinesthetic sensitivity in the maze habit. *Journal of Comparative Psychology, 9,* 71–105.

Lashley, K. S., & McCarthy, D. A. (1926). The survival of the maze habit after cerebellar injuries. *Journal of Comparative Psychology, 6,* 423–432.

Lattal, K. A. (1969). Contingency management of toothbrushing behavior in a summer camp for children. *Journal of Applied Behavior Analysis, 2,* 195–198.

Layng, T. V. J., & Andronis, P. T. (1984). Toward a functional analysis of delusional speech and hallucinatory behavior. *The Behavior Analyst, 7,* 139–156.

Leary, D. E. (1980). One hundred years of experimental psychology: An American perspective. *Psychological Research, 42,* 175–189.

Lee, V. L. (1981). Terminological and conceptual revision in the experimental analysis of language development: Why. *Behaviorism, 9,* 25–53.

Lee, V. L. (1983). Behavior as a constituent of conduct. *Behaviorism, 11,* 199–224.

Lee, V. L. (1984). Some notes on the subject matter of Skinner's *Verbal Behavior* (1957). *Behaviorism, 12,* 29–40.

Lee, V. L. (1985). Scientific knowledge as rules that guide behavior. *The Psychological Record, 35,* 183–192.

Lee, V. L. (1986). Act psychologies and the psychological nouns. *The Psychological Record, 36,* 167–177.

Lee, V. L. (1987). The structure of conduct. *Behaviorism, 15,* 141–148.

Lee, V. L., & Sanderson, G. M. (1987). Some contingencies of spelling. *Analysis of Verbal Behavior, 5,* 1–13.

Leigland, S. (1984). Can radical behaviorism rescue psychology? *The Behavior Analyst, 7,* 73–74.

Lemaine, G., MacLeod, R., Mulkay, M., & Weingart, P. (1976). Problems in the emergence of new disciplines. In G. Lemaine, R. MacLeod, M. Mulkay, & P. Weingart, (Eds.), *Perspectives on the emergence of scientific disciplines* (pp. 1–23). The Hague: Mouton.

Lichtenstein, P. E. (1980). Theoretical psychology: Where is it headed? *The Psychological Record, 30,* 447–458.

Lipsey, M. W. (1974). Psychology: Preparadigmatic, postparadigmatic, or mis-paradigmatic. *Science Studies, 4,* 406–410.

Llewelyn, S., & Kelly, J. (1980). Individualism in psychology: A case for a new paradigm? *Bulletin of the British Psychological Society, 33,* 407–411.

Lloyd, K. E. (1985). Behavioral anthropology: A review of Marvin Harris' *Cultural Materialism. Journal of the Experimental Analysis of Behavior, 43,* 279–287.

Lott, B. (1985). The potential enrichment of social/personality psychology through feminist research and vice versa. *American Psychologist, 40,* 155–164.

Lowe, C. F. (1979). Determinants of human operant behavior. In M. D. Zeile & P. Harzem (Eds.), *Advances in analysis of behavior: Vol. 1. Reinforcement and the organization of behavior* (pp. 159–192). Chichester, England: Wiley.

Lowe, C. F., & Higson, P. J. (1981). Self-instructional training and cognitive behavior modification: A behavioral analysis. In G. Davey (Ed.), *Applications of conditioning theory* (pp. 162–188). London: Methuen.

Lowe, C. F., & Horne, P. J. (1985). On the generality of behavioral principles: Human choice and the matching law. In C. F. Lowe, M. Richelle, D. E. Blackman, & C. M. Bradshaw (Eds.), *Behavior analysis and contemporary psychology* (pp. 97–115). London: Lawrence Erlbaum Associates.

Luchins, A. S., & Luchins, E. H. (1965). *Logical foundations of mathematics for behavioral scientists.* New York: Holt, Rinehart & Winston.

Lundh, L. G. (1981). The mind considered as a system of meaning structures: Elementary meaning structures. *Scandinavian Journal of Psychology, 22,* 145–160.

Luria, A. K. (1971). Towards the problem of the historical nature of psychological processes. *International Journal of Psychology, 6,* 259–272.

Lykken, D. T. (1968). Statistical significance in psychological research. *Psychological Bulletin, 70,* 151–159.

MacCorquodale, K. (1969). B. F. Skinner's *Verbal Behavior:* A retrospective appreciation. *Journal of the Experimental Analysis of Behavior, 12,* 831–841.

MacCorquodale, K. (1970). On Chomsky's review of Skinner's *Verbal Behavior. Journal of the Experimental Analysis of Behavior, 13,* 83–99.

MacFarlane, D. A. (1930). The role of kinethesis in maze learning. *University of California Publications in Psychology, 4,* 277–305.

MacKay, D. G. (1982). The problems of flexibility, fluency and speed-accuracy trade-off in skilled behavior. *Psychological Review, 89,* 483–506.

MacKenzie, B. D. (1977). *Behaviorism and the limits of scientific method.* Atlantic Highlands, NJ: Humanities Press.

MacLeod, R. B. (1965). The teaching of psychology and the psychology we teach. *American Psychologist, 20,* 344–352.

Malagodi, E. F. (1986). On radicalizing behaviorism: A call for cultural analysis. *The Behavior Analyst, 9,* 1–17.

Malcolm, N. (1970). Wittgenstein on the nature of mind. *American Philosophical Quarterly Monograph Series, 4,* 9–29.

Malcolm, N. (1971). The myth of cognitive processes and structures. In T. Mischel (Ed.), *Cognitive development and epistemology* (pp. 385–392). New York: Academic Press.

Malcolm, N. (1978). Thinking. In E. Leinfellner, W. Leinfellner, H. Berghel, & A. Hubner (Eds.), *Wittgenstein and his impact on contemporary thought* (pp. 411–419). Vienna: Holder-Pichler-Tempsky.

Manicas, P. T., & Secord, P. F. (1983). Implications for psychology of the new philosophy of science. *American Psychologist, 38,* 399–413.

Mapel, B. M. (1977). Philosophical criticism of behaviorism: An analysis. *Behaviorism, 5,* 17–32.

Marr, M. J. (1984). Conceptual approaches and issues. *Journal of the Experimental Analysis of Behavior, 42,* 353–362.

Martin, W. W. (1945). Some basic implications of a concept of organism for psychology. *Psychological Review, 52,* 333–343.

Masters, J. C. (1981). Developmental psychology. *Annual Review of Psychology, 32,* 117–151.

Mawhinney, V. T., Bostow, D. E., Laws, D. R., Blumenfeld, G. J., & Hopkins, B. L. (1971). A comparison of students' studying-behavior produced by daily, weekly, and three-week testing schedules. *Journal of Applied Behavior Analysis, 4,* 257–264.

Mayr, E. (1972). The nature of the Darwinian revolution. *Science, 176,* 981–989.

McCall, R. J. (1972). Beyond reason and evidence: The metapsychology of Professor B. F. Skinner. *Journal of Clinical Psychology, 28,* 125–139.

McDougall, W. (1912). *Psychology, the study of behavior.* New York: Holt.

McDougall, W. (1922). Prolegomena to psychology. *Psychological Review, 29,* 1–43.

McDougall, W. (1928). Men or robots? In C. Murchison (Ed.), *Psychologies of 1925* (pp. 273–291). Worchester, MA: Clark University Press.

McFall, R. M. (1982). A review and reformulation of the concept of social skills. *Behavioral Assessment, 4,* 1–33.

McKay, M., Davis, M., & Fanning, P. (1983). *Messages: The communication books.* Oakland, C.A.: New Harbinger Publications.

McKearney, J. W. (1977). Asking questions about behavior. *Perspectives in Biology and Medicine, 21,* 109–119.

Meehl, P. E. (1967). Theory-testing in psychology and physics: A methodological paradox. *Philosophy of Science, 34,* 103–115.

Meldon, A. I. (1970). Physiological happenings and bodily actions. In M. Brand (Ed.), *The nature of human action* (pp. 22–26). Glenview, IL: Scott, Foresman.

Michael, J. (1980). Flight from behavior analysis. *The Behavior Analyst, 3,* 1–22.

Michael, J. (1984). Verbal behavior. *Journal of the Experimental Analysis of Behavior, 42,* 363–376.

Midgley, M. (1978). *Beast and man: The roots of human nature.* New York: Cornell University Press.

Miner, J. B. (1929). The procedure of thinking about mind. *Psychological Review, 36,* 332–340.

Mischel, T. (1976). Psychological explanations and their vicissitudes. In J. K. Cole & W. J. Arnold (Eds.), *Nebraska Symposium on Motivation* (Vol. 23, pp. 133–204). Lincoln: University of Nebraska Press.

Mishler, E. (1979). Meaning in context. Is there any other kind? *Harvard Educational Review, 49,* 1–21.

Mohr, H. (1977). *Structure and significance of science.* New York: Springer-Verlag.

Molm, L. D. (1981). The legitimacy of behavioral theory as a sociological perspective. *American Sociologist, 16,* 153–165.

Molm, L. D., & Wiggins, J. A. (1979). A behavioral analysis of the dynamics of social exchange in the dyad. *Social Forces, 57,* 1157–1179.

Moore, O. K., & Lewis, D. J. (1953). Purpose and learning theory. *Psychological Review, 60,* 149–156.

Morris, E. K., Hursh, D. E., Winston, A. S., Gelfand, D. M., Hartmann, D. P., Reese, H. W., & Baer, D. M. (1982). Behavior analysis and developmental psychology. *Human Development, 25,* 340–364.

Morris, J. M. (1977). Biomechanics of the foot and ankle. *Clinical Orthopaedics and Related Research, 122,* 10–17.

Mueller, C. G. (1979). Some origins of psychology as science. *Annual Review of Psychology, 30,* 9–29.

Muenzinger, K. F. (1927). Physical and psychological reality. *Psychological Review, 34,* 220–223.

Muenzinger, K. F. (1928). Plasticity and mechanization of the problem box habit in guinea pigs. *Journal of Comparative Psychology, 8,* 45–69.

Mulkay, M. (1978). Consensus in science. *Social Science Information, 17,* 107–122.

Murray, H. A. (1938). *Explorations in personality.* New York: Oxford University Press.

Murray, H. A. (1951). Toward a classification of interactions. In T. Parsons & E. A. Shils (Eds.), *Toward a general theory of action* (pp. 434–464). Cambridge, MA: Harvard University Press.

Mursell, J. L. (1922). The stimulus-response relation. *Psychological Review, 29,* 146–162.

Neuringer, A. (1981). Self-experimentation: A call for change. *Behaviorism, 9,* 79–94.

Neuringer, A. (1984). Melioration and self-experimentation. *Journal of the Experimental Analysis of Behavior, 42,* 397–406.

Nevin, J. A. (1980). Editorial. *Journal of the Experimental Analysis of Behavior, 33,* i–ii.

Nevin, J. A. (1982). Editorial. *Journal of the Experimental Analysis of Behavior, 37,* 1–2.

Newtson, D., & Engquist, G. (1976). The perceptual organization of ongoing behavior. *Journal of Experimental Social Psychology, 12,* 436–450.

Newtson, D., Engquist, G., & Bois, J. (1977). The objective basis of behavior units. *Journal of Personality and Social Psychology, 35,* 847–862.

Nissen, H. W. (1950). Description of the learned response in discrimination behavior. *Psychological Review, 57,* 121–131.

Norman, D. A. (1980). Twelve issues for cognitive science. *Cognitive Science, 4,* 1–32.

Norman, D. A. (1981). Categorization of action slips. *Psychological Review, 88,* 1–15. (query R-359)

Northrop, F. S. C. (1947). *The logic of the sciences and the humanities.* New York: Macmillan.

Notcutt, B. (1953). *The psychology of personality.* London: Methuen.

Novikoff, A. B. (1945a). Continuity and discontinuity in evolution. *Science, 102,* 405–406.

Novikoff, A. B. (1945b). The concept of integrative levels and biology. *Science, 101,* 209–215.

Oppenheimer, R. (1956). Analogy in science. *American Psychologist, 11,* 127–135.

Packard, R. G. (1970). The control of "classroom attention": A group contingency for complex behavior. *Journal of Applied Behavior Analysis, 3,* 13–28.

Palermo, D. S. (1971). Is a scientific revolution taking place in psychology? *Science Studies, 1,* 135–155.

Parmelee, M. F. (1924). *The science of human behavior: Biological and psychological foundations.* New York: Macmillan.

Parrott, L. J. (1983). Perspectives on knowing and knowledge. *The Psychological Record, 33,* 171–184.

Parsons, J. A., Taylor, D. C., & Joyce, T. M. (1981). Precurrent self-prompting operants in children: "Remembering". *Journal of the Experimental Analysis of Behavior, 36,* 253–266.

Parsons, T., & Shils, E. A. (Eds.), (1951). *Toward a general theory of action.* Cambridge, MA: Harvard University Press.

Pear, J. J. (1983). Relative reinforcements for cognitive and behavioral terminologies. *The Psychological Record, 33,* 20–25.

Peele, S. (1981). Reductionism in the psychology of the eighties. *American Psychologist, 36,* 807–818.

Pepitone, A. (1981). Lessons from the history of social psychology. *American Psychologist, 36,* 972–985.

Peters, R. S. (1960). *The concept of motivation.* (2nd ed.). London: Routledge & Kegan Paul.

Phillips, D. C., & Orton, R. (1983). The new causal principle of cognitive learning theory: Perspectives on Bandura's "reciprocal determinism". *Psychological Review, 90,* 158–165.

Pierce, W. D., & Epling, W. F. (1980). What happened to analysis in applied behavior analysis? *The Behavior Analyst, 3,* 1–9.

Pisacreta, R. (1982). Some factors that influence the acquisition of complex, stereotyped, response sequences in pigeons. *Journal of the Experimental Analysis of Behavior, 37,* 359–369.

Platt, J. R. (1964). Strong inference. *Science, 146,* 347–353.

Polanyi, M. (1962). Tacit knowing: Its bearing on some problems of philosophy. *Reviews of Modern Physics, 34,* 601–616.

Poppen, R. (1982). The fixed-interval scallop in human affairs. *The Behavior Analyst, 5,* 127–136.

Potter, J. (1982). " . . . Nothing so practical as a good theory." The problematic application of social psychology. In P. Stringer (Ed.), Confronting social issues. *European Monographs in Social Psychology, 28,* 23–49.

Pratt, C. C. (1939). *The logic of modern psychology.* New York: Macmillan.

Pryor, K. W., Haag, R., & O'Reilly, J. (1969). The creative porpoise: Training for novel behavior. *Journal of the Experimental Analysis of Behavior, 12,* 653–661.

Purton, A. C. (1978). Ethological categories of behavior and some consequences of their conflation. *Animal Behaviour, 26,* 653-670.

Quine, W. V. (1957). The scope and language of science. *British Journal for the Philosophy of Science, 8,* 1-17.

Rachlin, H. (1977). A review of M. J. Mahoney's *Cognition and Behavior Modification. Journal of Applied Behavior Analysis, 10,* 369-374.

Rasch, P. J., & Burke, R. K. (1971). *Kinesiology and applied anatomy: The science of human movement* (4th ed.). Philadelphia: Lea & Febiger.

Rayfield, D. (1970). On describing actions. *Inquiry, 13,* 90-99.

Reason, J. (1979). Actions not as planned: The price of automatization. In G. Underwood & R. Stevens (Eds.), *Aspects of consciousness* (pp. 67-89). London: Academic Press.

Redd, W. H., & Wheeler, A. J. (1973). The relative effectiveness of monetary reinforcers and adult instructions in the control of children's choice behavior. *Journal of Experimental Child Psychology, 16,* 63-75.

Richelle, M. (1976). Formal analysis and functional analysis of verbal behavior: Notes on the debate between Chomsky and Skinner. *Behaviorism, 4,* 209-221.

Rincover, A. (1978). Sensory extinction: A procedure for eliminating self-stimulatory behavior in psychotic children. *Journal of Abnormal Child Psychology, 6,* 299-310.

Rincover, A., Cooke, R., Peoples, A., & Packard, D. (1979). Sensory extinction and sensory reinforcement principles for programming multiple adaptive behavior change. *Journal of Applied Behavior Analysis, 12,* 221-233.

Rincover, A., & Devany, J. (1982). The application of sensory extinction procedures to self-injury. *Analysis and Intervention in Developmental Disabilities, 2,* 67-81.

Ringen, J. (1976). Explanation, teleology, and operant behaviorism: A study of the experimental analysis of purposive behavior. *Philosophy of Science, 43,* 223-253.

Rippere, V. (1977). Commonsense beliefs about depression and antidepressive behavior: A study of social consensus. *Behavior Research and Therapy, 15,* 465-473.

Roback, A. A. (1923). *Behaviorism and psychology.* Cambridge, MA: Harvard University Bookstore.

Roberts, D. A., & Russell, T. L. (1975). An alternative approach to science education research: Drawing from philosophical analysis to examine practice. *Curriculum Theory Network, 5,* 107-125.

Rubinstein, D. (1977). The concept of action in the social sciences. *Journal for the Theory of Social Behavior, 7,* 209-236.

Russell, B. (1931). *The scientific outlook.* London: Allen & Unwin.

Russell, E. S. (1938). *The behavior of animals: An introduction to its study* (2nd ed.). London: Edward Arnold.

Russell, W. M. S., Mead, A. P., & Hayes, J. S. (1954). A basis for the quantitative study of the structure of behavior. *Behavior, 6,* 153-205.

Ryle, G. (1966). *The concept of mind.* Middlesex, England: Penguin Books. (Original work published 1949)

Ryle, G. (1979). *On thinking.* Oxford: Basil Blackwell.

Sampson, E. E. (1981). Cognitive psychology as ideology. *American Psychologist, 36,* 730–743.

Sampson, E. E. (1983). Deconstructing psychology's subject. *Journal of Mind and Behavior, 4,* 135–164.

Sanford, N. (1965). Will psychologists study human problems? *American Psychologist, 20,* 192–202.

Sarason, S. B. (1981). An asocial psychology and a misdirected clinical psychology. *American Psychologist, 36,* 827–836.

Savory, T. H. (1967). *The language of science* (rev. ed.) London: Andre Deutsch.

Schacht, T., & Nathan, P. E. (1977). But is it good for the psychologists? Appraisal and status of DSM-III. *American Psychologist, 32,* 1017–1025.

Schafer, R. (1976). *A new language for psychoanalysis.* New Haven: Yale University Press.

Schick, K. (1971). Operants. *Journal of the Experimental Analysis of Behavior, 15,* 413–423.

Schmitt, D. R. (1984). Interpersonal relations: Cooperation and competition. *Journal of the Experimental Analysis of Behavior, 42,* 377–383.

Schnaitter, R. (1975). Between organism and environment. A review of B. F. Skinner's *About Behaviorism. Journal of the Experimental Analysis of Behavior, 23,* 297–307.

Schoen, M. (1927). Instinct and man. *Psychological Review, 34,* 120–125.

Schoenfeld, W. N. (1972). Problems of modern behavior theory. *Conditional Reflex, 7,* 33–65.

Schoenfeld, W. N. (1976). The "response" in behavior theory. *Pavlovian Journal of Biological Science, 11,* 129–149.

Schoenfeld, W. N., & Farmer, J. (1970). Reinforcement schedules and the "behavior stream." In W. N. Schoenfeld (Ed.), *The theory of reinforcement schedules* (pp. 215–245). New York: Appleton-Century-Crofts.

Schoenfeld, W. N., Harris, A. H., & Farmer, J. (1966). Conditioning response variability. *Psychological Reports, 19,* 551–557.

Schutte, R. C., & Hopkins, B. L. (1970). The effects of teacher attention on following instructions in a kindergarten class. *Journal of Applied Behavior Analysis, 3,* 117–122.

Schutz, A. (1954). Concept and theory formation in the social sciences. *Journal of Philosophy, 51,* 256–273.

Schwartz, B. (1981). Control of complex, sequential operants by systematic visual information in pigeons. *Journal of the Experimental Psychology: Animal Behavior Processes, 7,* 31–44.

Schwartz, B. (1982). Failure to produce response variability with reinforcement. *Journal of the Experimental Analysis of Behavior, 37,* 171–181.

Scriven, M. (1956). A possible distinction between traditional scientific disciplines and the study of human behavior. In H. Feigl & M. Scriven (Eds.), *Minnesota studies in the philosophy of science* (Vol. 1, pp. 330–339). Minneapolis: University of Minnesota Press.

Scriven, M. (1964). Views of human nature. In T. W. Wann (Ed.), *Behaviorism and phenomenology: Contrasting bases for modern psychology.* (pp. 163–183). Chicago: University of Chicago Press.

Sederberg, P. V., & Sederberg, N. B. (1975). Transmitting the nontransmissable: The function of literature in the pursuit of social knowledge. *Philosophy and Phenomenological Research, 36,* 173–196.

Segal, E. F. (1972). Induction and the provenance of operants. In R. M. Gilbert & J. R. Millenson (Eds.) *Reinforcement—Behavioral analysis* (pp. 1–34). New York: Academic Press.

Segal, E. F. (1975). Psycholinguistics discovers the operant: A review of Roger Brown's *A first language: The early stages. Journal of the Experimental Analysis of Behavior, 23,* 149–158.

Shapere, D. (1964). The structure of scientific revolutions. *Philosophical Review, 73,* 383–394.

Sherif, C. W. (1979). Bias in psychology. In J. A. Sherman & E. T. Beck (Eds.), *The prism of sex* (pp. 93–133). Madison: University of Wisconsin Press.

Shimoff, E. (1986). Post-session verbal reports and the experimental analysis of behavior. *The Analysis of Verbal Behavior, 4,* 19–22.

Shimp, C. P. (1984). Cognition, behavior, and the experimental analysis of behavior. *Journal of the Experimental Analysis of Behavior, 42,* 407–420.

Shotter, J. (1980). Men the magicians: The duality of social being and the structure of moral worlds. In A. J. Chapman & D. M. Jones (Eds.), *Models of man* (pp. 13–34). Leicester: British Psychological Society.

Shulman, L. S. (1970). Reconstruction of educational research. *Review of Educational Research, 40,* 371–396.

Shulman, A. D., & Silverman, I. (1972). Profile of social psychology: A preliminary application of "reference analysis." *Journal of the History of the Behavioral Sciences, 8,* 232–236.

Shwayder, D. S. (1965). *The stratification of behavior.* London: Routledge & Kegan Paul.

Sidman, M. (1956). Verplanck's analysis of Skinner. *Contemporary Psychology, 1,* 7–8.

Sidman, M. (1960). *Tactics of scientific research.* New York: Basic Books.

Sidman, M. (1978). Remarks. *Behaviorism, 6,* 265–268.

Sidman, M. (1986a). Functional analysis of emergent verbal classes. In T. Thompson & M. D. Zeiler (Eds.), *Analysis and integration of behavioral units* (pp. 213–245). Hillsdale, NJ: Lawrence Erlbaum Associates.

Sidman, M. (1986b). The measurement of behavioral development. In N. A. Krasnegor, D. B. Gray, & T. Thompson (Eds.), *Developmental behavioral pharmacology* (pp. 43–52). Hillsdale, NJ: Lawrence Erlbaum Associates.

Skinner, B. F. (1938). *The behavior of organisms.* Englewood Cliffs, NJ: Prentice-Hall.

Skinner, B. F. (1953). *Science and human behavior.* New York: Free Press.

Skinner, B. F. (1957). *Verbal behavior.* New York: Appleton-Century-Crofts.

Skinner, B. F. (1967). B. F. Skinner (An autobiography). In E. G. Boring &

G. Lindzey (Eds.), *A history of psychology in autobiography* (Vol. 5, pp. 387–413). New York: Appleton-Century-Crofts.

Skinner, B. F. (1968). *The technology of teaching.* New York: Appleton-Century-Crofts.

Skinner, B. F. (1969). *Contingencies of reinforcement: A theoretical analysis.* New York: Appleton-Century-Crofts.

Skinner, B. F. (1971). *Beyond freedom and dignity.* New York: Knopf.

Skinner, B. F. (1972). *Cumulative record* (3rd ed.). New York: Appleton-Century-Crofts.

Skinner, B. F. (1973). Answers for my critics. In H. Wheeler (Ed.), *Beyond the punitive society.* (pp. 256–266). London: Wildwood House.

Skinner, B. F. (1974). *About behaviorism.* London: Jonathan Cape.

Skinner, B. F. (1975). The steep and thorny way to a science of behavior. *American Psychologist, 30,* 42–49.

Skinner, B. F. (1976). *Walden Two.* New York: Macmillan. (Original work published 1948)

Skinner, B. F. (1977). Why I am not a cognitive psychologist. *Behaviorism, 5,* 1–10.

Skinner, B. F. (1980). *Notebooks* (Edited by Robert Epstein). Englewood Cliffs, NJ: Prentice Hall.

Skinner, B. F. (1981). Selection by consequences. *Science, 213,* 501–504.

Skinner, B. F. (1982). Contrived reinforcement. *The Behavior Analyst, 5,* 3–8.

Skinner, B. F. (1986). Some thoughts about the future. *Journal of the Experimental Analysis of Behavior, 45,* 229–235.

Sloane, E. H. (1945). Reductionism. *Psychological Review, 52,* 214–223.

Smedslund, J. (1978). Bandura's theory of self-efficacy: A set of common sense theorems. *Scandinavian Journal of Psychology, 19,* 1–14.

Smith, T. L. (1983). Skinner's environmentalism: The analogy with natural selection. *Behaviorism, 11,* 133–153.

Snoeyenbos, M. H., & Putney, R. T. (1980). Psychology and science. *American Journal of Psychology, 93,* 579–592.

Somerville, J. (1941). Umbrellaology or methodology in social science. *Philosophy of Science 8,* 557–566.

Spence, K. W. (1956). *Behavior theory and conditioning.* New Haven: Yale University Press.

Sprinthall, N. A. (1975). Fantasy and reality in research: How to move beyond the unproductive paradox. *Counselor Education and supervision, 14,* 310–322.

Staats, A. W. (1981). Paradigmatic behaviorism, unified theory, unified theory construction methods, and the zeitgeist of separatism. *American Psychologist, 36,* 239–256.

Staddon, J. E. R. (1973). On the notion of cause, with applications to behaviorism. *Behaviorism, 1,* 25–63.

Staddon, J. E. R., & Simmelhag, V. L. (1971). The "superstition" experiment: A re-examination of its implications for the principles of adaptive behavior. *Psychological Review, 78,* 3–43.

Sundberg, M. L., & Partington, J. W. (1982). Skinner's *Verbal behavior:* A reference list. *Verbal Behavior News, 1*(1).

Sundberg, M. L., & Partington, J. W. (1983). Skinner's *Verbal behavior:* An update of the reference list. *Verbal Behavior News, 2,* 10–13.

Swartz, P. (1959). Perspectives in psychology IX. Literature as art and as knowledge. *The Psychological Record, 9,* 7–10.

Tennant, L., Cullen, C., & Hattersley, J. (1981). Applied behavior analysis: Intervention with retarded people. In G. Davey (Ed.), *Applications of conditioning theory* (pp. 29–59). London: Methuen.

Thelen, E. (1981). Rhythmical behavior in infancy: An ethological perspective. *Developmental Psychology, 17* 237–257.

Thompson, E. N. (1974). A plea for replication. California *Journal of Educational Research, 25,* 79–86.

Thompson, T. (1984). The examining magistrate for nature: A retrospective review of Claude Bernard's *An Introduction to the Study of Experimental Medicine. Journal of the Experimental Analysis of Behavior, 41,* 211–216.

Todd, J. T., & Morris, E. K. (1983). Misconception and miseducation: Presentations of radical behaviourism in psychology textbooks. *The Behavior Analyst, 6,* 153–160.

Tolman, E. C. (1932). *Purposive behavior in animals and man.* New York: Century.

Tolman, E. C. (1958). *Behavior and psychological man.* Berkeley & Los Angeles: University of California Press.

Tolman, E. C. (1959). *Principles of purposive behavior.* In S. Koch (Ed.), *Psychology: A study of a science: Vol.2. General systematic formulations, learning, and special processes* (pp. 92–157). New York: McGraw-Hill.

Tolman, E. C., & Brunswik, E. (1935). The organism and the causal texture of the environment. *Psychological Review, 42,* 43–77.

Tulving, E. (1985). How many memory systems are there? *American Psychologist, 40,* 385–398.

Turvey, M. T., & Carello, C. (1981). Cognition: The view from ecological realism. *Cognition, 10,* 313–321.

Tyler, F. B. (1970). Shaping of the science. *American Psychologist, 25,* 219–226.

Uttal, W. R. (1973). *The psychobiology of sensory coding.* New York: Harper & Row.

Vale, J. R., & Vale, C. A. (1969). Individual differences and general laws in psychology: A reconciliation. *American Psychologist, 24,* 1093–1108.

Van Melsen, A. G. (1961). *Science and technology.* (Duquesne Studies. Philosophical Series, 13). Pittsburg: Duquesne University Press.

Vargas, E. A. (1985). Cultural contingencies: A review of Marvin Harris's *Cannibals and Kings. Journal of the Experimental Analysis of Behavior, 43,* 419–428.

Vaughan, M. E., & Michael, J. L. (1982). Automatic reinforcement: An important but ignored concept. *Behaviorism, 10,* 217–227.

Verhave, T. (1967). Contributions to the history of psychology: IV. Joseph Buchanan (1785–1829) and the "Law of Exercise" (1812). *Psychological Reports, 20,* 127–133.

Vitulli, W. F. (1971). A quest for balance: Enough "No black scorpions" for a while. *American Psychologist, 26,* 106–107.

Vogel, R., & Annau, Z. (1973). An operant discrimination task allowing variability of response patterning. *Journal of the Experimental Analysis of Behavior, 20,* 1–6.

von Bertalanffy, L. (1951). Theoretical models in biology and psychology. *Journal of Personality, 20,* 24–38.

von Cranach, M. (1982). The psychological study of goal-directed action: Basic issues. In M. von Cranach and R. Harré (Eds.), *The analysis of action: Recent theoretical and empirical advances* (pp. 35–73). Cambridge: Cambridge University Press.

Wahler, R., Berland, R. M., & Coe, T. (1978). Generalization processes in child behavior change. In B. Lahey & A. Kazdin (Eds.), *Advances in Clinical Child Psychology* (Vol. 2, pp. 35–69). New York: Plenum.

Wahler, R. G., & Fox, J. J. (1982). Response structure in deviant child-parent relationships: Implications for family therapy. In D. J. Bernstein (Ed.), *Nebraska Symposium on Motivation.* (Vol. 29, pp. 1–46). Lincoln: University of Nebraska Press.

Walker, K. F. (1942). The nature and explanation of behavior. *Psychological Review, 49,* 569–585.

Waller, B. (1977). Chomsky, Wittgenstein, and the behaviorist perspective on language. *Behaviorism, 5,* 43–59.

Warren, H. C. (1930). The organic world and the causal principle. *Science, 71,* 204–208.

Warren, N. (1971). Is a scientific revolution taking place in psychology? Doubts and reservations. *Science Studies, 1,* 407–413.

Warren, N. C. (1922). The significance of neural adjustment. *Psychological Review, 29,* 481–489.

Watson, J. B. (1913). Psychology as the behaviorist views it. *Psychological Review, 20,* 158–177.

Watson, J. B. (1919). *Psychology from the standpoint of a behaviorist.* Philadelphia: Lippincott.

Watson, R. I. (1973). Psychology: A prescriptive science. In M. Henle, J. Jaynes, & J. J. Sullivan (Eds.), *Historical conceptions of psychology* (pp. 13–28). New York: Springer.

Weingarten, K., & Mechner, F. (1966). The contingency as an independent variable of social interaction. In T. Verhave (Ed.), *The experimental analysis of behavior: Selected readings* (pp. 447–459). New York: Appleton-Century-Crofts.

Weisberg, P., & Waldrop, P. B. (1972). Fixed-interval work habits of congress. *Journal of Applied Behavior Analysis, 5,* 93–97.

Welford, A. T. (1976). *Skilled performance: Perceptual and motor skills.* Glenview, IL: Scott, Foresman.

Wessells, M. G. (1982). A critique of Skinner's views on the obstructive character of cognitive theories. *Behaviorism, 10,* 65–84.

Wetherell, M., Potter, J., & Stringer, P. (1983). Psychology, literature and texts.

Bulletin of the British Psychological Society, 36, 377–379.

White, O. R. (1971). *A glossary of behavioral terminology.* Champaign, IL: Research Press.

Whitehead, A. N. (1953). *Science and the modern world.* Cambridge: Cambridge University Press.

Wickens, D. D. (1938). The transference of conditioned excitation and conditioned inhibition from one muscle group to the antagonistic muscle group. *Journal of Experimental Psychology, 22,* 101–123.

Wiener, N. I. (1972). Relevance. *American Psychologist, 27,* 241–242.

Williams, K. A. (1931). Five behaviorisms. *American Journal of Psychology, 43,* 337–360.

Woodger, J. H. (1967). *Biological principles: A critical study.* London: Routledge & Kegan Paul. (Original work published 1929)

Woodworth, R. S. (1930). Dynamic psychology. In C. Murchison (Ed.), *Psychologies of 1930* (pp. 327–336). Worcester, MA: Clark University Press.

Woodworth, R. S. (1958). *Dynamics of behavior.* New York: Holt.

Wyatt, W. J., Hawkins, R. P., & Davis, P. (1986). A survey of editors of behavioral journals. *The ABA Newsletter, 9.*

Zettle, R. D., & Hayes, S. C. (1982) Rule-governed behavior: A potential theoretical framework for cognitive-behavioral therapy. *Advances in Cognitive-Behavioral Research and Therapy, 1,* 73–118.

Ziman, J. M. (1971). Information, communication, knowledge. *American Psychologist, 26,* 338–345.

Ziman, J. (1976). *The force of knowledge.* Cambridge: Cambridge University Press.

Ziman, J. (1978). *Reliable knowledge: An exploration of the grounds for belief in science.* Cambridge: Cambridge University Press.

Zuriff, G. E. (1975). Where is the agent in behavior? *Behaviorism, 3,* 1–21.

AUTHOR INDEX

A

Abelson, R. P., 54, 154, *173*
Ackoff, R. L., 54, 108, 115, 135, *177*
Ades, T., 1, 154, *173*
Akers, R. L., 66, *176*
Alcock, J., 97, *174*
Allport, D. A., 1, *173*
Allport, F. H., 57, 108, *173*
Allport, G. W., 119, *173*
Alston, W. P., 47, 105, 158, *173*
Ames, A., Jr., 5, 11, *176*
Andronis, P. T., 108, *185*
Angell, J. R., 9, *173*
Annau, Z., 67, 164, *195*
Antonitis, J. J., 67, 164, *173*
Arrington, R. L., 78, 96, 108, *178*
Atkinson, C. J., 68, *181*
Ausubel, D. P., 1, *173*
Averill, J. R., 110, *173*
Ayllon, T., 140, *173*
Azrin, W. H., 140, *173*

B

Baer, D. M., 85, *188*
Baerends, G. P., 99, *173*
Ball, J., 54, *185*
Balz, A. G. A., 2, 10, 30, *173*
Bandura, A., 24, 74, *173*
Barlow, D. H., 148, *173*
Baron, A., 140, 141, 150, *174*
Baron, J., 121, *174*
Bass, B. M., 70, 73, 143, 147, *174*
Bates, E., 154, *174*
Beeighly-Smith, M., 154, *174*
Beer, J. J., 143, 147, *174*
Beers, J. W., 164, *174*
Beers, C. S., 164, *174*
Beidel, D. C., 40, *174*
Bentley, A. F., 84, 90, *174*
Bergmann, G., 99, *174*
Berland, R. M., 51, *195*
Bermant, G., 97, *174*
Bernard, C., 64, *174*
Best, D., 44, 69, 95, 136, *174*
Bethlehem, D., 4, *174*

197

SUBJECT INDEX

A

actions
    as abstract entities, 41–42
    analysis of, 68–69
        and extinction, 68
    and contingencies, 61, 73–75
    and bodily activities, 48–49, 92, 97
    and bodily happenings, 97
    as means-end units, 56–57, 60
    as natural units, 38–39
    refraining from, 44, 69
    as subject matter, 60, 81, 87–88
    synthesis of, 67–70
    terminology of, 41
        and *actor,* 53
        and *observer,* 53
    as transdermal, 90–91
acts
    as concrete particulars, 41, 132
    as ephemeral, 121
    as events, 38
    kinds of
        inchoate, 44, 94

    private, 44–45, 94
    public, 43–45
    terminology of, 40–41
awareness
    and conduct, 42–43
    and contingency-shaped behavior,
        138–139
    of contingencies, 62, 138–140
    of self, 141–143

B

behavior
    ambiguity of, 42, 95–98
    conglomerate meaning of, 102, 172
    as equifinal classes, 61
    as jargon, 24
    as *operant behavior,* 73
behavior
    amorphous formulation of, 153, 169,
        172
    as defined by movements *vs.* conse-
        quences, 96–97
    and environment, 50–52, 65

205